MARRIAGE IN CHANGING JAPAN

Marriage in Changing Japan

Community and Society

Joy Hendry

CHARLES E. TUTTLE CO.: PUBLISHERS
Rutland, Vermont & Tokyo, Japan

Published by the Charles E. Tuttle Company, Inc.
of Rutland, Vermont & Tokyo, Japan
with editorial offices
at Suido 1-chome, 2-6, Bunkyo-ku, Tokyo

© 1981 Joy Hendry

Library of Congress Catalog Card No. 85-051781
International Standard Book No. 0-8048-1506-2

First Tuttle edition, 1986
Second printing, 1989

PRINTED IN JAPAN

CONTENTS

PLATES, TABLES, DIAGRAMS, PLANS AND MAPS

Plates *following page* 144

Tables

Diagrams

Plans

Maps

INTRODUCTION

A favourite topic of conversation in Japan is the question of what factors go towards creating a good marriage. The subject seems to hold great fascination for young and old alike, whether discussed from the standpoint of theoretical preferences or the practical details of a specific match. Nor is the interest merely academic. The sums of money associated with weddings and the establishment of a marriage are enormous, often representing the savings of years, and they seem to exceed by far the outlay expected for other ceremonial occasions. Over the centuries, various government attempts to limit such extravagence have met with little success. It was this apparently extraordinary interest in marriage which provided the inspiration for this book and I hope that the book in turn goes at least part of the way to explaining it.

The Japanese laws which concern family and marriage were changed completely after the Second World War and discussion about marriage often centres around the advantages or otherwise of the Western influence which helped to bring this about. An extremely modern couple may see their marriage as differing in no way from a Western one, but many marriages are still arranged largely by families through a go-between, which was the practice in pre-war Japan. Writings on the topic suggest that though modifications have been made to behaviour in response to the legal changes and imported ideology, many of the previous customs and attitudes persist. People getting married in Japan today usually have been brought up entirely in the post-war period and, even for old people, as much time has passed since the war as they lived through before and during it. It is the aim of this book to examine just how far marriage has changed during the lifetime of these older people, and, in areas where there has been little change, to attempt to explain why this should be so.

The basic method employed was the intensive field work of social anthropology which most successfully approaches institutions such as family and marriage in their total social context. As the investigation proceeded it became clear that this method was well suited even to an industrial and technologically highly-developed country such as Japan. The result is a book in which the greater part is devoted to a detailed and descriptive analysis of the social organisation of one community and the place of marriage in that community. I feel that this provides the most successful answer to the question posed. However, I hope that the material from other parts of Japan, to be found in the text and in footnotes, will indicate the extent to which this community illustrates patterns to be found in Japan as a whole; and the structural principles expressed in the conclusion may provide the basis of cross-cultural comparison. In fact it could be argued that the community chosen is rather atypical. There is material here which is of folkloric interest as unique to the region. Nevertheless, the basic principles involved in marriage are common to Japan. Indeed, in my view, an understanding of them goes no small way towards providing an explanation of some of those Japanese qualities which we in the West have found so hard to fathom. The book is thus offered not only as a contribution to studies of marriage, or social anthropology more generally, but also, perhaps as a reflection of the initial inspiration, as a contribution to the wider field of Japanese studies.

Not a great deal has been written in Western languages specifically on the topic of marriage in modern Japan. Much time was spent during the research for this book ferreting out information for comparative purposes from a wide variety of sources. The first chapter is a summary of such work which also provides a general setting for the subsequent more specific analysis. It is based entirely on an eclectic range of material of varying quality, from scholarly work in Japanese to the rather casual observations of Western travellers. Some attempt has been made to evaluate the relevance of such comments to a general picture of change in Japanese marriage over the period in question, but many of them are presented almost verbatim and they have not been interpreted in the light of my own findings. Rather, this chapter seeks to provide a starting point and a control, so that the reader is free to assess the significance of the ensuing study for Japanese society in general. For that reason detailed references are provided in the notes.

There should also be enough information in the first chapter to convince anyone seeking a definition of marriage in Japan of the difficulties that might be encountered were one to be attempted. The problem resembles that facing someone trying to define marriage in a society such as Britain or America. Does one use criteria acceptable in a court of law or does one consider the views of members of the community? If the latter is chosen, care must be taken to define the community. Clearly 'the eyes of God' would be sufficient witness for some but not for others. In Japan a person married by a ceremony acceptable to the community may not yet be married in the eyes of the law; one married only in the eyes of the law may equally be regarded as married. Again, community ideas vary regionally and, within a single community, traditional die-hards may not accept a Westernised definition of marriage which appears perfectly reasonable to younger members of it. To take only the problem of legitimacy, steps have been taken to avoid stigmatising children born before their parents' legal marriage as the word 'illegitimate' is no longered entered after their name in the family register. It is not disputed that the law be clear on the matter, merely that the law coincides necessarily with public opinion. Further problems arise in the Japanese case when one considers the variety of words which may be translated as 'marriage'. In cities, amongst the younger generation, the word *kekkon* and *kon'in* are used, which share the common element *kon*, defined in a standard Japanese dictionary (Nihon Kokugo Daijiten) as 'the making of the *engumi* of a husband and wife'. *Engumi* is 'the joining of *en*', where *en* is a notion of Karmic destiny involving a relationship (see the glossary), and the word *engumi* itself is frequently used in all areas of society in a sense which would again be translated as 'marriage'. However, it may also refer to the creation of a relationship of adoption, a fact which is not insignificant of a more complex aspect of marriage concerning ideas of descent (see Chapter 3). More clearly concerned with descent and the continuity of a House are the words used in rural communities for 'marriage', such as *yomeiri*, 'the entering of a *yome*', and *yometori*, 'the taking of a *yome*' where *yome* means 'daughter-in-law' as much as it means 'wife', literally 'woman of the House' (see p. 16). I hope that instead of a definition the flavour of marriage in Japan will be accessible in Chapter 1. The chapter is divided into two parts: the first attempts to paint a general picture of the institution of marriage in various parts of society in pre-war Japan; the second describes the clear break which was made with tradition in the new Constitution of 1947 and indicates some of the effects of the subsequent innovations.

The following chapter plunges straight into the field study. A word should be said about the selection of the community for intensive research. No attempt was made to be representative since even in a country as homogeneous as Japan there are considerable regional variations to say nothing of rural-urban differences. It was possible, however, to avoid extremes. The community chosen is administratively part of a provincial city although it has a marked rural atmosphere. Over half of the households are concerned with agricultural or horticultural pursuits but it is by no means part of the depopulated countryside. It has had a fairly constant population size this century and is within commuting distance of a number of urban areas. There is plenty of work available for young people, a feature which commended the area since this ensured current examples of matchmaking procedure. It would probably be regarded as backward by some modern city dwellers, as any provincial community would, but a great number of urban people still have families in the country and, at times of ceremony and crisis, many draw upon the traditions of their house and village of origin. This community, like most, maintains links with relatives who have moved away to the more varied opportunities of big cities. Indeed, it was possible through such links, as well as through the proximity of other communities where occupations were more diversified, to gain access to a wider range of details about marriages and weddings than were available in the community itself. On the other hand, the size of the unit — some 54 households — made it possible to examine the actual marriages of all the married inhabitants so that a picture emerged of the way these had changed over the period of living memory. Since a large part of the work was carried out within this community it was also possible in time to achieve the degree of intimacy essential to penetrate the veneer of stereotypical responses to questions about areas of personal involvement. The most extended period spent living continuously in the area was from March 1975 to January 1976, but a return in 1979 provided a chance to check some of the analysis, bring figures up to date, and incorporate a few changes which had taken place. Some of the ethnographic present still refers to the 1975/6 period, especially where a particular point was being made, but dates are given where changes were observed and, as far as possible, tables include the 1979 figures.

Common abbreviations for family relationships found in anthropological works are used in this book as well. These are H = husband, W = wife, F = father, M = mother, S = son, D = daughter, B = brother, Z = sister, e = elder, y = younger. These letters are used in sequences to show more complicated relationships. For example FBSDH means "father's brother's son's daughter's husband," and HFeZDHyBWF means "husband's father's elder sister's daughter's husband's younger brother's wife's father."

Research in the field was made possible by the Social Science Research Council, which also supported me during a period after my return. The Japan Foundation provided funds which allowed me to carry out a good deal of comparative library research, and I am also indebted to my college, Lady Margaret Hall, Oxford, which awarded me a Henrietta Jex-Blake Research Scholarship, as well as a number of smaller sums, to help pay the fees and other expenses while I was a student there.

For academic advice, discussion and comments on earlier drafts of this work, I would like to thank I. J. McMullen, P.G. Riviere, N.J. Allen, R.P. Dore, R.H. Barnes, H. Befu, T. Yoshida, K. Matsunaga, D.C. Kay and M. Rawlings, although I take full responsibility for any errors that may remain. Plates 8 and 10 are courtesy of Alan Smith. For the processing of the photographs, I am indebted to A. Pugh, and for cheerful co-operation as well as typing skill, to S. Pusey.

During field-work, I incurred a multitude of debts which I can never repay. Professor Matsunaga gave up a great deal of time to visit me from Fukuoka and help with innumerable practical problems. Mr T. Nishie helped me to locate a suitable village for research in the first place, as well as introducing me to Mr Sasabuchi, who made available a splendid house for my use. Hospitality was offered and accepted in many homes, but for extended periods I must thank the Kumagae family, my next-door neighbours, and the Baba family, where I stayed in 1979. Finally, but by no means least, I must thank all the inhabitants of Kurotsuchi, as well as several in other nearby villages, and a number of Yame city employees, who gave so generously of their time and company during my investigations. Without their magnificent co-operation, this book could never have been written.

1 HISTORICAL CONTEXT

This chapter is intended to provide a summary of changes affecting family life in Japan during the period under consideration, as a background to the more specific study which is to follow. Based almost entirely on a wide range of literary sources, it has deliberately been made general in order to provide a framework within which the ensuing study can best be interpreted. A large number of references are included so that the chapter also provides possible access to more detailed work on topics mentioned here only briefly.

The period with which this book is most concerned falls within the living memory of the older members of today's population. Within this chapter the period is divided into two parts, considered separately. First, that preceding and including the Second World War, then the post-war period. This division is based on the assumption that the greatest single factor to have influenced the Japanese way of life in this century was defeat in the Second World War with the consequent US Occupation and introduction of democracy and other Western ideals into the legal and educational systems of the nation. Modern Western influence actually dates back much further, from the opening of the country before the Meiji Restoration in 1868 after two and a half centuries of almost complete isolation from foreign contacts, and reference will also be made to this earlier period. The Meiji Restoration marked the end of the long rule of the House of Tokugawa, after which the previous period is often named; it also marked the beginning of what is usually called Japan's 'modern' period. Japanese names for historical periods are sometimes used in the text and their approximate Western dates are provided at the end of the glossary. The more general term 'traditional' may be taken to apply to the Japan which was in existence before, or which has persisted through, the enormous Western influence of the modern period.

Family Life in Pre-war Japan

Today's old people in Japan were brought up at a time when the previous *samurai* family system, which had been formed and developed over some six hundred years, was being disseminated throughout all parts of society. Schools had been introduced throughout the nation from 1872, enrolment rose to 98 per cent during the first decade of this century, and it was chiefly by means of the government education policy, which crystallised during this period,[1] that the Confucian-coloured values of the *samurai* system were propagated. The Imperial Rescript on Education,[2] issued on 30 October 1890, had to be learned by heart by schoolchildren and this taught that filial piety should be second only to loyalty to the Emperor. Unless one was called upon to serve the nation, one's primary loyalties were to the family unit, the *ie*, and an individual was expected to find 'his *raison d'être* by contributing towards the maintenance and continuance of the family'.[3]

This *ie* is a Japanese concept which has been discussed and described by many writers on Japan including Ariga (1954), Befu (1971), Fukutake (1972), Isono (1964), Nakane (1967), Pelzel (1970) and, in particular detail, Dore (1971). It seems nevertheless essential to attempt a general explanation here, although a more detailed description of how it operated in the community studied is to be found in chapter 3. Several English words which are similar in meaning have been used to translate *ie*. They include 'family', 'house', 'household', 'stem family' and 'genealogy'.[4] Like the English concept of 'house', the *ie* means both 'family' and 'dwelling', and perhaps the closest English idea is that of 'House' as in 'House of Windsor'.[5] The importance of the memory of the ancestors was emphasised by Hearn, who described the *ie* as a 'religious society', which he thus compared to the classical Greek and Roman family.[6]

Its chief characteristic is one of continuity, independent of the individuals who pass through, and the primary duties of the living members are to honour the ancestors who went before them and ensure that descendants will follow after them. Rites held for the recently dead are said to ensure their welfare in the after life, but even after these cease, previous permanent living members join the general ranks of ancestors (*senzo*), most revered members of the *ie*. In pre-Meiji Japan, property was regarded as belonging to the *ie* as a whole;[7] there was often a common occupation — indeed this is sometimes emphasised as the basis for its existence — and the *ie* held a certain standing in the community to which it belonged. Each member contributed labour as he or she was able, received the common benefits without individual remuneration, and was expected to avoid all behaviour which might bring disgrace or disrepute on the whole *ie*. At any one time the affairs of the *ie* were managed ultimately by its head, although he could delegate duties to the other members. He was the representative of the *ie* to the outside and legally responsible for all its members, who were subordinate to him. Ideally the head took pride of place at table, was served the best food and went first to bathe. However, if a particular head was for some reason incompetent, or if his actions were detrimental to the *ie* as a whole, there were various means by which he could be replaced by a more suitable member.

Kinship was the first criterion for membership, but employees in the sense of retainers could also belong, and a totally unrelated person could be adopted into the household to ensure succession. Not even residence was a necessary criterion for membership, since a member temporarily living elsewhere would be held to belong to the *ie* of his family until he formally joined or created another *ie*, usually by marriage. Ideally there would only be one permanent member of the *ie* born in each generation, since all children but the successor were expected to marry and move out,[8] although unmarried siblings of the permanent members always had the right to return to the *ie*. Primogeniture became predominant during the Tokugawa period and was institutionalised in the Meiji Civil Code (Article 970),[9] but previously other types of succession had also been customary, particularly in certain regions.[10] The successor was accorded deferential treatment next only to that of the house head, and when he came of age, he would receive a wife from another household. This couple would form the generation to provide heirs for the succeeding one. Other sons sometimes formed new households which were regarded as branch houses of the main one from which they had departed (see Chapter 3, p. 104). In the absence of sons a common procedure was to adopt as head a man who also became the husband of a daughter, but a close male relative or even a total stranger could be adopted if there were no children at all. This provided another possibility for non-inheriting sons of households with many children. An adopted head is called a *yōshi*, and since he is taken into the *ie* rather than born into it, his position rather resembles that of the *yome*, a woman who marries in (see Chapter 3, p. 99). The word *yome* means 'daughter-in-law' as well as 'wife', and the Chinese character used to write it (嫁) is a combination of those for 'woman' (女) and *ie* (家), which illustrates well the way a woman 'married' the whole household, not just an individual.

Each member of the *ie* was expected to subordinate his or her individual interests to those of the *ie* as a whole, and the needs of parents and even children were to be considered before those of a wife. Love (*aijō*)[11] between spouses was not consistent with filial piety and marriages were usually arranged by heads of houses, often through a go-between.[12] The principals were expected to agree with the choice of their elders, and it was 'not considered quite proper for a son, and particularly for a daughter, to express too strong an opinion on the selection of the parents'.[13]

Diagram 1: Elements of the *Ie*

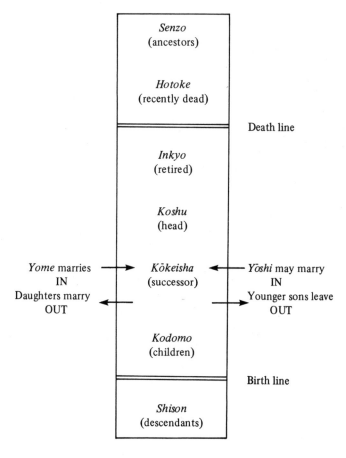

Moreover, from the Meiji period, a legal marriage required the permission of the house head (Meiji Civil Code, Article 750), and of parents for a man under 30 and a woman under 25 (Meiji Civil Code, Article 772). As Steiner has pointed out, these ages are beyond those at which it was customary to marry.[14] Some older couples in Japan describe meeting for the first time at their wedding, but it became usual for the go-between to arrange an occasion for each party to view the other, and this is characterised rather aptly by a Western observer of the late Meiji period as 'a meeting at which the lovers (if persons unknown to each other may be so styled) are allowed to see, sometimes even to speak to each other, and thus estimate each other's merits'.[15] This meeting is called a *miai*,[16] literally 'mutual viewing', and may take one of several forms (see Chapter 4, p. 122). The word is used to characterise arranged marriages, sometimes even when no such meeting actually occurred, to distinguish them from more modern 'love' matches.

Strong objections on the part of a son or daughter were possibly respected in some cases but, in general, the demands of the family were considered more important than any personal love and affection. The social standing of the household was one of the factors at stake, and in order to secure a suitable alliance upper-class families would sometimes betroth children at quite an early age.[17] Economic reasons were also important, especially in the lower classes, where it was vital for the new member of the family work-force to be industrious, and again a Westerner makes an apt comment: 'If you love your wife you spoil your mother's servant; it is almost as bad as flirting with your housemaid in England.'[18] But it is most frequently asserted that the main object of marriage was the perpetuation of the family line, not love, but the provision of an heir:[19] 'the purpose is to supply the ancestors with those who will faithfully serve them, a son and heir being the greatest blessing sought.'[20]

Much of this idea of marriage is of Chinese origin and, according to Hozumi, a combination of the teachings of Mencius and Confucius, taught in Japan for over 1,000 years, makes it the greatest crime a man can commit to remain single.[21] It was the duty of parents to see that their children married, and the alternative was disgrace to the family.[22] It seems that they usually succeeded, however, for other writers comment on the inevitability of marriage, especially for women: 'Marriage is as much a matter of course in a woman's life as death, and is no more to be avoided.'[23]

Another aspect of the serious nature of marriage is to be found in a consideration of the combination of Taoist and Shinto ideas on the topic. Thus marriage was regarded as a union of the two elements of the universe, the *in* and *yō* (yin and yang), 'considered by the people, to speak strictly, as a sacred course of humanity, indicated by the Deities of the nation'.[24] These yin/yang ideas in Japan date from at least as early as the sixth to eighth centuries AD, and in Tokugawa law the importance of the harmonious blending of these two elements was codified.[25] In 1933, Erskine wrote that the Japanese Almanac instructs: 'the marriage of two people affects the health and morale of the Empire . . . and therefore should not be entered into lightly without a full study of the fate and the compatibility of the two parties.'[26] Some detail about the calculation of such compatibility is given in Fujisaki's manual on marriage, but by then the writer regards this as superstition.[27] Traditionally it was said 'that the myriad of divine spirits that guard the Japanese assemble annually to assort the aspirants to matrimony'.[28] This gathering was supposed to take place at Izumo, where resides the deity regarded as supreme protector of marriages. Elsewhere the month of the meeting used to be called 'godless month' (*kannazuki*), and marriages were not to be held while the gods were away.[29]

Even sexual gratification was supposed to be separate from marriage and this is part of the wider idea pointed out by Benedict 'that "human feelings" should not intrude upon serious affairs of life'.[30] Love was indistinguishable from passion and 'brutal attachment on the same plane'.[31] 'Love' was considered to be on the same level as the casual mating of animals, and marriages based on it were generally considered to lead to unhappiness — witness the proverbial expression: 'those who come together in passion stay together in tears.'[32] Sex outside marriage was not regarded as sinful for men, however, until the Western condemnation of the hitherto widespread practices of concubinage and prostitution.[33] Until the Meiji Restoration things had changed little from the description of a foreign observer of the 1630s:

One man hath but one Wife, though as many Concubines as he can keep; and if that Wife do not please him, he may put her away, provided he dismiss her in a civil and honourable way. Any man may lie with a Whore, or common Woman, although he be married, with impunitie; but the Wife may not so much as speak in private with another Man, as is already said, without hazarding her life.[34]

In pre-Meiji times men took concubines to symbolise their success, and they and their issue were recognised legally as possible providers of succession to the *ie*.[35] After the Meiji Restoration concubines were first given greater legal status than they had had, which was in effect a return to the legal code of the eighth century, but such was the opposition to this move that their existence was legally abolished in 1882.[36] Kawashima talks of the previous system as polygamy (*ippu-tasai*), but the word for concubine (*mekake*) was distinct from that for wife, the status of the former was in no way comparable with that of the latter, and concubines frequently did not shave their eyebrows or blacken their teeth as wives were expected to do.[37]

Even before the 1882 change in the law, the traveller, Mrs Bishop, received the following answer when she asked her servant how many wives a man could have: 'Only one lawful one, but as many others . . . as he can support, just as Englishmen have.'[38] At the turn of the century, Chamberlain wrote similarly that a man who could afford it probably had a concubine, but, from the beginning of this century, the illegitimacy figures gradually began to decline and attitudes to sex began to change.[39]

Prostitution was also condemned from time to time after the Restoration, but the red-light district continued not only to survive but also to flourish. The more exalted *geisha* had held an important place in the lives of officials of the Tokugawa period and in earlier times, dancing girls, who also provided sexual services, used to be found in temples and shrines.[40] In Japan it is said that a man's heart is like an autumn sky,[41] and Bishop commented at the turn of the century, 'even apparent fidelity on the part of the husband is not regarded either as a virtue or a conventional requirement'.[42]

Things were very different for women, however. Chastity was expected, and, until the law was repealed in 1908, a husband who discovered his wife in an adulterous act could kill her and her lover without fear of prosecution.[43] Women were taught from an early age that their prime duty should be obedience: first to their father, then to their husband and husband's parents, and finally, when widowed, to their son. Many writers have quoted from the famous seventeenth-century treatise of the male neo-Confucianist Kaibara Ekken, *Onna Daigaku*, translated in Chamberlain as '*The Greater Learning for Women*'.[44] It laid out the principles by which women should order their lives. According to this, 'The only qualities that befit a woman are gentle obedience, chastity, mercy and quietness.' A woman should honour her father and mother-in-law more than her own parents, and in all dealings with her husband, she should be 'courteous, humble and conciliatory'. As a woman she was prone to be afflicted with the maladies of 'indocility, discontent, slander, jealousy and silliness' and 'Such is the stupidity of her character that it is incumbent on her, in every particular, to distrust herself and to obey her husband.'

In poor families it was a supreme example of filial self-sacrifice for a girl to sell herself into a house of ill fame for a period of years to aid the family.[45] Even after marriage, as a female commentator has pointed out, a girl was often little more than an apprentice for sometimes as much as twenty years, until her mother-in-law died.[46] The attitude of some men to women is illustrated in a quotation from a novel written during the Meiji period: 'In fact, as she's a woman, you can persuade her into doing anything.'[47]

The idea of women's basic inferiority was emphasised in other ways. According to the yin/yang classification they were to men as earth was to heaven, as human is to deity.[48] In the Five Classes of Relationship (*Gotōshin*) system, which classed relatives in order of proximity and importance, imported from Chinese law in the eighth century and readopted in early Meiji, wives were second-class relatives while husbands were first class.[49] Further, in Japanese mythology the divine founding couple, Izanami and Izanagi, failed in their first attempt to conceive a child because the woman spoke first, an act which was regarded by the superior heavenly beings as improper.[50]

The ease with which a woman could be divorced illustrates her low status, although in part this was due to her position as outsider in the household and a man adopted as *yōshi*, to marry the daughter of a house with no sons, was in a similar position. An annulment of the adoption was easy to effect and this constituted sufficient grounds for divorce. Thus both *yome* and *yōshi* could be sent home if they failed to suit their parents-in-law, even if their spouses were quite satisfied. It was usually said that they 'did not fit into the ways of the house' (*kafū ni awanai*). However, the law was more explicit about the divorce of women. During the Tokugawa period and in early Meiji it was merely necessary for a husband to state his intention to divorce in a letter, whose brevity was indicated by the usual term for this missive: *mikudarihan* ('three-and-a-half lines').[51] The wife, on the other hand, had no legal recourse in case of maltreatment, and in desperation could only run away to a convent at Kamakura where men were not admitted or, more picturesquely, she could resort to the supposed magical powers of a 'divorce nettle tree' at Itabashi.[52] Chamberlain comments that divorce was practised mostly by the lower classes, since men of the upper classes could have any number of mistresses and any wife was too inferior to be a serious nuisance.[53] Alliances created on marriage between upper-class families were also often too important to break.

The written law in early Meiji gave seven grounds on which a man was justified in divorcing his wife. They were sterility, adultery, disobedience to parents-in-law, loquacity, larceny, jealousy and bad disease. There were various qualifications in the original law, and a wife who had nowhere to go could not be sent away; also for certain reasons a wife was able to leave her husband, and this type of qualification replaced the absolute authority of the husband which had existed in the Tokugawa period. In 1873 a woman, accompanied by her father, elder brother or other close relative, was given the right to appeal directly to the court for a divorce on the following grounds: (1) desertion by the husband for more than two years; (2) imprisonment of the husband for one year or more; (3) profligacy of husband; (4) illness, especially malignant or acute mental illness.

In 1898 the principle that mutual consent was sufficient for divorce was made law (Meiji Civil Code, Article 808). In fact it is said that many women were still driven out or forced to agree to a divorce if demanded. Also marriages often were not legally registered until after a period of adjustment, perhaps until a baby was due to be born, so the *yome*, or indeed the *yōshi*, could be sent home without legal recourse.[54] Women could apply for a judicial divorce on grounds of cruelty, desertion and some serious misconduct (Meiji Civil Code, Article 813), but children remained in the *ie*, and in general, judicial divorces were rare, and represented less than 1 per cent of those registered.[55] Adultery was still only a crime and grounds for divorce if commited by a wife (Article 813). Gradually, however, the divorce figures did decline, just as the illegitimacy figures had done.[56]

During the Meiji period, extraordinary innovations had become commonplace in Japan. Western clothes, food and furniture had appeared everywhere, travel had become much easier, schools and post offices were built in every area and new ideas were spreading at a rate which many traditionalists found alarming. In particular, ideas which would undermine the basic tenets of the family system were seen by some as especially dangerous, and there was great controversy over the issue of how family and inheritance should be treated legally. This issue was postponed in the Civil Code of 1890, and after years of tortuous discussion, a compromise, which retained much of the patriarchal system, was brought in in 1898.[57] The discussions continued, however, and were aggravated by social problems such as delinquency and neglect, which were cited by conservatives as reasons for maintenance of family discipline and authority.

After the First World War, a rise in popular support for democracy and a basic incompatibility of its ideals with those of the family system provoked fears of a total collapse of the social structure and further reactionary efforts to strengthen it. Educationalists were especially traditional, and, while at high levels discussions were unresolved, the Confucianist values of the *samurai* system were, through education, still influencing all classes. Japanese mythology was taught as history in schools, along with Shinto as the national religion, and the extreme view portrayed the whole Japanese nation as descended from the divine ancestors through the Emperor's family as main line and all his subjects as members of branch lines of descent. History was compulsory from 1907 and all children were taught from the same textbooks, which were compiled by the Ministry of Education.[58] Regulations for teachers advocated their main aim to make students 'feel the joy of having been born in the Imperial land and comprehend the true meaning of reverence and public service.'[59] Filial piety was thus also the basis of loyalty to the Emperor, and the government, in his name and under the auspices of the patriotic state Shinto organisation, could claim unconditional obedience from the people as long as these values were emphasised.

Thus, while at high levels traditionalists were threatened by new ideas, the strength of their teachings increased among commoners. The marriage arranged through a go-between, common before the Restoration only among *samurai* families, who often needed to arrange unions across some distance to match their social standing, now spread to most levels of society. The new freer transport services and the national markets based on the new capitalist economy opened up the sphere of possibility for marriage partners for people who had previously sought spouses within the close community to which they had been confined.[60] Matches arranged through a third party began to replace the unions of free choice and mutual attraction which had been usual among commoners. In villages it was often the Youth Group which had had an important function with regard to arranging marriages, aided in many areas by the existence of a Youth Lodge which provided the venue for romance and sexual exploits amongst the members. In some areas it was said that the Youth Groups disapproved of promiscuity and their leaders took steps to arrange the marriages of lovers, while elsewhere free sexual relationships were encouraged for a period, and illegitimate children merely incorporated into their mother's natal *ie* should a marriage fail to develop. In many areas the Youth Groups responded to the new exogamous marriages in irresponsible harassment of families involved, and, according to Kamishima, this so tarnished their image that they soon lost their traditional role with regard to marriage.[61]

Where there were no Youth Lodges, a man would visit the girl of his choice at home, and if her parents approved of the match, they sometimes let her sleep near the door to receive her lover at night in the hope that a formal marriage would soon be agreed between the two families. The girl concerned was free to consent to such a union or to refuse a suitor and, in general, country women were less subservient and dependent than they were later taught they should be. Either partner could halt the proceedings in the early stages of a marriage, so that divorce was fairer for women, and Yanagida suggests that divorce actually increased in the Meiji period, as people were taught Confucian ideals.[62] A woman would also expect to share her husband's authority when the couple inherited the household, and she would often receive the family rice ladle from her mother-in-law as a token of this. Even in 1904, Lorimer commented that 'the humbler the wife is socially, the more she is on a footing of equality with her husband'.[63]

Two other Western writers describe nineteenth-century customs whereby a suitor in higher classes could determine his chances of success with a girl,[64] but as the *samurai* ethic spread, personal choice in marriage came to be viewed as 'barbaric or backward', 'a disruptive act, rebellious against both family and nation'.[65] The visit of a suitor to his lover's house was called a *yobai*, and according to scholars the meaning of the word changed from a legitimate expression of marriage proposal to a derogatory term with the folk etymology 'night-creep', which had distinctly illicit overtones. This was so effective a change that in 1948 Ariga wrote that people would be surprised the word had ever been applied to a proper means to marriage.[66]

Gradually the marriage arranged by parents through the offices of a go-between became the normal and proper way to proceed. If parents were particularly 'understanding' they might ask a go-between to help stage an arranged marriage to make a 'love match' look respectable, but on the whole mate selection through love came to be thought 'immodest, or even immoral'.[67] In 1930, one writer wrote that 'According to the traditional moral ideas, it is deemed a sign of mental and moral weakness to "fall in love" ' and Kawashima maintains that in the army and navy, until the end of the war, love was thought 'effeminate and unmanly' (*memeshii*).[68] A marriage based on such a foundation could only cause scandal, as Chamberlain noted of the only love match he claimed to have heard of in 28 years.[69] In contrast to this dearth of breakaway marriages, the alternative for smitten couples was 'commonplace': 'Numberless are the tales of men who, being unable to wed the object of their passion . . . have bound themselves tightly to her with a rope, and then precipitated themselves into the water.'[70]

In 1904 Tamura wrote that there was no such thing as courtship in Japan, as boys and girls were segregated, and indeed this principle was enforced in schools, by the police in cinemas, and by custom in social gatherings.[71] Love affairs between workmates were sufficient cause for dismissal, and during the war travelling couples were arrested — even in one case a university professor of fifty who was taking his wife to visit a family grave.[72] A new kind of Youth Group grew up, but it had no marriage function and often it was limited to boys with no corresponding group for girls.[73]

However, as the mores hitherto traditional in the upper classes spread to the peasant, new ideas continued to affect the behaviour and attitudes of the more sophisticated members of Japanese society. The decline in the practice of concubinage and a consequent reduction in the illegitimacy figures have already been mentioned; similarly the divorce rate was reduced and women given greater legal resources in the case of mistreatment. In general, women were gradually becoming better educated, more were able independently to go out to work, and their status was improving in consequence. As early as 1904, Sladen quoted Gubbins as follows: 'In no respect has modern progress in Japan made greater strides than in the improvement of the position of women.'[74] In 1915, at the coronation of the Emperor Taishō, the Empress was given a throne for the first time. As Crown Prince, the Emperor had previously made a point of allowing his wife to enter a carriage before him, and it was known that the couple habitually took meals together, actions which Sladen describes as 'an astounding revolution in Japan'.[75]

The age at which young people were marrying was gradually increasing. In early Meiji it was not uncommon for girls to be married off at 16, but by the early twentieth century, their average age at marriage was nearly 23 and still rising.[76] In 1931, a female scholar, Iwasaki, interpreted the decline in divorce figures as directly related to this increase in the age and status of women at marriage. With greater opportunities to work and support themselves, women are able to be more selective about their husbands, she argues, and in a separate article she comments that although young people were not yet free to choose their own marital partners, their opinions were more often respected than previously.[77]

With increased literacy, papers, magazines and books multiplied to keep up with demand, and through this medium, as well as through films and plays, ideas about Western romantic love as a noble emotion leading to a greater understanding between married couples began to spread and affect attitudes.[78] One ideal image projected was that of the 'good wife and wise mother' (*ryōsaikenbo*), a better half on the European model, a companion and friend to her husband, equal to him and able to discuss his work rather than wait on him like a servant.[79] The idea of seeking happiness in marriage was a new one, and it was consistent with another new idea, that of the husband and wife setting up their own home. The movement of people to work in industry often required young couples to do this already, but the idea that it would be preferable to the old extended family was now also being expressed.[80] A few brave people began to defy scandal and publicly to make marriages based on love. In effect it was often elopement, and merely added fuel to the fire of the traditionalists' cry for maintenance of a strong family system,[81] but with defeat in the Second World War, these tearaways became pioneers of a new age.

The Family in Post-war Japan

As agreed in the Potsdam Declaration of surrender, the Occupation brought democracy to Japan. The new ideas, which had previously shocked society, were now codified, and with regard to marriage the new Constitution of May 1947 read:

> Marriage shall be based only on the mutual consent of both sexes and it shall be maintained through mutual cooperation with the equal rights of husband and wife as a basis. With regard to choice of spouse, property rights, inheritance, choice of domicile, divorce and other matters pertaining to marriage and the family, laws shall be enacted from the standpoint of individual dignity and the essential equality of the sexes. (Article 24)

The laws based on this Constitution came into effect on 1 January 1948, and the overall theme is well illustrated in this extract. The foundations of the family system and the patriarchal authority of the head of the *ie* were abolished. Much discussion between conservative and radical elements ensued, and in particular the potential dangers of removing the household's authority were at issue, but the fundamentals of the family system were at odds with the basic tenets of democracy, and the conservatives were defeated at last.[82]

From this time, all children, male and female, have had a right to equal inheritance, and a widow has a right to one-third of the estate (Article 900). The children also share equal obligation to support their parents when aged. This replaces the inheritance of all property by the eldest son. Each nuclear family was now to have, and still has, a separate registration sheet, initiated on marriage, at the local registration office. This replaces the old system whereby a new head of the house was the reason for starting a new sheet for any household. The couple may now choose either of their surnames, which sounds very equal, but in fact makes provision for the old practice of adoption of a *yōshi* as a daughter's husband into a house with no sons. Parental consent is no longer legally necessary for persons of majority, that is over 20 years of age, who desire marriage, and those under this age but over 18 for a boy and 16 for a girl need the consent of only one parent (Article 731, 737). The age of majority is usually 20, but marriage overrides this rule and is an alternative means of attaining this status (Article 753).

The education system, which had played such a part in inculcating the values of pre-war society, was completely reorganised under the Occupation. One of the first acts of the Allied Forces was to sever the links between the government and Shinto, and in December of 1945 a directive was issued banning the teaching of Shinto in schools. On the last day of the same year, another directive suspended the teaching of morals, Japanese history and geography, and on the first day of 1946, the Emperor renounced his own divinity. History teaching was now to lay greater emphasis on the lives of the people than on the works of emperors, and the first post-war history textbook omitted the well-known legends and stories of Japanese mythology:

The findings of archaeologists, sociologists, and evidence from Chinese records were to provide facts, now regarded as the basis of history teaching. Myths and legends, drawn from the ancient Japanese histories the Kojiki and the Nihon Shoki, were excluded so that they would not be confused with historical fact.[83]

The Imperial Rescript, which had made explicit the virtues of loyalty and filial piety, was withdrawn, and for some years moral values were not taught at all as a formal subject in school. Textbooks must still be approved by the Ministry of Education, and the present morals course in elementary schools propounds the basic principles of democracy and other Western ideals.

In 1946, women were first able to exercise their franchise, and, from that time, opportunities for higher education for women have increased, as have possibilities for them to take on prestigious and lucrative employment.[84] As stated in the Constitution, women have been given the legal status of full and equal partners in marriage, and 'an act of unchastity' on the part of the husband or wife has become a ground for judicial divorce (Article 770). According to court figures, women have been taking advantage of this, and since the war divorce figures in general have been gradually increasing, particularly those handled by the courts.[85] Kawashima reported that women were no longer afraid to display aggressive behaviour towards their husbands' lovers, and that an association of sin with prostitution was expressed soon after the war by a majority of men and women.[86]

However, prostitution continued, and the equality women received by law was slower to be reflected in behaviour. In 1961 it was reported that women were still frequently regarded as cheap temporary labour, those who worked at home were often exploited by middlemen, and some evidence continued of the attitude that wives and mothers should not work.[87] A more recent article talks of the guilt Japanese women with young children apparently feel if they go out to work, as well as reporting the small percentage of adolescent girls who want to have a job outside the home when they marry.[88] Rohlen reports that the bank he studied would discourage strongly a company wife from working, since 'this would take her from her primary roles of mother and wife'.[89] Japanese television illustrates well the supporting role women are expected to take. Innumerable are the shows which are presented by a man, accompanied by a woman who faithfully laughs at his jokes and insinuates a constant supply of appropriate exclamations and asides into his flow of chatter.

It is not only with regard to the status of women that practice fails to live up to the theoretical ideals of the post-war Constitution. The family system more generally has not crumbled away in accordance with the fears of the traditionalists and the hopes of the radicals. As Fukutake wrote in 1974, 'A revolution in legislation could not bring about a revolution in practice, and the *ie* system still survives in custom.'[90] A clause of the laws of succession admits of the necessity for an heir to be chosen to inherit the genealogical records and utensils of religious rites (Article 897), and several writers have described a practice whereby one son does in fact inherit particularly farm property because his siblings sign away their rights for the good of the *ie*.[91] It seems that there is less emphasis on this successor's being the eldest son than there used to be, and other siblings usually receive a share of the inheritance in the form of education, financial help with a house or business, or a bridal trousseau.[92] According to Morioka, the Shin sect of Buddhism, at least, has made every effort to maintain its system of hereditary succession for priests, and parishioners are still regarded as households requiring services for ancestors.[93] Nor does the old system exist only for matters concerned with ancestor worship. A modern Japanese commentator noted in 1969 that the strength of family unity is still demonstrated, particularly in the case of marriage 'which has to take into account various family considerations above everything else'.[94]

In early post-war Japan the term *kekkon* (marriage), which suggests a union of equals much more than did previous terms such as *yomeiri* (*yome*-entering), became widely used in urban areas.[95] Newspapers and magazines openly emphasised the association of love and happiness with marriage, and opinion polls were published to illustrate the importance love had taken on as an ideal.[96] Further polls in the fifties showed how a majority of people questioned thought individuals should choose their own marital partners rather than let their parents do it. Another poll claimed to illustrate the way the husband/wife relationship was becoming more important than that between parent and child in marriage and another still cited a preference expressed by young people in cities for even the eldest son to set up his own home.

However, writers citing these polls also noted that practice tended to show less innovation than ideals had done. Figures for actual marriages still leaned heavily towards a preference for arrangements involving parents and a third party as intermediary. Love was an ideal to be sought in marriage but in practice opportunity was lacking and parental approval was still sought. Kawashima's book was an attempt in 1954 to shed light on this discrepancy between ideal and practice, and he saw the previous strong segregation of the sexes as one of the chief causes.[97] In 1958, Baber wrote that boys he had interviewed were more bold about wanting to choose their own partners than girls were, most girls wanting to choose together with their parents, though some were apparently happy to rely entirely on the guidance of their parents.[98] In the same year, Sano wrote of parents in Tokyo and Hokkaido: 'parental attitude toward the inauguration of marriage has not been changing at any spectacular rate, and is not likely to change much in the near future.' She claimed that parents had always been concerned for the happiness of their children, as well as for the household, and their part in the choice of partner was mostly a protection from the consequences of possible faulty judgement at such an early age.[99]

Field-workers in country villages commented during the fifties and sixties that the number of arranged marriages was far in excess of those based on 'love matches' and some note that these had replaced the previous arrangements of mutual attraction.[100] Devos found a distrust of free choice in marriage through psychological testing, though some people had openly expressed positive attitudes to the concept. Elsewhere he calls this phenomenon a 'psychological lag', and he also uses this phrase to refer to the way many young people were found to support 'love matches' in principle while expecting themselves to bow to the pressures of family and community and make a marriage arranged with parents.[101] Befu, too, has talked of a lag in practices with regard to the new form of 'romantic marriage', especially in rural areas, and he also cites reasons such as the lack of opportunities for meeting people.[102]

Even in an urban sample of young nuclear families, Blood found a substantial proportion of arranged marriages in the 1960s, and he quotes the saying of a number of old people he talked to: 'arranged marriages start out cold and get hot, whereas love matches start out hot and grow cold.'[103] A Japanese writer has described the *miai* as a 'rational utilization of a traditional practice'. She comments that immediately after the war girls were against such meetings, but by 1961, a survey among college students showed 80 per cent in favour because of the wider range of choice offered than through random meetings.[104] In 1974, Fukutake wrote of Japan in general that *miai* marriages still predominate over 'love' marriages, though he adds that it is common for the first meeting to be supplemented by 'dating'.[105] A 1976 report of a rural area in Shikoku mentions a preference of parents and young people for 'modified versions of the arranged marriage' despite opportunities for male/female contact in school and Youth Groups, 'because it is commonly believed that marriage partners chosen by one's parents in consultation with respected, experienced go-betweens, have greater chance of success'.[106]

It is evident, then, that though the arranged marriage may have changed in form, it is still very much in existence, and furthermore still accounts for a large number of marriages. Figures are sometimes published, but these are notoriously unreliable due to the difficulty of classifying actual marriages as arranged or 'love'.[107] In subsequent chapters of this book the intention is to present in detail a description of marriage and family life in a particular community, indicating just how these institutions have changed during the period under consideration, and to offer some kind of an explanation of why changes have or have not taken place.

Notes

1. A discussion of the experiments and debates over education until policy was decided is to be found in Herbert Passin, *Society and Education in Japan*, (Columbia University, New York, 1965), pp. 62-99. and further detail about the introduction of schools in Keizō Shibusawa, *Japanese Life and Culture in the Meiji Era*, (trans. and adapted by Charles S. Terry (Obunsha, Tokyo, 1958), pp. 294-303.

2. An English translation appears in full in Passin, *Society and Education*, pp. 226-8.

3. Kizaemon Ariga, 'The Family in Japan', *Marriage and Family Living*, vol. 16 (1954), p. 362.

4. The first three are used fairly frequently, the last two were suggested by Harumi Befu, *Japan, an Anthropological Introduction* (Chandler, San Francisco, 1971), p. 38, and Chōshū Takeda, 'Ancestor Worship', *Proceedings of the 8th International Congress of Anthropological and Ethnographical Sciences*, Vol. 3 (1968), p. 124.

5. Tadashi Fukutake, *Japanese Rural Society*, trans. R.P. Dore (Cornell University Press, London, 1972), p. 40.

6. Lafcadio Hearn, *Japan: an Attempt at Interpretation* (Macmillan, New York, 1924), p. 67.

7. In Meiji law it became necessary to register property as legally belonging to the head of the *ie* as an individual.

8. According to Nobushige Hozumi, *Ancestor Worship and Japanese Law* (Maruzen, Tokyo, 1913), p. 138, younger sons could not lawfully contract marriage before Meiji since they had no chance of becoming head of the household. They were thus expected to remain single members of the *ie*, but he adds that although *samurai* families observed the rule, others would usually allow their younger sons to set up new households. This would solve the problem since a man could marry if he expected to be head of a household (cf. Thomas C. Smith, *Nakahara* (Stanford University Press, Stanford, 1977), p. 105). *Samurai* influence in some parts of the country led to the exclusion of younger sons from the youth organisations which helped to arrange marriages (Richard E. Varner, 'The Organised Peasant', *Monumenta Nipponica*, vol. 32 (1977), p. 467).

9. References to the Meiji Civil Code indicate consultation of the 1934 translation by W.J. Sebald of the 1898 Code.

10. Takashi Maeda, *Summary of Ane Katoku* (Kansai University Press, Osaka, 1976); Michio Suenari, 'First Child Inheritance in Japan', *Ethnology*, vol. 11 (1972), pp. 122-6; Donald Philippi, *Kojiki* (trans., University of Tokyo Press, Tokyo, 1969), p. 184; Kanji Naito, 'Inheritance Patterns on a Catholic Island', *Social Compass*, vol. 17 (1970), pp. 21-36; Seiichi Izumi and Nobuhiro Nagashima, 'Katoku Sōzoku kara mita Nihon no Higashi to Nishi' ('East and West Japan and the Succession System'), *Kokubungaku Kaishaku to Kanshō*, vol. 28, no. 5 (1963), pp. 121-6.

11. There is no word in Japanese to correspond exactly to the Western concept of 'love', with its Christian connotations, a point which is discussed in more detail in Chapter 4, where the two most common words used to translate love, *aijō* and *ren'ai*, are analysed. *Ren'ai* is used particularly to characterise the 'love match' of recent times, but the meanings and connotations of both words were undergoing such changes during the period considered here that usage will be confined to the references of commentators.

12. Takeyoshi Kawashima, *Kekkon (Marriage)*, (Iwanami Shoten, Tokyo, 1954), p. 101; Tarō Nakayama, *Nihon Kon'in Shi (A History of Marriage in Japan)* (Shunyō-dō, Tokyo, 1928), p. 906; Jirō Kamishima, *Nihonjin no Kekkonkan*

(*The Japanese View of Marriage*) (Chikuma Sôsho, Tokyo, 1969), pp. 81-2.

13. Daigoro Goh, 'Family Relations in Japan', *Transactions and Proceedings of the Japan Society*, vol. 2 (1895), p. 133.

14. Kurt Steiner, 'Revisions of the Civil Code of Japan', *Far Eastern Quarterly*, vol. 9, no. 2 (1950), p. 178.

15. Basil Hall Chamberlain, *Things Japanese*, 4th edn (John Murray, London, 1902), p. 309.

16. According to Kunio Yanagida, *Japanese Manners and Customs in the Meiji Era*, trans. and adapted by Charles S. Terry (Obunsha, Tokyo, 1957), p. 174, this word was originally *me-ai* ('meeting the bride'), a name of the principal marriage ceremony.

17. Ariga, *The Family*, p. 366.

18. Douglas Sladen and Norma Lorimer, *More Queer Things About Japan* (Anthony Treherne, London, 1904), p. 384.

19. Itsue Takamure, *Nihon Kon'in Shi (A History of Marriage in Japan)* (Nihon Rekishi Shinsho, Tokyo, 1963), p. 230; Naomi Tamura, *The Japanese Bride* (Harper and Bros., New York and London, 1904), p. 6; Jukichi Inouye, *Home Life in Tokyo* (Tokyo, 1910), p. 195.

20. William Erskine, *Japanese Customs* (Kyo Bun Kwan, Tokyo, 1925), p. 131.

21. Hozumi, *Ancestor Worship*, pp. 129-31.

22. Goh, 'Family Relations in Japan', p. 126; Tamura, *The Japanese Bride*, pp. 7-8.

23. Alice M. Bacon, *Japanese Girls and Women* (Gay and Bird, London, 1891), p. 57; cf. Inouye, *Home Life in Tokyo*, pp. 176-7.

24. Goh, 'Family Relations in Japan', p. 139.

25. Tsutomu Ema, *Kekkon no Rekishi (History of Marriage)* (Yûzan-kaku, Tokyo, 1971), p. 24; Nakayama, *Nihon Kon'in Shi*, p. 550; G.B. Sansom, *Japan: a Short Cultural History* (revised, The Cresset Press, London, 1952), p. 462. Before the Meiji Restoration, it was necessary for people desiring marriage to petition for permission. In the case of princes or court nobles they had to apply to the Emperor himself, feudal lords had to apply to the *shogun*, and *samurai* to their respective overlords (L.W. Küchler, 'Marriage in Japan', *Transactions of the Asiatic Society of Japan*, vol. 13 (1885), p. 116).

26. William Erskine, *Japanese Festivals and Calendar Lore* (Kyo Bun Kwan, Tokyo, 1933), pp. 181-2.

27. Hiroshi Fujisaki, *Kankonsôsai Jiten (Dictionary of Ceremonial)* (Tsuru Shobo, Tokyo, 1957), pp. 32-41; some of these details are reproduced in the appendix of this book.

28. C. Pfoundes, 'On Some Rites and Customs of Old Japan', *Journal of the Anthropological Institute*, vol. 12 (1882), p. 223.

29. Ernest Clement, 'Calendar (Japanese)' in James Hastings (ed.), *Encyclopaedia of Religion and Ethics* (Edinburgh, 1910), vol. 3, p. 115; Erskine, *Japanese Festivals*, p. 132. It is interesting that it has apparently become fashionable for couples on their honeymoons to visit this shrine at Izumo, although the young people concerned may laugh off their actions as superstition. The two couples of my acquaintance who held perhaps the most Westernised weddings I heard about, in Tokyo and Hiroshima, made Izumo the chief destination of their honeymoon journeys.

30. Ruth Benedict, *The Chrysanthemum and the Sword* (Secker and Warburg, London, 1947), p. 184.

31. Tamura, *The Japanese Bride*, p. 3.

32. Fukutake, *Japanese Rural Society*, p. 44.

33. Kawashima, *Kekkon*, pp. 143, 163-70; R.P. Dore, *City Life in Japan*

(University of California Press, Berkeley, Los Angeles and London, 1971), pp. 158-60.

34. This is a quotation of Francois Caron, reprinted in Bernard S. Silberman (ed.), *Japanese Character and Culture* (University of Arizona Press, Tucson, 1962), pp. 282-3.

35. Kawashima, *Kekkon*, pp. 166-7; Zenotsuke Nakagawa, 'A Century of Marriage Law', *Japan Quarterly*, vol. 10, no. 2 (1963), p. 185; Sōkichi Tsuda, *An Inquiry into the Japanese Mind as Mirrored in Literature* trans. Fukumatsu Matsuda (Japan Society for the Promotion of Science, Tokyo, 1970), p. 185. The status value of concubines was described by Chinese writers of third-century Japan. According to an extract quoted by Sansom, *Japan*, p. 30, four or five wives indicated a man of high rank, two or three one of lesser importance.

36. Ryōsuke Ishii, *Japanese Legislation in the Meiji Era*, trans. and adapted by William J. Chambliss (Pan-Pacific Press, Tokyo, 1958), pp. 666-7.

37. Ibid.; Tsuda, *An Inquiry into the Japanese Mind*, p. 186; T. Yokoyama, personal communication. In the Heian period, from the tenth to the twelfth centuries AD, marriage was uxorilocal so that a man moved into his wife's house. It may have been the case that a practice closer to polygamy existed at that time, since one man could divide his time between two or three different houses (Ivan Morris, 'Marriage in the World of Genji', *Asia*, vol. 11 (1968), pp. 54-77; William H. McCullough, 'Japanese Marital Institutions in the Heian Period', *Harvard Journal of Asian Studies*, vol. 27, (1967), pp. 103-67).

38. I.L. Bishop, *Unbeaten Tracks in Japan* (John Murray, London, 1900), p. 210.

39. Chamberlain, *Things Japanese*, p. 311; S.F. Hartley, 'The Decline of Illegitimacy in Japan', *Social Problems*, vol. 18 (1970), pp. 79-81; R.P. Dore, 'Japanese Rural Fertility', *Population Studies*, vol. 7 (1953), p. 69; Kawashima, *Kekkon*, p. 175.

40. Kamishima, *Nihonjin no Kekkonkan*, pp. 53, 8-13, 49; cf. Tsuda, *An Inquiry into the Japanese Mind*, p. 208.

41. Ema, *Kekkon no Rekishi*, p. 12.

42. Bishop, *Unbeaten Tracks in Japan*, p. 216.

43. Ishii, *Japanese Legislation*, pp. 670-1.

44. Chamberlain, *Things Japanese*, p. 498; cf. Dore, *City Life*, p. 158; Nakayama, *Nihon Kon'in Shi*, pp. 884-8; Küchler, 'Marriage in Japan', pp. 125-7. The ensuing quotations are taken from Chamberlain, pp. 498-505. The Japanese original is reproduced, with *furigana* (phonetic script alongside the Chinese characters), in Itsuo Emori (ed.), *Nihon no Kon'in (Japanese Marriage)* (Gendai no Esupuri No. 104, Tokyo, 1976), pp. 124-7.

45. Sladen and Lorimer, *More Queer Things about Japan*, pp. 331, 468, 483.

46. Fujiko Isono, 'The Family and Women in Japan', *The Sociological Review* (University of Keele), vol. 12, no. 1(1964), p. 42.

47. Shimei Futabatei, *An Adopted Husband*, trans. Buhachiro Mitsui and Gregg M. Sinclair (Greenwood Press, New York, 1969), p. 22.

48. Tsutomu Himeoka, 'Hōken Dōtoku ni arawareta Fūfu no jōge Kankei' ('Husband-Wife Vertical Relationship according to Feudal Morals'), *Shakaigaku Hyōron*, vol. 4, no. 3 (1954), pp. 2-3.

49. Goh, 'Family Relations in Japan', pp. 122, 154; Nakagawa, 'A Century of Marriage Law', p. 183.

50. Ema, *Kekkon no Rekishi*, p. 14; Philippi, *Kojiki*, pp. 51-2.

51. This discussion of divorce is based on the following works in particular: Goh, 'Family Relations in Japan', p. 149, Hozumi, *Ancestor Worship and Japanese Law*, p. 144, Küchler, 'Marriage in Japan', pp. 130-1, Nakagawa, 'A Century of Marriage Law', pp. 184-9, and Yozo Watanabe, 'The Family and the Law' in

A.T. von Mehren (ed.), *Law in Japan* (Harvard University Press, Cambridge, Mass., 1963), pp. 365-7. In the Heian period, divorce was simply a cessation of relations and apparently no legal papers were required (McCullogh, 'Japanese Marital Institutions', p. 139, Morris, 'Marriage in the World of Genji', pp. 73-4).

52. Mock Jōya, *Japanese Customs and Manners* (The Sakurai Shoten, Tokyo, 1955), p. 183.

53. Chamberlain, *Things Japanese*, p. 312; cf. Tsuda, *An Inquiry into the Japanese Mind*, p. 197; Inouye, *Home Life in Tokyo*, p. 208.

54. Dore, 'Japanese Rural Fertility', p. 73; Toshio Fueto, 'The Discrepancy Between Marriage Laws and Mores in Japan', *American Journal of Comparative Law*, vol. 5 (1956), p. 257; Takeyoshi Kawashima and Kurt Steiner, 'Modernisation and Divorce Rate Trends in Japan', *Economic Development and Cultural Change*, vol. 9, no. 1 (1960), p. 219.

55. As Dore has put it, 'the go-between, assisted by various relatives and friends of both families, would work with quasi-judicial formality' (Ronald Dore, *Shinohata* (Allen Lane, London, 1978), p. 165; cf. *City Life*, p. 183).

56. Dore, *City Life*, p. 182.

57. Takamure, *Nihon Kon'in Shi*, pp. 251-2; Ishii, *Japanese Legislation*, p. 661; Dore, *City Life*, p. 92.

58. John Caiger, 'The Aims and Content of School Courses in Japanese History 1872-1945' in Edmund Skrzypczak (ed.), *Japan's Modern Century* (Sophia University and Tuttle, Tokyo, 1968), pp. 60-1.

59. Ibid., p. 77.

60. Kamishima, *Nihonjin no Kekkonkan*, pp. 81-2; Yanagida, *Japanese Manners and Customs*, pp. 166-7; Kizaemon Ariga, *Nihon Kon'in Shiron (A Study of the History of Marriage in Japan)* (Nikko Shoin, Tokyo, 1948), p. 23.

61. Kamishima, *Nihonjin no Kekkonkan*, pp. 83-4; cf. Yanagida, *Japanese Manners and Customs*, p. 168. The function of Youth Groups with regard to marriage is also discussed in a number of other places, among them Ariga, *Nihon Kon'in Shiron*, pp. 5-201; Kamishima, pp. 82-3, 144; Yanagida, *Japanese Manners and Customs*, pp. 165-6, 217-42; Edward Norbeck, 'Age-Grading in Japan', *American Anthropologist*, vol. 55 (1953), pp. 376-9; Tokuzō Omachi, 'Kon'in' ('Marriage'), 'Seinenshiki' ('Coming of Age') and 'Konrei' ('Marriage Ceremony') in T. Omachi *et al.* (eds.), *Nihon Minzokugaku Taikei (An Outline of Japanese Folklore)* (Heibonsha, Tokyo, 1962), vol. 3, pp. 197-9, and vol. 4, pp. 235-9 and pp. 268-73; and Varner, 'The Organized Peasant', pp. 478-80.

62. Yanagida, *Japanese Manners and Customs*, p. 182. Much of this paragraph is based on Yanagida's work, for example, ibid., pp. 118-19, 161, 165, 242-5.

63. Sladen and Lorimer, *More Queer Things about Japan*, p. 27.

64. Bishop, *Unbeaten Tracks in Japan*, p. 213; J.M. Dixon, 'Japanese Etiquette', *Transactions of the Asiatic Society of Japan*, vol. 13 (1885), p. 13.

65. Hiroshi Wagatsuma and George Devos, 'Attitudes toward Arranged Marriage in Rural Japan', *Human Organization*, vol. 21 (1962), p. 187.

66. Ariga, *Nihon Kon'in Shiron*, p. 5; cf. Yanagida, *Japanese Manners and Customs*, pp. 164-6; Dore, *Shinohata*, p. 166; Itsuo Emori, 'Yobai to Tsumadoi' in Emori (ed.), *Nihon no Kon'in*, pp. 68-9. According to scholars, the use of the word in ancient literature referred to an exchange of names, from *yobu* which means 'to call (a name)', when a man would give his name to a girl as a proposal, and, if the girl agreed, she would give her name. This would lead to visiting, sometimes referred to by the same word, *yobai*, although it seems that the practice is closely associated with a type of marriage known as *tsumadoi-kon* (wife-visiting marriage), and the line dividing the two is thin (Emori, 'Yobai to Tsumadoi', pp. 68-79; Takamure, *Nihon Kon'in Shi*, pp. 43-4; Ariga, *Nihon*

Kon'in Shiron, p. 5). Yanagida refers to a noun *yobau*, with the meaning 'continuous call', as the origin of the word, however (Kunio Yanagida, *Kon'in no Hanashi (On Marriage)* (Iwanami Shoten, Tokyo, 1948), p. 71; *Japanese Manners and Customs*, p. 164). In both cases the word refers to a proposal, but it can also be used for subsequent visiting, hence the recent folk etymology of 'night-creep'. The *yobai* in recent times will be discussed again in Chapter 4.

67. Isono, 'Family and Women in Japan', p. 41.

68. Yasu Iwasaki, 'Divorce in Japan', *American Journal of Sociology*, vol. 36 (1930), p. 444; Kawashima, *Kekkon*, p. 173; cf. Dore, *City Life*, p. 158.

69. Takamure, *Nihon Kon'in Shi*, p. 230; Chamberlain, *Things Japanese*, p. 312.

70. Chamberlain, *Things Japanese*, p. 222.

71. Tamura, *The Japanese Bride*, pp. 11, 13; Kawashima, *Kekkon*, p. 11, 12, 16; cf. Dore, *City Life*, p. 159. Segregation of the sexes for reasons of pollution was common in many parts of Japan before this period of dissemination of new ideas (Toshiaki Harada, 'Nyonin Kinsei' ('Prohibitions on Women'), *Shakai to Denshō*, vol. 2, no. 4 (1958), pp. 162-71.

72. Kawashima, *Kekkon*, p. 14-15.

73. Kamishima, *Nihonjin no Kekkonkan*, p. 84.

74. Sladen and Lorimer, *More Queer Things about Japan*, pp. 329-30.

75. Ibid., pp. 431-2.

76. Iwasaki, 'Why the Divorce Rate has Declined in Japan', *American Journal of Sociology*, vol. 36 (1931), p. 581; Bishop *Unbeaten Tracks in Japan*, p. 213; Bacon, *Japanese Girls and Women*, p. 57; Dore, 'Japanese Rural Fertility', p. 64; R.E. Baber, *Youth Looks at Marriage and the Family* (International Christian University, Tokyo, 1958), pp. 45-6.

77. Iwasaki, 'Divorce in Japan', p. 445; 'Divorce Rate Decline', pp. 580-3; cf. Dore, *City Life*, p. 182; Kawashima, *Kekkon*, p. 107-8.

78. Iwasaki, 'Divorce in Japan', pp. 444-5; Dore, *City Life*, p. 161; Kamishima, *Nihonjin no Kekkonkan*, pp. 91-2.

79. Kamishima, *Nihonjin no Kekkonkan*, pp. 15 and 201-9, where he quotes from female writer Haruko Hatoyama and a male commentator Giichi Masuda; Takamure, *Nihon Kon'in Shi*, p. 255.

80. Iwasaki, 'Divorce Rate Decline', p. 569.

81. Kamishima, *Nihonjin no Kekkonkan*, pp. 88-9.

82. In this section I am indebted in particular to Watanabe, 'The Family and the Law', Nakagawa, 'A Century of Marriage Law', and Steiner, 'Revisions of the Civil Code' for their analyses of the post-war legal changes.

83. John Caiger, 'Ienaga Saburo and the First Post-War Japanese History Textbook', *Modern Asian Studies*, vol. 3, no. 1 (1969), p. 11. This paragraph is based on this work by Caiger (pp. 4-11), as well as on Robert J. Smith, *Ancestor Worship in Contemporary Japan* (Stanford University Press, Stanford, 1974), p. 37; and H. Byron Earhart, *Japanese Religion: Unity and Diversity* (Dickenson, Belmont, California, 1969), p. 90.

84. Baber, *Youth Looks at Marriage*, pp. 16-7; Takashi Koyama, *The Changing Social Position of Women in Japan* (Unesco, Paris, 1961), pp. 26-32.

85. Kawashima, *Kekkon*, p. 180; Koyama, *Social Position of Women*, pp. 49-50; Nakagawa, 'A Century of Marriage Law', p. 191; *Japan Statistical Yearbook* (Bureau of Statistics, Tokyo, 1977), pp. 36-7.

86. Kawashima, *Kekkon*, pp. 181, 188.

87. Koyama, *Social Position of Women*, pp. 111-16, 125-9; Chiye Sano, *Changing Values of the Japanese Family* (The Catholic University of America Press, Washington, DC, 1958), p. 103.

88. Helmut Morsbach, 'Aspects of Japanese Marriage' in Marie Corbin (ed.),

The Couple (Penguin Books, Harmondsworth, 1978), p. 98.

89. Thomas P. Rohlen, *For Harmony and Strength* (University of California Press, Berkeley, Los Angeles and London, 1974), p. 242.

90. Tadashi Fukutake, *Japanese Society Today* (University of Tokyo Press, Tokyo, 1974), p. 34.

91. Baber, 'Youth Looks at Marriage', p. 90; Watanabe, 'The Family and the Law', p. 386; Dore, 'Japanese Rural Fertility', p. 72; Fueto, 'Laws and Mores', p. 258; E.C. Masuoka *et al.*, 'Role Conflicts in the Modern Japanese Family', *Social Forces*, vol. 41 (1962), p. 3; Gail Bernstein, 'Women in Rural Japan' in Joyce Lebra *et al.* (eds.), *Women in Changing Japan* (Westview Press, Boulder, Colorado, 1976), p. 49.

92. Y.S. Matsumoto, 'Notes on Primogeniture in Postwar Japan' in R. Smith and R. Beardsley (eds.), *Japanese Culture: its Development and Characteristics* (Viking Fund Publications in Anthropology No. 34, Wenner Gren Foundation, New York, 1962), pp. 67-8; Watanabe, 'The Family and the Law', p. 385; Fukutake, *Japanese Rural Society*, p. 55; Dore, *City Life*, p. 101; see also Chapter 3, p. 97 of this book.

93. Kiyomi Morioka, *Religion in Changing Japanese Society* (University of Tokyo Press, Tokyo, 1975), p. 103.

94. Ichiro Kawasaki, *Japan Unmasked* (Tuttle, Tokyo, 1969), p. 185.

95. Chie Nakane, *Kinship and Economic Organization in Rural Japan* (University of London, The Athlone Press, London, 1967), p. 154, fn 1. The etymology of *Kekkon* is to be found in the Japanese index.

96. These opinion polls and those referred to in the next few lines are reproduced and discussed in Koyama, *Social Position of Women*, pp. 41-3; Jean Stoetzel, *Without the Chrysanthemum and the Sword* (Columbia University Press, New York, 1955), pp. 182-4; and Kawashima, *Kekkon*, pp. 71-3, 120-1, 183-4; cf. Dore, *City Life*, pp. 163-4.

97. Kawashima, *Kekkon*, p. 8-17.

98. Baber, 'Youth Looks at Marriage', pp. 55-7. Dore reported a corresponding greater concern among parents to arrange the marriages of their daughters than those of their sons (*City Life*, pp. 139-40).

99. Sano, *Changing Values*, pp. 72, 76; cf. Dore, *City Life*, p. 141.

100. Theodore Brameld, *Japan: Culture, Education and Change in Two Communities* (Holt, Rinehart and Winston, New York, 1968), p. 58; Edward Norbeck, *Takashima* (University of Utah Press, Salt Lake City, 1954), p. 175; Robert J. Smith, 'Kurusu: A Japanese Agricultural Community' in J.B. Cornell and R.J. Smith (eds.), *Two Japanese Villages* (Greenwood Press, New York, 1969), p. 77.

101. George Devos, 'Social Values and Personal Attitudes in Primary Human Relations in Niiike' in R.K. Beardsley *et al.* (eds.), *Studies in Japanese Culture* (Centre for Japanese Studies, Ann Arbor, 1965), pp. 61-2; *Socialization for Achievement* (University of California Press, Berkeley, Los Angeles and London, 1973), pp. 18-9; Wagatsuma and Devos, 'Attitudes toward Arranged Marriage', p. 200.

102. Befu, *Anthropological Introduction*, p. 51; cf. Robert O. Blood, *Love Match and Arranged Marriage* (The Free Press, New York, 1967), p. 9.

103. Blood, *Love Match*, p. 6.

104. Isono, 'Family and Women in Japan', p. 53.

105. Fukutake, *Japanese Society Today*, p. 35.

106. Bernstein, 'Women in Rural Japan', p. 46.

107. Bob Horiguchi, 'Inside the Weeklies', *Japan Times Weekly*, vol. 17, no. 8, p. 4, for example, cf. Blood, *Love Match and Arranged Marriage*, p. 14. A detailed discussion of the difficulties of such classification is to be found in Chapter 4.

2 THE COMMUNITY

The unit chosen for a focus during research was a community which, like many others in rural Japan, has remained relatively self-contained for as long as there are records. After the household, it is without doubt the primary and most important social unit of its inhabitants. Many of the households are related to one another and two surnames account for nearly 80 per cent of them. The reasons for this phenomenon will emerge in subsequent chapters, but the continuity of relationships possible in such a community probably helps to account for the high degree of co-operation which will be the concern of this chapter. Residence in such a community involves a number of obligations, and a person marrying in must participate as a representative of a household, if not necessarily as an individual. For many village purposes, the household is the more important unit and an inquiry about the population of a village is frequently given as a number of households.[1] Groups of households are assigned certain responsibilities for certain periods and these will be discussed in this chapter. They have been classified as administrative and religious, but there is considerable overlap in these functions.[2] Groups joined on an individual basis are generally based on age and these form a separate section. The geographical, socio-economic and historical setting is described first to provide a framework for the detail of community activity which follows. It is not intended to include a comprehensive account of each topic mentioned, but to build a foundation for the theme to be developed in subsequent chapters, and to present a picture of the people with whom we are concerned.

Geographical Location

Topographical Features

This study took place in Kyūshū, the most southerly of Japan's four main islands, in a village called Kurotsuchi. Like the rest of Japan, much of Kyūshū is mountainous, but Kurotsuchi lies on the edge of the most extensive area of low relief on the island. The area is known as Tsukushi, and the plain of this name is surrounded by mountains and hill lands in the north and east, and itself surrounds the Ariake Sea, which is enclosed to the north and west by the Nagasaki Peninsula

37

Map 1: A Relief Map of Kyūshū

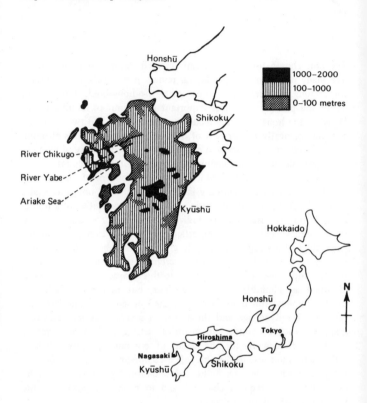

(see Map 1). Its occupation goes back to prehistoric times, and Kurotsuchi is not far from the site of one of the keyhole-type tomb mounds (*kofun*), which date back to the Tomb Period which started in about AD 250.[3] Evidence of the Jōri system of land subdivision, practised in the seventh and eighth centuries, is still to be seen in the rectangular pattern of canals and fields.[4] The Tsukushi Plain is drained by the Chikugo River, and, until the Meiji Restoration, the area of concern was known as Chikugo Province (Chikugo *no kuni*).

Kurotsuchi lies in the southern part of this plain, close to the head

Map 2: Kyūshū with Chief Cities and Prefectures

of the valley of the smaller Yabe River, at a point where the flat alluvial paddy land begins to give way to foothills. The vista is one of rice fields, divided by a network of paths and small canals, and here and there a village stands out like an island, especially when the land is flooded after transplanting. From a vantage point a few hundred yards into the hills, a town can be seen only two or three kilometres away to the west, but in every other direction, mountains obscure a clear view. The local residents are proud of their situation. The land is fertile, with plenty of water and good drainage, and the mountains afford protection from the typhoons which cause such havoc elsewhere in southern Japan.

Climate

The climate of this region is classified with the rest of central and south-western Japan as humid subtropical.[5] Summers are hot with the average temperature for August, the warmest month, being between 75 and 81 degrees Fahrenheit, accompanied by a high level of humidity. Winters are relatively mild with average temperatures in the low 40s. Snow falls occasionally, but it usually lies for no more than a few hours, and a winter wheat crop is possible in this area.

There are two peak periods of rainfall. The first, in June, brings some 30 cm. of precipitation over a period of one month, and coincides with rice transplanting. The second, in September, characterised also by high winds, is sometimes known as the 'typhoon season', and precipitation for the month is in the region of 20 cm. Least rain falls between the months of November and February.

Appearance and Facilities

The village of Kurotsuchi itself is laid out around a T-shaped tarmac thoroughfare. A cluster of wooden houses forms the residential nucleus, and large greenhouses trail away into the rice paddies which surround the village and separate it from other similar villages. The houses are quite close together, but plots of vegetables, seed-beds and an occasional greenhouse are frequently to be seen tucked in between the buildings, giving even the residential section a distinctly agricultural air. One or two houses still have the thatched roof which is said to have characterised the village ten years before the study, but most now sport the new blue tiles which reflect the recent prosperity of the whole nation. The main road has a tarmac surface, but grassy paths still lead between some houses to other houses, and a network of irrigation streams criss-crosses the whole village. Some of the houses have a tidy cultivated frontage, others a bare yard — Japanese gardens are very picturesque, but they are usually hidden from the view of the passer-by. The general atmosphere is pleasant, however, and since only a few cars pass through the village, it is quite quiet and peaceful.

The geographical centre of the village, at the T-junction (see Map 5 on p. 60) is also something of a social centre. Here is situated the village shop, which is styled 'the tobacconist's', though it is a well-equipped general store. It is a household concern, and remains open daily until 10 or 11 p.m., with the single exception of New Year's Day, and it forms part of the ground floor of the family's home. Opposite the shop is the village hall, which houses some communal equipment, and is available for meetings, classes, displays and social gatherings. Next to the hall is the bath-house, which is open every evening from 5 p.m., and since members of some 60 per cent of the 54 houses make use of its facilities daily, it is the scene of much activity from that time. There are two large baths, one for men and one for women, arranged either side of a wall which also separates the changing-rooms.

The usual procedure is to soak first for a few minutes in the hot water, often enjoying a chat with others doing the same, then to get out and wash thoroughly with soap at the side, rinse off with bowls of water, and finally to return to the bath for another long soak before drying oneself with a squeezed-out hot flannel. The bath-house is thus a good centre for the exchange of news and gossip, so that some families with bathrooms of their own prefer to make use of the more sociable village facility. The baths are run entirely by the co-operative efforts of the households which use them.

Also within a few steps of the T-junction is a hut which contains the village fire-fighting equipment, chiefly a rather antiquated pump, which is brought out for testing about once a month. There is also a look-out tower for locating the site of fires nearby. Opposite this tower is the fishmonger's, a newer shop than the general store, run by the younger wife of a family of carpenters in the village. The only other shop, which provides a rice-polishing service, is also run by a housewife, and is situated a few steps to the east of the T-junction. A group of women can often be seen chatting outside this building.

Further away to the east of the village is the spiritual heart of Kurotsuchi, the *miya* or village shrine, an impressive wooden construction set in a compound surrounded by a wall. There is a large arch at the entrance (*torii*), and a line of carved stone lanterns and guardian animals adorns either side of the walk up to the building. To one side, but still within the compound, a collection of swings and a slide have been erected for the use of the children, and mothers' remarks suggest that this is regarded as an especially safe place to play. This shrine is the place of worship of the guardian deity of the village who will be discussed later in the chapter.

Another small shrine in the west of the village is concealed from passers-by because it is situated behind two houses, and can only be approached by a narrow path which runs between them. A smaller arch marks entry to the sacred area, which is mostly bare space, with a raised dais at one side and a small stone shrine under a tree at the other. This shrine is dedicated to the deity of thunder and lightning (*kaminarisan*, or, more affectionately, the onomatopoeic *gorogorosan*), but on this site used to stand a huge camphor tree, which it is said required seven people standing with outstretched arms to encircle its trunk. The tree had been attributed divine properties, but, some fifty years previously, it was blown down during a severe thunderstorm. Two years before that, a house had been burned down by lightning and an old lady killed, so the villagers decided to build the new shrine and hold a festival there every year in the hope that no further accidents would occur. It is the only shrine in the district dedicated to this deity, and the village baseball team in 1975 had chosen the name 'The Flashers', inspired by this connection. By 1979, however, this team had been superseded by another called simply 'Kurotsuchi'. There could be no idea that the deity was offended to be associated with sport, however, since the site had in 1979 been floodlit for village volley-ball tournaments and was also used for the old people's 'gate-ball', a game resembling croquet. A new tree, also attributed divine properties, was planted to replace the old one and this has now reached quite a respectable size.

There is one more public place of worship in the village, and this comprises a collection of Buddhist images situated in a small compound away from the road. There is a gold-leaf image of the female bodhisattva, Kannon, locked into an altar set on a small raised dais, and stone images of 13 other Buddhas and bodhisattvas, in a fixed order, as well as a larger statue of Kōbō Daishi.[6] A similar collection of stone images appears in many villages in the area.

Administrative Units

The 'village'[7] of Kurotsuchi is now administratively one of 77 sections of the city (*shi*) of Yame, although by English standards the whole city rather resembles a provincial town surrounded by a large number of rural villages. The villages are within easy walking distance of their neighbours, however, and more sparsely populated rural areas in the region belong to the administrative unit of Yame County (*gun*), the whole area being part of Fukuoka prefecture. Yame City is still divided for some purposes into the eight previous administrative units which were amalgamated to form a city in 1954. These comprise the town of Fukushima in the centre and seven more rural areas, now known as 'school zones', since each has a separate primary school (see Map 3). Kurotsuchi is one of seven villages which make up the school zone known as Tadami.

Population

In the most recent census of 1975, Yame City, an area of 39.2 sq. km., had a population of 38,846 people living in 9,706 households. Of these, 9,050 resided in the 2,527 households of Fukushima, an area of 2.34 sq. km. Each of the other seven school zones covers a greater surface area, but comprises a smaller population, which illustrates the more rural nature of the outer zones. Tadami, which is an area of 6.2 sq. km., had a population of 3,454 people in 753 households; and Kurotsuchi, an area of 214,404 sq. m., including fields, 266 individuals residing in 54 households. Fukuoka prefecture had a total population of 4,292,994, and Yame County, which does not include the city, 62,395 in 14,548 households.

Table 1: Population of Yame City since 1920

1920	29,665 individuals	1950	40,651
1925	32,448	1955	42,220
1930	33,672	1960	41,195
1935	34,943	1965	39,312
1940	34,589	1970	38,848
1947	42,563	1975	38,846

Table 2: Population of Kurotsuchi and Tadami School Zone

Kurotsuchi	Households	Male	Female	Total
1965	53	134	147	281
1970	53	134	147	281
1975	54	124	142	266
Tadami				
1960	666	1,788	1,959	3,747
1965	690	1,683	1,828	3,511
1970	728	1,672	1,790	3,462
1975	753	1,665	1,789	3,454

Figures for the area now covered by Yame City have been calculated back to 1920, and these are shown in Table 1. In accordance with national trends, they show a sharp increase after the Second World War, then decline somewhat. They remained almost constant between the census reports of 1970 and 1975, and local records suggest that they have increased again since then. Records for Kurotsuchi are available only for the last three census reports, and for Tadami school zone for the last four. These are shown in Table 2. The gradual decrease in the population of Tadami, combined with an increase in the number of households, probably illustrates a trend towards smaller families, which will be discussed in the next chapter.

Table 3: Population of Kurotsuchi by Sex and Age, May 1975

	Men	Women	Total
Over 80	1	4	5
70 - 79	7	10	17
60 - 69	10	12	22
50 - 59	16	16	32
40 - 49	15	22	37
30 - 39	16	11	27
20 - 29	20	19	39
10 - 19	20	22	42
0 - 9	21	22	43
Totals	126	138	264

Table 4: Household Size in Numbers of Members

Number of people in household		8	7	6	5	4	3	2	1	Total
Number of households	1975		9	9	20	7	5	1	2	53
	1979	1	8	8	17	7	9	2	1	53

Average size of household = 264/53 = 4.98 (1975); 257/53 = 4.85 (1979)

An analysis of the population of Kurotsuchi by sex and age at the time of study is given in Table 3. The apparent shortage of people between the ages of 30 and 40 illustrates a drop in the birth rate during the war years. Of the 264 permanent residents in 1975, 128 were married couples, 112 children and unmarried people under 30, 17 widows, 3 widowers, 1 a divorced man, and another man and woman were unmarried. By 1979, there were 257 permanent residents in 53 households, but four babies were due to be born in the near future, and a nuclear family expected soon to move in with their parents, so it had not greatly changed. The number of individuals seems to have diminished slightly over the years, but older villagers say that there has been little change in the number of houses since their childhood, though a few families have moved away; and others have taken over or reconstructed the vacant homes. The new families are usually related to older ones, and the vast majority of Kurotsuchi households have existed in the same place for generations. Thirty-one of them share one surname, though they say they are not necessarily related, and 10, who share another, can trace back their common ancestry. The nature of these relationships will be considered in more detail in the next chapter. Since the war, there is only one family which has moved into Kurotsuchi in its entirety, and that was because of personal problems in their previous home. They rent their property and do not yet take a full part in village activities.

The average number of people in one house is almost five, and it can be seen from Table 4 that no less than 20 houses had exactly this number in 1975.[8] More households were bigger than smaller than this, and members of houses with three or fewer occupants either had health or economic problems, or expected soon to increase their numbers, perhaps by marrying or having children. Some of the reasons for this phenomenon have their place in the following chapter, but it is advantageous in village life to have several people available to help discharge the obligations which fall upon the household as a unit, as will become clearer in the following pages.

Historical Affiliations

Historically, the village of Kurotsuchi has remained relatively constant as the primary community of its inhabitants throughout several changes in its outside allegiances. The oldest reference in local literature seems to be a record of the construction of the village shrine in 1546.[9] At that time, the village belonged to Kawasaki Manor (*shō*).[10] This was ruled over by the Kawasaki family, with a castle situated on a hill to the east of Kurotsuchi in a school zone of the present city still known as Kawasaki (see Map 3). Nothing remains now of this castle, which was built according to local records in 1191,[11] but residents of the area know where it was situated, and refer to it as Dog's Tail Castle (*Inuojō*). They are aware that this was once the seat of higher secular powers, and many Kurotsuchi families are still connected with Kawasaki because this is the site of their Buddhist temple, and the resting place of the remains of their ancestors. The priest at this temple claims descent from the Kawasaki family, the present incumbent being the sixteenth generation since the temple was built in 1592.

The Kawasaki family, like those of many other local lords, was displaced as Toyotomi Hidetoshi brought the whole island under central control in 1587. For a short time an area called Kōzuma County, not much changed from Kawasaki Manor, was ruled by a Tanaka family, based in a castle in Fukushima, which was built in 1601.[12] In 1621, however, this area was incorporated into a wider unit ruled from Kurume by the Arima family, which was sent from Kyoto, and which remained in power throughout the Tokugawa period. The Arima Domain (*han*), together with the neighbouring Tachibana Domain, ruled by the family of that name from the city of Yanagawa, made up Chikugo Province.

During the Meiji Restoration, in 1889, Kurotsuchi became part of a rural unit centred on the neighbouring village of Tadami, owing higher allegiance to the newly created Fukuoka prefecture. This remained unchanged until the establishment of Yame City in 1954.

Communications

Kurotsuchi is today within easy access of the main arteries of communication which serve Kyūshū, and, indeed, the wider nation. Kurume, a city of 194,178 people, only 12 km. away, is the nearest truly urban area to Kurotsuchi, used for shopping, entertainment and some religious purposes. The prefectural capital, Fukuoka City, with a population of 871,717 people, is about 50 km. distant, but there are good road and rail connections from Yame. Kurotsuchi is but ten minutes, by car, from the Kyūshū Expressway, which runs from Fukuoka City in the north to Kumamoto City in the south, and it is even closer to the main national route 3, which provides access to the rest of Kyūshū. It is thus possible to make day-return journeys to several large cities. Most households in Kurotsuchi have one or more motor vehicles, but there is also a good bus service to Fukushima or Kurume, and thence to other places if necessary, which passes at regular intervals within a few minutes' walk of the village.

The main Kagoshima railway line, which runs the length of the island, can be reached by travelling to Kurume or Hainuzuka (in Chikugo City) by bus, or by taking a local train on the Yabe branch line. This runs from Hainuzuka up into the mountains to Kurogi, and has a station a few minutes walk from Kurotsuchi, though services are rather infrequent. There is also an efficient private railway service from Kurume to Fukuoka in the north, or to Yanagawa in the southwest. Fukuoka is linked to Tokyo and other parts of Japan by the *shinkansen*, the high-speed 'bullet train', which covers the thousand kilometres to the capital in 6 hours and 56 minutes. Fukuoka also has an international airport.

Map 3: Yame City with School Zones

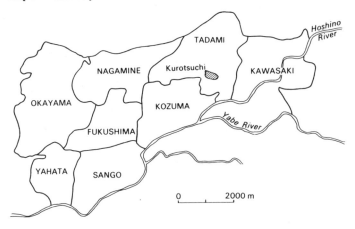

Economic Activity

Types of Employment

The Tsukushi Plain, in which Kurotsuchi is situated, has been described as 'lush', with rice yields among the highest in the nation.[13] Figures from Yame City Hall confirmed that this part of the plain was no exception, production in 1978 being an average of 535 kilos per 1,000 sq. m., a unit for which 499 kilos was the national average crop. Double cropping is climatically possible in this region, but most farmers prefer to leave their land fallow during the winter, although a few do grow a wheat crop.

A majority of Kurotsuchi families grows rice, at least for their own consumption, and there is a distinct festive air in the village during the two or three days in June that it takes to put out the seedlings.[14] Completion of the task is celebrated with a river festival, and even non-farming households participate. Nowadays, transplanting, as well as harvesting, is done by machine, and much agricultural work has been eased in other ways by modern technology which includes the use of fertiliser, weed-killers and insecticide.

Some fifty years ago, many Kurotsuchi families used to make hand-made paper in the slack agricultural season.[15] This industry has also been gradually mechanised over the years, so that now only

Map 4: Section of Kyūshū with Communications

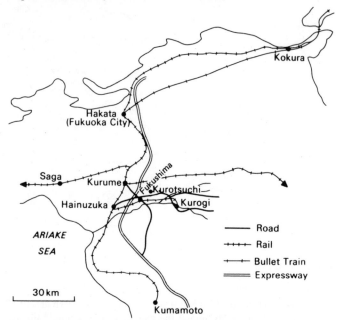

one household continues the old trade, but paper factories which have opened in the area have provided some outside employment. Other new supplementary occupations have involved the commercial production of vegetables and, in particular, greenhouses were built for the cultivation of tomatoes. About twenty years ago, some local people began experimenting with chrysanthemum plants in these greenhouses, and now cultivation of this luxury crop has brought a good deal of prosperity to many families in the area.

Each greenhouse is approximately 330 sq. m. in area, with a capacity for some 15,000 plants. They are mere frames in the summer, but are protected in the winter with a vinyl covering, which is put on after the 'typhoon season' is over. These houses have heaters and fans to keep them at a thermostatically controlled temperature of 15 to 20 degrees C. throughout the winter. They are also equipped with electric lights, which are kept on until midnight in September to produce a late crop from summer seedlings in time for the profitable New Year market. At this time, the flowers from Yame travel to shops in Tokyo and Osaka. According to details available in the City Hall, Tadami school zone is responsible for more than 55 per cent of Yame's chrysanthemum crop, of which Kurotsuchi alone produces 10 per cent, also having the greatest average area per household devoted to chrysanthemums in the city.

There is a good deal of skill involved in bringing these flowers to maximum beauty for the best market, since prices can halve or double in the space of a week, and some young people mentioned this challenge as part of the attraction involved in their cultivation. The cultivators are mainly young people, and this occupation has apparently provided an incentive in this area for sons to remain in the family home and pursue, as did their forbears, the cultivation of the land. In some households, the rice production is supervised by the older man, and the chrysanthemum or other newer venture by the inheriting son. In neighbouring villages other flowers such as roses and carnations are also being grown, and smaller greenhouses are sometimes constructed for the cultivation of strawberries.

Another relatively new source of income in this area, and again something of a challenge for young people, is the production of green tea. This has been grown in the mountainous regions of Yame county for many years, and a temple there claims to have on its premises the oldest tree in the land, brought from China 700 years ago. In 1967, a group of farmers in the Tadami school zone decided to invest in opening up a hill behind the villages, and this has been engineered into a massive area of tea fields known as the *pairotto*, from the English word 'pilot'. The first tea trees were planted in 1971, and as they began to produce, a factory was built to provide the drying process on the spot. By 1975, many trees were giving a full four crops a year, and a steady and lucrative source of income to those people who had had the foresight to invest in the project. Other mountain produce which is cultivated includes mandarin oranges, plums, peaches and grapes.

Apart from paper, manufactured goods associated with Yame are lanterns, both of volcanic rock for outdoor use and of bamboo and paper for funerals and festivals, other bamboo articles, Buddhist household altars (*butsudan*), *sake*, fireworks and wax. There is also some lumbering industry in the area. In Tadami, some work for local people is provided by a cement works, a cloth factory and three paper factories. It is also possible for residents of this area to commute to Kurume, and even to Fukuoka, for work, and there are many opportunities in Fukushima. Many younger sons, who are unable or unwilling to stay in the household, go off to cities as far afield as Tokyo, Osaka and Nagoya, and arrangements are sometimes made through a relative or a friend already living in the city concerned.

Actual Occupations

Kurotsuchi has the air of an agricultural community and a journalist who visited it during the period of study was given by residents a rough estimate of 80 per cent as the number of families involved in agricultural work. Most households take part in festivals associated with the agricultural cycle, but, in fact, only 50 per cent of the houses are full-time farmers in that all the permanent members are involved in farming. Most of these houses grow chrysanthemums, but four of them supplement their income with non-agricultural pursuits including bamboo work, part-time business ventures and, in the case already mentioned, paper-making.[16]

There are another eight households whose members do some farming, but in which at least one permanent member has a different full-time occupation. For example, in one case, the chief breadwinner runs a paper-marketing business together with his son, whom he is training to succeed him, and his brother, who has formed a new household and lives across the road. The wives do the farming. Another household has a crippled man who is trained to do electrical maintenance and repair, which he does while his wife and mother do most of the farming, aided occasionally by his brother, who takes a holiday from his work elsewhere to help with the rice harvest. Sometimes it is the older generation which does the farming while the inheriting son goes out to work elsewhere, and hope is expressed in such cases that the son's wife will show an interest in agriculture. Most of these part-time farmers cultivate their own rice and sometimes vegetables too, turning at busy times for extra help to members who have other occupations.

Several men go out from the village to work in factories, and, of these, no less than six are employed making paper, so it can be seen that the old skill has not been entirely forgotten. Four families in the village have carpenters among them, and three of these are descendants of one man who came to Kurotsuchi in the early part of this century, the fourth being the trainee of one of the others. Two of these now have facilities for apprentices and this provides an occupational possibility for Kurotsuchi school-leavers. Five Kurotsuchi men are employed as drivers, one family has a honey business, and another runs the village shop. Most wives who are not involved in a family concern have some other source of income. Several work in a local weaving factory,

Table 5: Occupations of Members of Kurotsuchi Not Exclusively Engaged in Farming

House Number	eH	eW	H	W	yH	yW	S	S	S	D	D
2			F	F			K	K	C		
3	R	R			Dr	K	Dr				
4											
6			F	F						Y	
6A			F/Z	F/Z			C			K	
7	N	N			K	Y					
8			Dr	We							
9		—				F	K			K	
13		F			Z/E	F	K				
13A			Dr	Y							
16	PK	—			K	K					
18			PK	Sh/F			K				
22	F	F			F/P	F/P				F/P	
23		PK			PK	Y					
24			PK	Y						K	K
25			PK	F			K				
26		F			Dr	Y					
26A			Dr	Y							
27			PK	We							
28	R	F			C	Sh					
29			Sh	Sh			Sh			T	
31	—				B	F	F				
34		Ho/Y			Ho	Ho/Y					
35	F	F			F/B	F					
36	C	F			K	Y					
40A			C	—							
41			—	We			K				
42		—	PB	F			PB				
42A			PB	F/P							
47A							K				

KEY

H = husband	B = own business	N = home work
W = wife	C = carpentry	P = paper making
e = elder	Dr = driver	R = retired
y = younger	E = electrical work	Sh = shop
S = son (unmarried)	F = farming	T = teacher
D = daughter (")	Ho = honey production	We = weaver
	K = company employee	Y = sewing
		Z = bamboo work

S and D may be of any couple

e and y are used to qualify H and W in households with more than one generation of conjugal pairs but many take in sewing or other work that they can do in the home. This is often craft work such as doll- or lantern-making. The care of young childen is left to grandparents where possible, but these may also do part-time work. Girls between school-leaving age and marriage often spend some time studying, but they may also join in with household work or go out to a factory or office in Kurume or Fukushima. Some such girls go away to work in a city for a spell before they settle down.

Occupation as a Basis for Social Ranking

Most households maintain a standard of living above that which could be described as subsistence level, and many show definite signs of affluence. There is, for example, a large number of splendid new houses which have been built in the village in the last few years, and there had been a great turnover in motor vehicles between 1975 and 1979. In general, farming families are better off than the others, but this is not always the case, an exception being when a man has decided to pursue his education in preference to agricultural work. Many of the non-farming families changed their occupation because of some difficult situation in the past, but some are branches of older farming households who stayed in the village but took up some other occupation. Non-farming families are classified within the village according to their various occupations to some extent, but amongst farming families too, certain distinctions are made. All farming families own at least some of their land, usually all of it, and the majority of the work is done by family labour. Table 6 lists the area of farming land owned by each family in the village, and an indication is also made of the crops grown, since cash crops such as chrysanthemums require a much smaller area than others, and mountain land less labour than the paddy fields around the village. It can also be seen from this table that rented land is only a small amount of the total,[17] although there is no great stigma attached to tenancy. Some prestige is still accorded to the older farming families who have worked the same land for generations, especially where they have managed to maintain this property in good order. The phrase 'households with property' is sometimes heard in reference to such people, particularly by those whose assets are less. It can be seen from the table, however, that even families with most land have not a great area by international standards, the maximum holding, including mountain land, being only 24,000 sq. m. The property of one household is also likely to be scattered somewhat around the village, and the size of the fields is small. The 214,404 sq. m. of Kurotsuchi's own land is divided into no less than

Table 6: Land Ownership, Kurotsuchi, 1975 (non-residential)

	Land in *tan* $\cong$ 1,000 sq. m.			Crops Grown			
	Near Village		In Mountains		Chrysanth. and/or		Fruit (oranges
House	Owned	Rented		Rice	Tomato	Tea	and plums)
1	10			x	x		
2	5			x	x		
5	10			x	x		
6	8			x	x		
6A	2.5	+1.5		x			
9	1 + ?			x			
11	1.2			x			
12	2.2		7	x	x	x	
13	5			x			
14	9.5		13	x	x	x	
17	15	+0.6	5	x			x
18	2.4			x			
19	3.7		10	x	x	x	
20	15			x	x	x	x
21	10			x	x		
22	13	-3^a		x			
23	0.6	−0.6		x			
25	1.3			x			
26	2.5	−2.5					
28	2.5			x			
30	14			x	x		
31	4	+0.7	10	x	x	x	
32	6			x	x		
33	6.5			x	x		
35	8			x	x		
36	2			x			
37	10	−3	5	x	x	x	
37A	1	+3		x	x		
39	13		11	x	x	x	
40	2	+1		x	x		
42	3			x			
42A	1.6			x			
43	4		12	x	x	x	
44	14		3	x	x		x
45	10			x	x		
46	8	+2		x	x		
47	10		2.5	x		x	

These figures are approximate, since land records at the City Hall gave areas in square metres, whereas farmers frequently gave them in *tan*, and for convenience, the conversion 1 *tan* = 993 sq. m. was rounded off to 1,000 sq. m. in all conversions. This seems justifiable since the farmers also made frequent use of the same conversion figures, and areas in sq. m. were anyway taken to the nearest 100 sq. m. once they had been added up for a single owner.

Note: a. The minus sign indicates land rented out to someone else and therefore not being cultivated by the owner.

267 individual plots. Fifty-three of these plots are classified as residential, and they are usually owned by the families which live on them. These have not been included in the table. A few farmers own land over the boundaries into neighbouring villages, and the total area of farmland in the vicinity of the residential area is about 235,500 sq. m., which is accounted for by 37 owner-households.

Co-operation

There is little hiring of labour except at occasional busy periods such as the first tea harvest, which is picked by hand, or at peak times in the chrysanthemum cultivation cycle. Then some housewives may leave their usual employment to help another household and earn a little extra cash. In the past there was more exchange of labour, especially for rice transplanting, but machines have made it possible for each household to be almost self-sufficient. At harvest time, sons, daughters and siblings with other usual occupations may take time off to help, and sometimes more distant city relatives put in a few days' work at busy periods in exchange for a measure of rice for their own purposes. Some machines were shared at first, it is said, but most households can now afford their own, and in general, co-operation in agriculture operates at higher levels. The traditional example of this is the way whole villages must co-operate with one another at rice-transplanting time to ensure even distribution of water, so that dates for transplanting vary from village to village and all members of one village must work on the same days. This is arranged by the irrigation union which covers the whole Yame area as well as that of the neighbouring city of Chikugo. Members pay a subscription to finance the mechanics of the system which is operated by ten paid representatives of the various regions involved.

Otherwise, co-operation is now exemplified by the highly efficient and active national organisation known as the Agricultural Co-operative (*nōgyō kyōdō kumiai*).[18] This operates in all rural areas, and, indeed, affects the lives of more than just the farmers. It serves, for example, as the most frequently used bank for many individuals as well as for families and innumerable savings groups in the area. It has a local branch in Tadami, and a more central office in Fukushima. It also provides a city-wide broadcasting and telephone service to which most households in the rural areas subscribe. Once rent has been paid, this service includes free calls to anywhere in the network, broadcasts four times a day of national and local news as well as local events and features, and an emergency service which is used especially for directing fire auxiliaries to the scene of a disaster. The Co-operative also runs a shop at each branch office, is able to obtain wholesale supplies of goods required by farmers, and markets their produce through national channels.

There are subsidiary co-operatives for each speciality well represented in the area, and, at meetings of these, production figures are discussed, experiences pooled, and plans made for the future. Results are announced for production for each village, so if someone fails to prepare his produce properly, he brings shame on the whole community. These speciality co-operatives usually operate for a unit larger than the village since only those households involved in their production are included, but the general Agricultural Co-operative usually has a branch at village level. This is called a 'production union' (*seisan kumiai*) and everyone who grows rice and wheat belongs. The chief functions at this level are the ordering of equipment and fertiliser, and the advance estimation of quantities of goods to be sold through the union. Practical co-operative ventures such as crop-spraying are organised through even smaller divisions called 'practice unions' (*jikkōkumiai*).

A women's section (*fujinbu*) also exists at village level, and more housewives belong to this than there are farmers in the village. The main function of the organisation is to co-ordinate orders for domestic supplies through the Co-operative, but the profit made is enough to finance a celebration feast once a year when the officials are elected. There is also a savings bank run by this section for the exclusive use of women, so that the housewife can, if she so desires, keep her own savings apart from those of the household.

Marketing

Agricultural produce may be marketed through the Agricultural Co-operatives, but some growers prefer individually to seek the best open market for their wares. Chrysanthemum growers, for instance, travel to flower markets in Fukuoka, Kumamoto, Saseho, Kokura and Kurume, depending on the prices in those cities at any one time. This involves something of a gamble, of course, as prices vary from day to day, but members of Kurotsuchi co-operate with one another, so that several sellers can soon take advantage of news from one particular market. This co-operation is quite well organised, and a representative of the group involved is picked each year to perform certain tasks.

These markets are profit-making concerns and they employ an auctioneer to do the actual selling. The producers merely deposit their goods, and, at a fixed time, the auctioneer leads round a group of buyers who bargain for each lot separately. The buyers must belong to a union, and they must pay a monthly sum to be present at the sales as well as a large fee to become a member initially. They must also be sharp, for, here as elsewhere, the auctioneer is slick, and his speech consists almost entirely of the jargon of his trade. An assistant follows him round, making a note of the price at which each lot was sold, and the farmers are paid later. Usually they register themselves at the market so that they can pick up payment for a period at their own convenience rather than waiting for the outcome of each day's sales. The market retains a percentage. This is a system which involves a certain amount of trust, but the Kurotsuchi farmers said that they doubted there would be any malpractice, for the markets are anxious to maintain their supply.

Education

Even the older residents in Kurotsuchi attended school for the six years which were compulsory in pre-war days, and many attended for the full eight years offered by the local elementary school in Tadami. This school celebrated its centenary in 1976, and records of its graduates are available from 1910. They include almost every member of Kurotsuchi also included in the family records at the local registry office, which is consistent with the figure quoted in Chapter 1, that 98 per cent of the population was attending school by the first decade of this century. A few of the more able and better-off boys went on to the agricultural college in Fukushima, which was founded in 1909, but most of them joined the family work-force after elementary school. A number of the older women had also gone on after school to study dress-making or other domestic accomplishments, but, on the whole, children nowadays tend to stay at school longer than their parents did.

The present state school system is uniform throughout the country. It is comprehensive and coeducational, frequently described as a 6-3-3 arrangement, indicating that primary school involves six years of schooling, middle school three, and high school a further three. The vast majority of children enter at six and move up each year with the class, so this also corresponds usually to the number of years spent at school. However, only nine years are compulsory, and entry into high school is competitive, although a number of private schools provide three years of further education for pupils who fail to gain admission to state high schools.

In Yame there is one primary school for each of the previous administrative units, which are thus often referred to as school zones. Two such zones combine for middle schools, and Tadami graduates join those of the Kawasaki zone at Misaki Middle School, where this name — Misaki — is a combination of the second parts of the names of the primary schools. Choice of primary and middle school is thus determined by residence, but high schools are attended on the bases of merit and special interest. There are four state high schools of different academic standing, comprising two general, one agricultural and one commercial. In Yame-*shi* there is also a private girls' school which concentrates on cooking, sewing and other domestic accomplishments, and a privately owned general high school. There is a prestigious high school in Kurume with very competitive entry, and some Yame students commute there if they are able to gain a place. The nearest university is in Kurume too, but there are several more, both state and private, in Fukuoka City.[19]

Even in rural areas, Japanese children are encouraged in their studies, and Kurotsuchi is no exception. Family celebrations often accompany the progress of an individual child at his or her school, and many children are given their own desks for homework. Most children attend municipal nursery schools for two or three years before entering the primary school, and, after the compulsory period, all but one or two students enter one or other of the high schools. Many of the boys attend the agricultural college, and a few of the girls too. It divides its pupils by sex, and while the boys study topics such as agricultural machinery, the girls are given a grounding in domestic skills such as cooking and sewing. The agricultural college has a proportion of two to one, boys to girls, so it does not ignore the role played by women in farming, but most Kurotsuchi girls actually seem to attend the private girls' high school.

Those children who leave school on completion of compulsory attendance usually transfer to some kind of practical training and, typically, this is apprentice carpentry for boys and dressmaking for girls. Some students take up such practical training after high school, and girls especially often take further training of some sort. A few Kurotsuchi residents manage to enter the more academically orientated high schools, and then to move on to university or perhaps business school. These are usually boys. Girls in the Yame area who go on to higher education seem to choose the two-year colleges, and this apparently mirrors a national trait.[20]

In Yame there are also good facilities for adult education, especially since a central meeting hall (*chūōkōminkan*), which provides classrooms and demonstration facilities, was built in the mid-sixties. Many young women study the feminine arts of flower arrangement and tea ceremony in the years between school and marriage, but there is also a group called the 'youth university' (*seinen daigaku*) for members of both sexes of this age group to study together, once a week, many matters of general interest. The hall facilities are also used by village groups such as the Housewives' Association and the Youth Group, which also arrange classes in village halls if there is sufficient demand. During the period of study, instructors were engaged to come to Kurotsuchi to give regular classes in two different types of traditional singing and in the art of dressing in kimono.

Administration

Village Assembly

As residents of the city of Yame, members of Kurotsuchi have the right to vote in elections for the 24 seats on the city council, which sits in chambers in the City Hall in Fukushima. However, the area is not represented directly and it is only a tendency for people to support local candidates which provides councillors from most parts of the city. In general, the affairs of villages such as Kurotsuchi are settled internally, with a good deal of autonomy, and the village head is the chief means of liaison with the bureaucratic structure in the City Hall. Taxes and rates are paid through him for the village as a whole, and information from the City Hall is distributed through him to the villagers.

The head is elected, together with his committee of deputy, treasurer and three councillors, every other March by the village assembly (*chōnaikai*).[21] This comprises one representative of each household in the village, irrespective of size. Each household pays a fixed sum into village funds which are used to maintain public buildings such as the village hall and shrine, occasionally to purchase property such as the children's slides and swings, for the upkeep of village paths and streams, and to provide a small amount of remuneration for the officers, as well as for groups and individuals who carry out certain specific tasks. Sometimes a sum is also assigned to school improvements or to a national charity appeal.

The maintenance of village paths is a task undertaken once a year by a work-force comprising one member of each household. This lasts a morning or a little longer, and is quite a festive occasion. A household which fails to send a member is fined, and one which sends a woman where a man could be sent must pay a quarter of the same sum; for a woman, be she twice as fit as the grandfather sent from her neighbours' house, is counted as only three-quarters of his work value, and unless there is no man in the house to come, the difference must be made up in cash. The care of streams is carried out by groups of farmers who use the water and surrounding land, as is that of paths between fields and greenhouses used only by the owners.

Another task of the village head and his committee is to arbitrate in the case of quarrels in the community. Where possible these are resolved within the village, if necessary by calling a meeting of the whole assembly, and only one boundary dispute in living memory found its way to the City Hall and another family problem to the courts. Much co-operation is required from each household if village affairs are to run smoothly, and the ultimate sanction which can be applied is a form of ostracism, when relations with the offending household are virtually severed. This is a rare occurrence, however, and no one could remember a case in Kurotsuchi, though a man in the neighbouring village of Inobu described vividly how, as a child, he had had to walk alone to school each day when the punishment was applied to his family.

Elected committee members of the village assembly are generally heads of old families in the village, and usually farmers. The head has always been such a person, and it is quite permissible for the same man to be re-elected several times. The oldest man in the village had held the position for a continuous period of twenty years, and another for six, but yet other previous heads said that two had been enough. The path to leadership usually involves other posts, and nowadays a man is close to retiring from public life by the time he becomes head. Members of poor families and those relatively new in the village seem not to be chosen for office.

Tonarigumi

For the actual mechanics of tax collection and the distribution òf information from the City Hall, the village is divided into three groups called *tonarigumi* (neighbourhood groups).[22] These are shown on Map 5. There is one councillor elected for each *tonarigumi*, known as east, west and central, but much of the communication between the elected committee and each household is carried out by the head of each group, a task which circulates in the order shown on the map. This order is also followed by the local news-sheet and other information

Map 5: Kurotsuchi: *Tonarigumi* and *Kairanban* Route

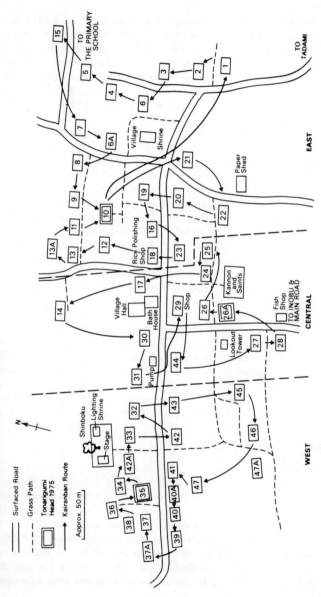

bulletins, known as the *kairanban* ('circulating notice board'). The head of the *tonarigumi* receives such information, removes that intended only for the head, and passes on the rest to the next house, which in turn passes it on when it has seen it. The head remains in office for a year, but the actual task of tax collection is delegated to a different household each month, again following the same order, and the money is finally brought to the head, who takes it to the appropriate committee member. If there is to be a village meeting at short notice, the head of the *tonarigumi* is responsible for notifying each household. At the end of the year a gathering is held at the head's house, food and drink is served to a representative of every other household, and the task is officially passed on. The task is assigned to a household rather than to an individual, and any member can share the burdens involved, but it is compulsory, and differs from the position of elected councillor in a way similar to the difference between bureaucrats and politicians.

The *tonarigumi* also has functions other than administrative ones: for example, every year after the rice seedlings have been transplanted it is this group which celebrates a river festival (*kawa matsuri*).[23] One member of each household meets in one of the houses, again decided by rotation, and straw models of fish, octopus and fishing baskets are fashioned, then to be hung as an offering over the waterways of the village. This is also the group within which the Agricultural Practice Union operates, though this only involves the farming families. Sometimes invitations to social gatherings are issued automatically to every member of the *tonarigumi*, and one example of such an occasion is a wedding, when all the households are invited to send a female member to a special reception. In 1979 there were also enthusiastic volleyball teams in each *tonarigumi* and during my visit they held an exciting and well-supported tournament.

Housewives' Association

Some of the administrative tasks of the village are accomplished in practice by an association made up of a female representative of each household. This is the Housewives' Association[24] (*fujinkai*), and the village group is a local branch of the national organisation. It organises a rota for cleaning the village hall and the public area around the Buddhist images, and for these services the group receives a sum of money from the village funds. It also organises events of interest to its members, such as demonstrations of craft work or the art of dressing in kimono, and once a year there is a day's outing to some place of interest. Members pay a small sum into the group's funds each month towards this day out, and if they are unable to go, they receive the whole sum back. Further activities are arranged at school-zone or city level, and during 1975 these included visits to the city council and law courts, a cooking demonstration, a display of handicrafts and a sports day. Members of the group may also help at other meetings for children or old people, and, before I left the village, they organised a splendid farewell luncheon party for me.

The Housewives' Association shares a committee for *tonarigumi* representatives with the Women's Section of the Agricultural Co-operative, though each has a different head and deputy. These are elected for a term of two years in March of the year the village head does not change.

The Fire Brigade and Road Safety Corps

The fire-fighting corps (*shōbōdan*) is a small group responsible for village safety in times of disaster and, in particular, for putting out fires. The members keep the village pump in good order and, as part of a national organisation, they attend occasional training sessions with the professional fire brigade in Yame-*shi*. They must be ready to drop anything they are doing at the sound of sirens, and usually turn out to any fire in the school zone and other nearby villages, receiving reciprocal aid for a fire in Kurotsuchi. For this service they receive a small remuneration, but the leader explained that they do it not for financial reward but because it is a duty that their fathers discharged before them and that they must do in turn. There are eight men in the Kurotsuchi group which is like a kind of age-grade through which all able male villagers pass for a few years, usually in their late twenties and early thirties. One or two join each year, as the leader and possibly another senior member drop out, leaving the leadership to the next most senior member. There is a certain social function attached to this group, for, after the pump has been checked each month, the members enjoy a few glasses of beer together in the pump shed.

A similar but shorter duty occurs later in life for two years when men join a group of three from Kurotsuchi to take part in road safety activity at school zone level. Apart from occasional patrols, these men are only on duty at school functions such as sports day.

Religious Activity

Religious activity in Kurotsuchi can sometimes be classified as Buddhist, sometimes Shinto, and, sometimes, as with the river festival, as folk religion. In fact, the syncretic nature[25] of the sum total of religious activity of these villagers is in itself a type of folk religion, and it can be considered to form a coherent system, as will be seen subsequently. However, religion has often been involved with politics in Japan,[26] and some aspects of it are publicised and therefore regarded in a more self-conscious manner than others. For example, the strong association of Shinto with wartime nationalism, and its subsequent disrepute, are probably responsible for the fact that nowadays Shinto observances are often referred to, with folk practices, as superstition.[27] They are nevertheless practised, and most Kurotsuchi households, like the majority of those in the nation,[28] owe allegiance to both Shinto and Buddhist establishments.

The village as a whole used to be associated with a Buddhist temple[29] in Kawasaki, but since the Meiji Restoration some households have broken away and changed their sect, and other new families have moved into the village, maintaining their previous allegiances to other temples. Buddhist rites are chiefly sought when someone dies, a priest visits the house for the funeral, and the ashes are taken to a *nōkotsudō* (place for remains) convenient for further attentions (see Chapter 6). Some villages have built their own *nōkotsudō*, as has Inobu, but since there is one at the temple in Kawasaki, and other Kurotsuchi families may use the Inobu one, there is no need for one in Kurotsuchi. There is anyway no necessary relationship between village and *nōkotsudō*, and the village close by which claims to have been the first to build *nōkotsudō* has several small ones, each for a group of families sharing the same surname. Ashes lie with others of the household, and it is the household which is the traditional and fundamental social unit of Buddhism.

In contrast, all residents of the village are entitled to the protection of the Shinto deity, and are expected to take part in shrine[30] activities. The guardian deity *(ujigami)*[31] of this village was once a well-known historical figure by the name of Sugawara Michizane.[32]

Zagumi

For attentions to the shrine, the village is divided into seven groups of seven or eight houses and these are called *zagumi*.[33] The care of the shrine rotates among them, each taking responsibility for a year at a time. One of the main tasks is for the women of the households concerned to take time on the 1st and 15th[34] of each month to tidy up the shrine compound, keep the weeds down, and change the flowers and water offered to the deity. In any one year, another of the *zagumi* groups performs the same function at the Lightning shrine. These groups must also celebrate the various rites of the ceremonial calendar at their respective shrines.

At the Lightning shrine there are two special events during the year, one in April for the Lightning deity, and the other in September for the *shinboku* tree.[35] The former is the biggest festival celebrated in the village, and much of the preparation is done by the Youth Group, which puts on entertainment and attracts visitors from elsewhere. The *zagumi* is responsible for the sale of talismans on this occasion, and for the co-ordination of events. In September, the men get up early to make a new *shimenawa* (a straw rope which marks a sacred area or object) for the entrance and another to go round the tree, while the women of the group prepare *sake* and plates of food to offer to the deity. A Shinto priest is called and he conducts a purification rite (*harai*) during which he may ask the deity to choose the house to lead the incoming group from names of those households which have not recently held this post. After the purification, the priest and representatives of the households concerned share *sake* and the offered food as a ritual feast. The flags and other equipment used on such occasions are later officially handed over to the new head household.

The village shrine (*miya*) has a handover day similar to this, but the annual events are more numerous, though rarely involving more than the seven houses of the group. The one exception is the summer *matsuri*, when the Youth Group again helps. First they construct the huge *shimenawa* for the entrance, and then make paper flowers to decorate long sticks which, after being offered to the deity, are sold to each house in the village for 'household protection'. Proceeds go to the funds of the Youth Group, as do those from the entertainment at the Lightning Festival. Again the priest is called and he conducts a purification rite. The *zagumi* puts up decorations at New Year before other villagers come to pay their first respects. They must also make offerings on certain days in the spring and autumn, determined by the old Chinese calendar (see Appendix), to welcome and see off respectively a deity of rice cultivation known as *Shanichi*, elsewhere called the earth spirit.[36] They also prepare rice with beans (*azuki gohan* or *sekihan*), which is used on all happy ceremonial occasions, and serve this with tea to people who come to pay their respects on the day of a little shrine within the *miya* compound to Bizaiten, a female deity said to be good for business. Usually these smaller events connected with the shrine provided an occasion for the women of the households concerned to enjoy a change and a rest from the daily round of chores, and an opportunity for a chat. Any food left over at the end is divided between them, carefully wrapped, and taken home to be shared out with other members of each household. This practice, common at any function attended by a representative of a household, seems to be a way to ensure that other members can partake if they wish.

There has apparently been little dissent in the past over the fulfilment of these tasks, and most households partake without complaint and without remuneration for the twice-monthly tidying up. This is not purely a religious matter, since it is regarded as a village obligation, just as the priests' fees and shrine expenses are taken out of the village funds. As Plath has commented, this is 'more a civic than religious obligation'.[37] Thus complaints and indignation were expressed when two households claimed dissent on the grounds that their Buddhist allegiances to the successful 'new' religion, Sōka Gakkai,[38] would not allow participation in Shinto rites. Other housewives saw this as a rather mean way of avoiding the cleaning duties, and village officials complained that they were also trying to avoid paying their full dues. One member of the village council gave a good illustration of the problem when answering an unrelated question about whether there had ever been a case of official ostracism in the village. He replied that there had not, but added immediately that these Sōka Gakkai houses tended to cut themselves off.[39]

Kinjo

There is another kind of neighbourhood group, sometimes associated with religious activity, where each household is linked by tradition with a number of others, usually those surrounding it, and the group varies according to which household is the focus of attention. The Sōka Gakkai houses are included here, as are all those in the village, and the purpose of the group is mutual aid in times of difficulty, particularly those associated with life crises. This group is referred to as *tonari* (neighbour) *kinjo* (vicinity), or just *kinjo*. On specific occasions, such as the sharing in rites to remember the dead, a word with religious connotations, *kōjū*[40] may also be used. Whatever its name, and whether or not one cares for the people involved, this is the group with which one shares in some way one's joys and one's sorrows. Particularly in the case of death, this group of neighbours takes over all the practical tasks involved with preparations for the wake that evening and the funeral (see Chapter 6, p. 210). In times of sickness, too, these are the people who will express concern and who will offer help if necessary. No doubt they were available at childbirth too, when this took place at home, but now they make the effort to visit the new family member and mother in hospital, and when these return home, a small gift will be brought to each *kinjo* household as a greeting from the baby. Similar gifts are sent on other occasions, for example from a new bride's home when she makes her first visit after marriage. The men of this group are invited to join the nuptial celebrations, and also to help out with house-building and repairs.

Kō

The *kō* of the name *kōjū* mentioned above is another word which means group, and it is applied in different parts of Japan to various associations of people, often religious, and frequently who collect money at regular intervals towards some future benefit.[41] According to Japanese writers, the word has a derivation associated with Buddhist practices, but many of these *kō* now meet to raise money to visit Shinto shrines and places sacred according to folk beliefs.[42] In Kurotsuchi, various groups call themselves *Ise-kō*, which indicate that they were formed with the aim of visiting the Ise shrine of the Shinto sun goddess Amaterasu, but their functions are now largely social, and recruitment based on age, so they will be considered in more detail in the following section.

One type of *kō* in Kurotsuchi which retains a more manifestly religious connection, though it also has an important social function, is the Kannon-*kō*. The bodhisattva Kannon is often regarded as the patron of women, and specific images of her are attributed special properties such as the ability to cure infertility or problems of lactation. Two small images of Kannon are kept in Kurotsuchi, as well as the large gold-leaf one, and they circulate among two separate groups which meet every month on or around the 17th to pass on the image. Membership of these groups is voluntary, though by household, and only women attend the meetings. The household which has taken care of the image for the past month hosts the occasion, which involves a snack after supper, though each member receives a handful of rice which has been offered to the saint. Each member pays a small sum each time, and an annual outing is made with the proceeds. The evenings are usually spent in conversation and laughter in all-female company, and members enjoy the evening out.[43] Households sometimes drop out of the groups, perhaps if they only have one woman who cannot spare the time, and while I was present, there was talk in one group of inviting relatively new houses to join, so membership seems to be quite fluid.

The village altar for Kannon receives special attention on two occasions during the summer, once on the evening of 17 July, and the other on the morning of 10 August. This is carried out by girls in their sixth year at primary school (or fifth and sixth if numbers are short), who at 11 or 12 are on the brink of puberty. They clean out the little building, decorate it with flowers and candles, and bring rice with beans and tea to serve to people who come to pray. All the visitors are again women, and when I was present, several grandmothers brought their granddaughters, some of whom had been loitering around earlier, curious to see what their tasks would later be. The prayers are said to concern chiefly women's problems, and the girls reported having asked for nice husbands when they are of age. In August preparations are made in the evening for morning prayers, and traditionally, it is said, the girls used to pass the night in the open wooden building, but recently fears of mosquitos and summer colds have done away with this custom.

The other stone images at this site are visited twice a year at the equinoxes as part of a pilgrimage to all such sites by members of the Shingon sect, which was founded by Kōbō Daishi, who is depicted in the largest statue. In Kurotsuchi there are no members of this sect, but a delegation of housewives serves refreshments to the pilgrims on each occasion, as do the owners of three private images also situated in the village and visited by the pilgrims at this time. Village children join in the fun, making something of a sport of collecting biscuits at the four strategic spots, and the fact that one of the images to whom attention is given is Jizō[44] and not Kōbō seems to bother no one at all. The pilgrims also pray to the other 13 saints at the main site.

Age Groups

Membership of most groups so far mentioned has been by household, and, although an individual may attend meetings, it is as a representative of the household. Villagers also have certain activities in which they participate as individuals, varying according to age, with two distinct types of group to which any person may belong. One is a group of age-mates who remain together throughout much of their lives, and the other is a group with members of a particular age range through which individuals pass. The first type has already been mentioned as they are often called *kō*, and a collection of 'same-age groups' (*dōnen-kō*) is recognised by Japanese scholars, although in some places these are distinct from Ise-*kō*.[45]

Same-age Groups

In Kurotsuchi, the men's 'same-age' groups are sometimes called Ise-*kō*, and members explained that the ostensible intention is to save money to visit Ise, but in fact only one or two such groups have actually been there as a group, though many members of such groups have been on a different basis. Instead, the money saved at regular social gatherings is used for shorter, more frequent trips to local resorts, perhaps hot springs. The number, variety and enthusiasm of these groups seems to be a characteristic of Kurotsuchi not necessarily found in neighbouring communities, and they are commonly referred to as *tomodachi-kō*,[46] where *tomodachi*, which is 'friend' in standard Japanese, means 'age-mate' in local dialect. A group of *tomodachi* do not always form a *kō*, but such a *kō* always involves *tomodachi*, though it may include more than one year's classmates if a particular year was rather sparse.

Children who will be in the same school year are encouraged by their mothers to play together almost as soon as they can run about, and during primary school a formal group may well be formed. These are separated by sex. The boys' group is called Hiko-*kō*, again because the ostensible aim is to make a pilgrimage to a mountain called Hiko, a word which also means 'male child'. This may once have been part of a puberty ordeal necessary for entry into the youth group.[47] Nowadays, however, the boys meet regularly throughout their school career, saving amounts which increase as they grow older, and, when they leave school, they spend the money on a week or a fortnight's pleasure trip. Some members leave the village at this stage, others go away to study, and usually there is a lapse in age-mate activities until men settle down and get married. Girls usually leave the village when they marry, but their groups often remain active until that time, even after school days are over, and the last meetings are farewell parties for brides. These groups are called *chimeguri* (literally, 'blood-round'), in recognition of the association of women with blood, and sometimes they meet to perform rites connected with female activities such as the *harikuyō* (needle memorial), also performed annually by women in sewing work.

The groups of adults are more varied in type. All male ones usually remain fairly small and close to school class groups, meeting monthly to dine together in each of their houses in rotation, and each paying a fixed sum into the kitty, which is banked with the Agricultural Co-operative. Groups of women meet less regularly and their activities vary more. Older women have more time to spend together as a rule, and are better able to take a day off to visit a hot spring resort; the youngest group, still very much encumbered with household obligations and small children, has had no meeting as yet, but they have started saving, and they hope at some stage to ask a cookery teacher to come to the village to demonstrate a type of ceremonial cookery. A few groups involve married couples, usually older people who can leave household affairs in the hands of the younger generation while they have a day out, but there are two younger, originally male, groups which include wives at their monthly dinners.

Apart from the social activities, these groups provide aid and support for members in times of need. The men help with each other's housebuilding; they all visit each other at times of sickness and celebration, such as wedding festivities, and, when one 37-year-old man died during this investigation, his age-mates were very active in helping his stunned family to settle his affairs and reorganise their farming activities.

Not every villager belongs to such a group, however, and sometimes through an accident of birth a man will have no age-mates close enough. Occasionally such people maintain ties with colleagues from high school or agricultural college, and men who work for companies may join a similar group of workmates, perhaps all those who joined the company at the same time. Two groups of young farmers, comprising all those from Tadami school zone who graduated from agricultural college together, meet once a month in this capacity and many of them also belong to Kurotsuchi age-mate groups as well. Groups may change their arrangements to suit circumstances. One man who married into the village was invited to join the men of his age, and another quite large group of married couples recently split into groups of men and women to save a widow from dropping out after the death of her husband. There is thus a certain amount of flexibility, but, on the whole, the groups are enduring and important in the lives of their members. About 70 per cent of adult males and just over 60 per cent of females were members at the time of the study.

Age Grades

The second type of group involving individuals recruited according to age may be compared to age grades, which exist in different parts of the country, though they are less comprehensive than they used to be and their functions have often changed in recent years.[48] The children's groups (*kodomogumi*) used to include children of varying ages who often had certain religious functions to perform.[49] The rites performed by girls for the image of Kannon in Kurotsuchi may have been such, and the group sometimes performs at a village festival, but otherwise the activities of today's group are non-religious. It is composed strictly of all the primary schoolchildren in the village. Organised by mothers of the final-year pupils, they go on an annual outing during the summer holidays, which the mothers seemed to enjoy as much as the children the year I joined them. At school, an identical group is called the Kurotsuchi *gakudan*. As such, they meet at the end of each term under the leadership of three final-year students, supervised by a teacher, to discuss plans for the holidays, lodge complaints about each other in public, and to decide what activities are annoying or dangerous and therefore to be prohibited. They print a catalogue of these decisions in the school printing room and distribute the result to all their members, which appears to be an effective form of self-discipline within the group.

Village identity is fostered in other ways at primary school. Swimming during the summer holidays is organised in village groups, but perhaps the most clear example of this is the inter-village relay race on the school sports day. This is the only event for which prizes are awarded, and the winning villages, for both boys' and girls' races, receive a certificate to display in the village hall and a flag to be kept for that year. Parents sit in village groups, marked out around the arena, and there is always a good attendance to cheer the youngsters on. Each girls' and boys' team has a runner from each of the six years, so many of the spectators have a relative in the race. Heats are interspersed with other events throughout the day, and excitement is thereby kept up until the final run-off. The winning teams are usually fêted by the adults of the village in the village hall the same evening or the following day, so it is no small occasion.

In 1979, these children's groups in different villlages were practising for a softball tournament which was to involve heats in each of the school zones, followed by city-level play-offs to find a champion village.[50]

The next age grade is the Youth Group (*seinendan*), which was extremely active and enthusiastic in 1975, although numbers had diminished somewhat in 1979. Membership, which is voluntary[51] and open to youths from the time they leave school until they are 25 for males and 23 for females, probably fluctuates, since it was reported in 1975 that the group had been without girls at all for several years prior to a successful recruiting drive that year. Apart from the festival activities already mentioned, the group holds regular meetings which often involve discussions or debates about specific topics, they organise

trips or classes of interest to members, and they send teams to participate in a variety of sporting events organised at school-zone and city
levels. The funds they raised in 1975 were sufficient to finance a few
days away at a resort for the group, and even some girls whose parents
were not usually keen for them to be out late in the evening were
allowed to go, the activities of the Youth Group apparently constitut-
ing a respectable exception. In 1979, however, its reputation had
slipped somewhat, and one girl claimed to have left the group because
its members stayed out too late in the evening. Such factors probably
vary from year to year.

The group under this name is, like the Housewives' Association and
the Fire Brigade, a twentieth-century organisation first formed on the
instructions and models of central government.[52] As such, it was used
to promote nationalism during the war and to disseminate new ideas
during the Occupation.[53] In some villages anthropologists have reported
a subsequent loss of interest in such groups.[54] Before Meiji, however,
youth groups, called by various names (*wakamonogumi, wakashū*, etc.)
had a wider variety of functions within villages, and sometimes included
men until they were in their 40s.[55] It seems that they have always had a
part to play in village festivals, and previously they carried out certain
protective functions which now come under the jurisdiction of the
police and the Fire Brigade. There was also an educative role and, in
many areas, the Youth Group provided the functions concerned with
marriages which were described in the previous chapter. There is no
evidence that such a function existed within living memory in Kurotsuchi, however, although two separate groups existed for boys and girls
when today's old people were young.[56]

There is a series of groups inspired by the American PTA, one for
each of primary, middle and high schools, though the last is not closely
related to the village, and these tend to throw together mothers of
children of the same age. Officially the committees of these groups are
supposed to include a male and female parent of village children in their
last year at the primary and middle schools, but men frequently send
their wives as substitutes, and this principle even applies on a day
specifically set aside for fathers to visit the school and see their children's work. Thus, though married women have no age grades as such,
the younger ones often find themselves together according to the age
of their children,[57] and the outing of the *kodomogumi* is a good specific
example of this. In the past, there used to be a young wives' group
(*wakazumakai*), it is said, but this no longer exists in that form. The
Housewives' Association activities frequently involve older women, and,

although there are no specific age grades, particular activities are appropriate for women of particular ages. The Fire Brigade has been mentioned as a kind of age grade through which men pass, but otherwise there are no formal groups for married men either.

When people reach the age of 61, they become eligible to join an Old People's Club (*rōjinkai*) which receives a grant from the government to encourage old people to perform light tasks of community value. In 1975, numbers in Kurotsuchi had not reached the 30 people required to form such a group, but in 1979 they had sufficient people and an extremely active 'gateball-club', which would meet at 5 a.m. to practise this game. A tournament held during my visit attracted many younger villagers and provided a hilarious afternoon's entertainment.

Villagers of 75 and over are entertained once a year together with old people from all the villages in the school zone. This event is held in the hall at the primary school, where the second-year children put on an entertainment and professional singers and dancers are hired for the occasion. Various city dignitaries including local councillors address the assembly and, together with the heads of all the villages represented, they join the old people for lunch, which is provided by the village committees of the Housewives' Association. The old people are also invited to the school sports day, when they sit in a specially reserved area, and are addressed after the presentation of prizes by a final-year child.

It has been illustrated, in this chapter, how residence in such a village involves a degree of participation in village affairs. A person marrying into the village is automatically drawn in, sometimes as an individual according to his or her age, but more often through membership in a household. The internal organisation of such a household, and again the implications of membership, form the subject-matter of the following chapter.

Notes

1. Cf. Richard K. Beardsley *et al.*, *Village Japan*, Phoenix edn (University of Chicago Press, Chicago, 1969), p. 216; John F. Embree, *Suye Mura* (University of Chicago Press, Chicago, 1939), pp. 19, 79; Chie Nakane, *Kinship and Economic Organisation in Rural Japan* (University of London, The Athlone Press, 1967), p. 2; Edward Norbeck, *Takashima* (University of Utah Press, Salt Lake City, 1954), p. 48. The household will be the subject-matter of the next chapter.

Throughout this chapter the term is applied to the current residential unit which is recognised by the village administration. References to the 'family' apply to the people living in one household. Japanese terms are discussed in the next chapter.

2. Most of the types of groups found in Kurotsuchi are also evident in other villages, although there appears to be a wide variation in the names of such groups, a different amount of overlap in their functions, and sometimes a lesser degree of co-operation, e.g. Robert Smith, *Kurusu* (Dawson, Folkestone, 1978), p. 203. E. Norbeck, 'Changing Associations in a Recently Industrialized Japanese Community', *Urban Anthropology*, vol. 6, no. 1 (1977), p. 59, describes a trend towards specialisation of association functions in his study of the urbanisation of Takashima, previously an island fishing community. General descriptions of such groups throughout Japan are to be found in Harumi Befu, *Japan: an Anthropological Introduction* (Chandler, San Francisco, 1971), pp. 82-93, and Tadashi Fukutake, *Japanese Rural Society*, trans. R.P. Dore (Cornell University Press, London, 1972), pp. 96-137.

3. Befu, *Anthropological Introduction*, p. 22.

4. Glenn T. Trewartha, *Japan: a Geography* (University of Wisconsin Press, Madison and Milwaukee; Methuen, London, 1970), p. 586. Trewartha is the source of most of the geographical information provided here, in particular pp. 571-94.

5. Trewartha, *Japan*, p. 64. Rainfall figures from ibid., p. 51.

6. Kōbō Daishi was a priest who travelled to China in the ninth century and returned to Japan to found the Shingon sect of Buddhism. More detail about him may be found in Byron H. Earhart, *Japanese Religion: Unity and Diversity* (Dickenson, Belmont, California, 1969), pp. 37-9; Joseph Kitagawa, 'Master and Saviour' in *Studies of Esoteric Buddhism and Tantrism* (Koyasan, Japan, 1965) and Noriyoshi Tamaru, 'Buddhism' in Hori *et al.* (eds.), *Japanese Religion*, trans. Yoshiya Abe and David Reid (Kodansha International, Tokyo and Palo Alto, 1972), pp. 55-8.

7. The translation of Japanese terms for administrative units can be rather confusing, for the usual English equivalents apply much more accurately to the system which was in existence at the time of the Restoration than to today's, and a number of changes since then have altered radically the meaning of some of the terms (cf. Nakane, *Rural Japan*, p. 43). For example, the terms for 'town' and 'city', *machi* and *shi* respectively, are now applied for administrative purposes to quite rural areas and, indeed, the region under study is a case in point. Kurotsuchi itself belongs to a *shi*, and several of the surrounding rural areas are classified as *machi*.

The term *mura*, traditionally 'village', is now no closer to the English meaning. Two administrative changes since the Restoration have applied the term to progressively wider areas, subsuming a number of previous *mura*. Kurotsuchi was officially a *mura* before 1889, but the administrative reorganisation at that time reapplied the term to a collection of such villages, in this case with the name of the largest, Tadami (*Fukuoka-ken Shichōson GappeiShi (A History of the Amalgamation of Cities, Towns and Villages in Fukuoka Prefecture* (Fukuoka, Kenchō, Fukuoka, 1962) p. 606). The previous *mura* became *buraku*, and this term, still used in everyday speech, is often translated as 'hamlet' (Befu, *Anthropological Introduction*, p. 67; Fukutake, *Japanese Rural Society*, p. 81; Dore *Land Reform in Japan* (Oxford University Press, Oxford, 1959), p. 31). Further administrative reorganisation in the 1950s amalgamated seven of the new *mura* with a *machi* by the name of Fukushima to form Yame-*shi*, and Kurotsuchi is now, officially, one of the 77 *chōnai* which comprise it. (For nation-wide detail of local government reorganisation, see Fukutake, *Japanese Rural Society*, Part IV).

The term *mura* is now only used administratively for rather remote rural areas, usually much larger than Tadami was, and I have decided to follow Nakane and use the term 'village' rather than 'hamlet' for the 'important social and economic unit' of which Kurotsuchi is an example (*Rural Japan*, p. 43). It is a collection of households, separated physically from other such collections, and with communal facilities for worship, meetings and even for bathing. It is the same type of *buraku* of which Embree's *Suye Mura* was composed and, like those of Embree's description, 'is largely self-contained socially with its own . . . headman and religious centre' (*Suye Mura*, p. 23). After the household, it is the primary and most important social unit of its inhabitants (cf. Fukutake, *Japanese Rural Society*, p. 82; Dore *Land Reform* p. 31fn), and since Kurotsuchi comprises 54 houses, two shops, a meeting hall, a bath-house and a shrine, it would even seem misleading to use in English the term 'hamlet', which is defined in the *OED* (s.v. hamlet): 'a group of houses or small village, esp. a village without a church, included in the parish belonging to another village or town'.

8. This is somewhat larger than the national average – in 1975, 3.44 (*Japan Statistical Year Book* (Bureau of Statistics, Tokyo, 1977), p. 28). Rather, it corresponds to the figure which remained relatively unchanged from that estimated for the mid-eighteenth century to about 1955, when a sudden decline is interpreted as corresponding to the decline in the number of people engaged in agriculture (ibid.; Chie Nakane, 'An Interpretation of the Size and Structure of the Household in Japan over Three Centuries' in P. Laslett and R. Wall (eds.), *Household and Family in Past Time* (Cambridge University Press, Cambridge, 1972), pp. 523, 532; Akira Hayami and Nobuko Uchida, 'Size of Household in a Japanese County throughout the Tokugawa Era' in Laslett and Wall, *Household and Family*, p. 473.

9. *Chikugo Kokushi* (*A History of Chikugo Province*) (Chikugo Iseki Kankokai, 1926), p. 293.

10. Japanese feudal terms are not necessarily accurately translated by the English words used, but where they will only be referred to in passing and are not important to the argument, a conventional translation will be made to avoid overloading the text with native terms. The Japanese word will be given in parentheses the first time the word is used.

11. *Yame-gunshi* (*A History of Yame County*) (Yame-gun Yakusho, 1917), p. 49.

12. Ibid., p. 80.

13. Trewartha, *Japan*, p. 586.

14. This festive air, noted also by Smith, *Kurusu*, pp. 89-90, in 1951, has not disappeared as he feared, despite the almost complete mechanisation of transplanting techniques.

15. Paper has been associated with Yame for some hundreds of years (Kunio Hirano and Hisao Iida, *Fukuoka-ken no Rekishi* (*History of Fukuoka Prefecture*) (Yamakawa, Tokyo, 1975), *furoku* (Appendix, p. 92), and, according to locals, its quality is enhanced by the water of the Yabe River.

16. According to a local newspaper article, this man was the first person in Japan to use bamboo shavings as the raw material for his paper, and these he obtained from a factory making chopsticks. More usually, rice straw is used for this purpose.

17. Before the Second World War there was more tenancy farming, but the post-war land reform measures removed much of the property at nominal cost from people who were not working it and sold it, at the same price, to the tenants who were (Befu, *Anthropological Introduction*, pp. 75-6; Fukutake, *Japanese Rural Society*, pp. 8-14; and for a detailed analysis: Dore *Land Reform*). Even before the war there were no big landowners in Kurotsuchi, and most farmers were owner-cultivators as they are now. However, some families owned enough

land to have some to rent out, sometimes on a temporary basis, perhaps until a son grew up (cf. Dore, *Land Reform*, p. 26). Some landowners were able to purchase land from people who had fallen into debt, but allow them to keep working it, as tenants. This was a way in which many landowners grew progressively richer before and during the Meiji period (ibid., pp. 12-19), and it is said that there were one or two such people in the neighbouring village of Hon. A study of the land records reveals no great changes in landholdings in Kurotsuchi during the Land Reform, which bears out the reports of the villagers. A few households, which were regarded as small-time landlords, lost any land they owned outside the village which was tenanted, since in the next village they were regarded as 'absentee landlords' (ibid., p. 23), and tenanted land within Kurotsuchi was usually divided between the landlord and the tenants. According to Dore, this arrangement was often made within a single village ('hamlet'), in order to preserve the peace of the community, especially where arbitration was needed between landlord and tenant, both of whom wanted to keep the land (*Land Reform*, pp. 161-2, 165). Even now, tenanted land in Kurotsuchi seems to be less than is found elsewhere (ibid., p. 371; Smith *Kurusu*, pp. 110-11).

18. The nature of rice cultivation has made co-operation an important characteristic of agriculture in Japan from time immemorial (cf. Dore, *Land Reform*, p. 351; Fukutake, *Japanese Rural Society*, p. 82), but the modern national organisation has developed since the Restoration. Previously the most intensive and important co-operation was at village level, but gradually advantage could be taken of national markets, government loans and improved techniques which could quickly be disseminated through this channel. During the war period, the organisation was also used for rationing and other government controls. See Dore, *Land Reform*, pp. 277-8 for details of the development of the modern co-operatives, and ibid., pp. 278-97; and *Shinohata* (Allen Lane, London, 1978), pp. 122-32 for more detailed descriptions of their operation.

19. Universities provide four-year degree courses, and junior colleges a two-year complete course. These establishments are ranked so that employment possibilities are frequently limited according to the status of one's institute of higher education. Thus some students spend years between school and university trying repeatedly to gain admission to the high-prestige establishments. Further details of the modern Japanese education system are to be found in Herbert Passin, *Society and Education in Japan* (Columbia University, New York, 1965), pp. 108-16; Ezra F. Vogel, *Japan's New Middle Class* (University of California Press, Berkeley, Los Angeles and London, 1963), pp. 40-67; R.P. Dore, *City Life in Japan* (University of California Press, Berkeley, Los Angeles and London, 1971), pp. 227-41; *Shinohata*, pp. 175-91.

20. Figures for 1974 showed that although almost as many girls as boys graduated from high school, 90 per cent of junior college enrolment was women, who represented only 18 per cent of the enrolment of four-year courses (Joy Paulson, 'Evolution of the Feminine Ideal', p. 21, and E. Knipe Mouer, 'Women in Teaching', p. 158 in Joyce Lebra *et al.* (eds.), *Women in Changing Japan* (Westview Press, Boulder, Colorado, 1976); cf. *Japan Statistical Yearbook*, 1977, p. 574.

21. *Chōnai* is the official classification of the village as a unit of the city (*shi*), and *kai* is a term which is used for several groups and may be translated 'association' or 'assembly'.

22. These are probably the descendants of the policing groups of the Tokugawa period (K. Asakawa, 'Notes on Village Government in Japan after 1600', *Journal of the American Oriental Society*, vol. 30, no. 3 (1910), pp. 267-8; Sir J. Barrow, 'Sketches of the Manners and Usages of Japan', *Quarterly Review*, vol. 52 (1834), pp. 293-317; Kunio Yanagida, *Japanese Manners and Customs in*

the Meiji Era, trans. and adapted by Charles S. Terry (Obunsha, Tokyo, 1957), p. 69), which were revived during the last war for government control and indoctrination of the people, 'moral training' and 'fostering of . . . spiritual solidarity' (Kurt Steiner, 'Popular Political Participation and Political Development in Japan: the Rural Level' in Robert Ward (ed.), *Political Development in Modern Japan* (Princeton University Press, Princeton, 1968), p. 240; also Ralph Brainbanti, 'Neighbourhood Associations in Japan and their Democratic Potentialities', *Far Eastern Quarterly*, vol. 7 (1948), pp. 136-64; Befu, *Anthropological Introduction*, pp. 82-3; Fukutake, *Japanese Rural Society*, pp. 96-9.

23. *Kawa* is 'river', though in this case the 'river' concerned is little more than a deep stream; *matsuri* is usually translated as 'festival', but it is derived from the verb *matsuru* which includes the ideas 'to worship' and 'to deify', so that it has a religious connotation which 'festival' lacks. A festival similar to this is described as characteristic of Okimachi, a town a few miles away from Yame, by Yutaka Chikushi, *Nihon no Minzoku (Folklore of Japan)*, no. 40 (Fukuoka, Tokyo, 1974), p. 127.

24. Names of organisations and other groups are given in Japanese where there is any possibility of confusion with similar groups, but if the English translation makes clear which Japanese group is meant, this will be used. Although the Housewives' Association is a national organisation it seems to have died out in villages where many women are employed outside the community (for example Norbeck, 'Changing Associations', pp. 49-51; Smith, *Kurusu*, p. 224).

25. Syncretism of Shinto and Buddhism in the wider nation went through a long period of official fusion from the seventh and eighth centuries until they were separated, by government order, in the early Meiji period (see, for example, Shigeru Matsumoto, 'Introduction' in Hori *et al.* (eds.), *Japanese Religion*, pp. 17-18.

26. See, for example, Robert J. Smith, *Ancestor Worship in Contemporary Japan* (Stanford University Press, Stanford, 1974), pp. 3-4.

27. Cf. Hitoshi Miyake, 'Folk Religion' in Hori *et al.* (eds.), *Japanese Religion*, p. 143; Norbeck, *Takashima*, p. 213.

28. Kiyomi Morioka, *Religion in Changing Japanese Society* (University of Tokyo Press, Tokyo, 1975), pp. 3-4.

29. This was called the *danka seido* (parishioner system), set up in connection with the suppression of Christianity during the time of Tokugawa Iemitsu in the seventeenth century, when every household had to be registered with a Buddhist temple (Earhart, *Unity and Diversity*, p. 71; Norihisa Suzuki, 'Christianity', p. 78, and Noriyoshi Tamaru, 'Buddhism', p. 51, in Hori *et al.* (eds.), *Japanese Religion*.

30. It is conventional to use the word 'shrine' for Shinto places of worship and the word 'temple' for those with a Buddhist foundation (cf. Earhart, *Unity and Diversity*, p. 18; Morioka, *Religion in Japanese Society*, p. 5).

31. *Ujigami* is made up of two elements, *uji* and *kami*. The second, *kami*, is often loosely translated as 'god' or 'deity', but it has a wider meaning in Japanese, including such concepts as 'powers of nature', 'revered human beings' and 'spirits of the dead' (H. Byron Earhart, *Religion in the Japanese Experience* (Dickenson, Belmont, California, 1974), p. 9). It has a variety of possible etymologies, which are summarised by D.C. Holtom, 'The Meaning of *Kami*', *Monumenta Nipponica*, vol. 3 (1940), pp. 1-27. The meaning of *kami* is sometimes compared with that of the Polynesian concept *mana* (Geoffrey Bownas, *Japanese Rainmaking and Other Folk Practices* (Allen and Unwin, London, 1963), p. 24; Holtom in Earhart, *Japanese Experience*, p. 10). *Uji* is another word whose origins are disputed (for example N. Hozumi, *Ancestor Worship and Japanese Law* (Maruzen, Tokyo, 1913), pp. 48-9; Smith, *Ancestor Worship*, pp. 7-8). It appears,

however, once to have applied to a kind of localised kin group, and in current usage it can mean 'family name'. The *ujigami* was the tutelary deity of the kin group, possibly an ancestor (Fukutake, *Japanese Rural Society*, p. 105; Kunio Yanagida, *About Our Ancestors*, trans. Fanny Mayer and Yasuyo Ishiwara (Japanese National Commission for Unesco, Tokyo, 1970), pp. 125-6), who protected the *ujiko* (*uji* children) or members of the group. As time went by, membership of such a group came to depend on territoriality rather than kinship, but this change seems to have occurred at different times in different places, and just how it changed still seems to be disputed (Hiroji Naoe, 'A Study of *Yashikigami*' in R.M. Dorson (ed.), *Studies in Japanese Folklore* (Kennikat Press, Port Washington, New York and London, 1973), pp. 198-9; Yanagida, *Japanese Manners and Customs*, p. 295. A cogent and convincing presentation of the process is to be found in Hall's study of Bizen province: John W. Hall, *Government and Local Power in Japan 500-1700* (Princeton University Press, Princeton, 1966), Chapter 1.

32. Sugawara Michizane was a ninth-century nobleman who worked to restore Imperial power in the time of the Fujiwara family hegemony. After a period of favour, he was betrayed and banished to Dazaifu in Kyūshū where he subsequently died. Much disaster in the capital city which followed his death was attributed eventually to the vengeful spirit of Michizane, and, to remove this course, a shrine was erected where he was to be worshipped as a deity. Over the years his popularity has increased and he is now widely worshipped and has many shrines dedicated to his name. He is often regarded as a god of learning. See, for example, Ivan Morris, *The Nobility of Failure* (Secker and Warburg, London, 1975), pp. 41-66, and G.B. Sansom, *Japan: a Short Cultural History*, revised edn (The Cresset Press, London, 1952), pp. 210-11. Kurotsuchi's residents sometimes visit the original shrine at Dazaifu.

33. *za* means 'group', as does *gumi*, but *za* is associated with shrine worship, used, for example, with *miya* (shrine) in *miyaza*, a group which sometimes differs from the *zagumi*, though both are associated with the shrine. See, for example, Ichiro Hori, *Folk Religion of Japan* (University of Chicago Press, Chicago, 1974), p. 62; Toshiaki Harada, 'Miya no za to Kabu' ('Shrine Organisations'), *Shūkyō Kenkyū*, vol. 36 (1963), pp. 1-12; Smith, *Ancestor Worship*, pp. 3, 154; Befu, *Anthropological Introduction*, pp. 83-4.

34. These are days which, according to the lunar calendar, used to be regarded as holy and particularly appropriate for holidays (Yanagida, *Manners and Customs*, p. 263). Festivals were often held on the 15th of the month, which would also be the night of the full moon (John F. Embree, 'Some Social Functions of Religion in Rural Japan', *American Journal of Sociology*, vol. 47 (1941), p. 185.

35. *Shin* is an alternative pronunciation of the character for *kami*, also used in the word *Shinto*, and *boku* is 'tree'.

36. Beardsley *et al.*, *Village Japan*, p. 189; cf. William Erskine, *Japanese Festivals and Calendar Lore* (Kyo Bun Kwan, 1933), p. 167. Shanichi is actually the name of the day, which is the *tsuchi no e* (see Appendix) nearest to the vernal and autumnal equinoxes (Miyake, 'Folk Religion', pp. 127-8; Toshijiro Hirayama, 'Seasonal Rituals Connected with Rice Culture' in Dorson (ed.), *Studies in Japanese Folklore*, p. 75.

37. David W. Plath, *The After Hours* (University of California Press, Berkeley, Los Angeles and London, 1964), p. 146.

38. Sōka Gakkai is the most successful and largest of a group of religious sects which have developed in recent times and are therefore termed 'new'. Together they had a conjectured 8 million members in 1972 (Shigeyoshi Murakami, 'New Religions in Japan', *East Asian Cultural Studies*, vol. 11, nos. 1-4 (1972), p. 26). Sōka Gakkai was developed in the 1930s from the teachings of Nichiren, whose original following is still a separate, traditional sect, and

this new body rejects all other religions as 'heresy' (ibid., p. 25). A political party which grew out of the religious movement was founded in 1964, and this is called Kōmeitō, sometimes referred to in English as the 'Clean Government Party' (ibid., p. 26). For more details see, for example, Kiyoaki Murata, *Japan's New Buddhism* (Walker, Weatherhill, New York, 1969); Noah S. Brannen, *Sōka Gakkai: Japan's Militant Buddhists* (John Knox Press, Richmond, Virginia, 1968); and, on new religions in general, Murakami.

39. A similar situation has been reported in villages where Christian families have refused to make contributions to community festivals (Mitsuru Shimpo, 'Impact, Congruence and New Equilibrium' in K. Morioka and W.H. Newell (eds.), *The Sociology of Japanese Religion* (Brill, Leiden, 1975), p. 68), although Norbeck reports that two Sōka Gakkai families in Takashima did continue to fulfil their traditional Shinto roles ('Changing Associations', p. 57).

40. In Niiike this word appears to have had a wider meaning (Beardsley *et al.*, *Village Japan*, p. 248).

41. Embree, *Suye Mura*, pp. 138-53; Beardsley *et al.*, *Village Japan*, p. 260; Fukutake, *Japanese Rural Society*, p. 106; Yanagida, *Manners and Customs*, p. 301.

42. Fukutake, *Japanese Rural Society*, p. 106; Hori, *Folk Religion*, p. 38; Lucy S. Itō, 'Kō, Japanese Confraternities', *Monumenta Nipponica*, vol. 8 (1952), pp. 412-15.

43. Cf. Itō, 'Kō', p. 414.

44. Details about the Jizō cult in Japan, as well as historical information about the character, are to be found in Yoshiko Dykstra, 'Jizō, the Most Merciful', *Monumenta Nipponica*, vol. 33 (1978), pp. 179-200.

45. Keigo Seki, 'Nenrei Shūdan' ('Age-groups') in T. Omachi *et al.* (eds.), *Nihon Minzokugaku Taikei* (Heibonsha, Tokyo, 1962), pp. 139, 154-6; Tokutarō Sakurai, *Kōshūdan Seiritsu Katei no Kenkyū* (*A Study of the Development of Kō Organisation*) (Yoshikawa Kōbunkan, Tokyo, 1962), pp. 346-55; Embree, *Suye Mura*, pp. 148-50.

46. According to Seki, pp. 154-5, this usage is also found in a district of Kyoto.

47. Chikushi, *Nihon no Minzoku*, p. 197; Kamishima, *Nihonjin no Kekkonkan* (*The Japanese View of Marriage*) (Chikuma Sōsho, Tokyo, 1969), p. 187; Omachi, *'Seinenshiki'* ('Coming of Age'), in Omachi *et al.* (eds.), *Nihon Minzokugaku Taikei*, pp. 236-7.

48. Edward Norbeck, 'Age-Grading in Japan', *American Anthropologist*, vol. 55 (1953), p. 373; Fukutake, *Japanese Rural Society*, pp. 102-3; Seki, 'Nenrei Shūdan'.

49. Seki, 'Nenrei Shūdan', p. 134; Fukutake, *Japanese Rural Society*, p. 103; Toshimi Takeuchi, 'Kodomogumi ni tsuite' ('The Children's Group'), *Minzokugaku Kenkyū*, vol. 21, no. 4 (1957), pp. 61-7.

50. Such activities help, no doubt, to maintain traditional village rivalry which has also been described elsewhere (Embree, *Suye Mura*, p. 29; Dore, *Land Reform*, pp. 343, 353).

51. Membership used to be compulsory for all youths of a certain age, and, even after the war, when it was made voluntary, reports seem to indicate that villagers felt obliged to join (Fukutake, *Japanese Rural Society*, pp. 110, 115; Dore, *Land Reform*, p. 362.

52. Dore, *Land Reform*, p. 360; Fukutake, *Japanese Rural Society*, p. 110.

53. Dore, *Land Reform*, pp. 486-9; Norbeck, 'Age-grading', p. 376.

54. John B. Cornell, 'Matsunagi' p. 193, and R.J. Smith, 'Kurusu', p. 7, in J.B. Cornell and R.J. Smith, *Two Japanese Villages* (Greenwood Press, New York, 1969); Norbeck, 'Changing Associations', p. 49; Fukutake, *Japanese Rural Society*, p. 115.

55. Richard E. Varner, 'The Organised Peasant', *Monumenta Nipponica*, vol. 32 (1977), pp. 464-5.

56. A map of the distribution of youth lodges associated with this does not include the Yame area (Seki, 'Nenrei Shūdan', pp. 170-1), nor does a description of where these institutions are found in Fukuoka prefecture (Chikushi, *Nihon no Minzoku*, pp. 119-20).

57. Elsewhere even childless women attend meetings of the PTA, which appears to have taken over some of the functions of a more generalised women's society (E. Norbeck, *Changing Japan* (Holt Rinehart and Winston, New York, 1965), p. 53). Vogel reports that in the city the PTA provides almost the only avenue for women new to the district to see each other regularly (*Middle Class*, pp. 110-12).

3 THE HOUSEHOLD AND MARRIED LIFE

The word 'household' has been used so far to apply to the members of a single residential unit. In Japanese this is the *setai* or *ko*, where *setai* (or *shotai*) means exclusively 'household' in this sense, while *ko* may also have other meanings, such as 'door' and 'house'. The extent to which this household displays the characteristics of the traditional *ie*, which were outlined in Chapter 1, will be under consideration in this chapter. The chief differences between the *setai* and the *ie* is that the former is an actual representation at any time of the *ie*, which itself includes an ideology of continuity, a diachronic element of remembrance of preceding generations and, indeed, of the importance of ensuring future ones. The word *ie* can also be used in reference to the present household, to the building which houses it, and, in writing, it appears in compound words which use an alternative reading of the character, *ka*, for example: *kagyō* (household occupation), *kafū* (ways of the house), *kamon* (house crest) and *kazoku* (family).[1]

The characteristics of the *ie* as described in Chapter 1 were those of the samurai which were being disseminated through education at the turn of the century. After the Second World War, legal support for the old system was removed, the importance of the individual was advocated, and families are now registered on marriage as nuclear families, though all those resident at one address are filed together. In this chapter present practices will be described and compared with informants' recollections of pre-war ones. Previous practices can also be inferred in some cases from documentary evidence. It is thus hoped to give an idea of how far national change has affected the operations of households in Kurotsuchi.

The chapter is divided into a number of sections. First there are details of the house itself, then the people in it and their activities, and then the relations between members of the household. After this, the developmental cycle of the household is considered in sections on succession and inheritance, marriage and adoption, and branch households. Finally, a few words on the relations between households will pave the way for subsequent chapters.

The Building

Japanese houses are usually built of wood, and it is the carpenter who designs them and fashions their components, though some of the construction may be done by relatives and neighbours (see Chapter 6, p. 216). The carpenter has been described as the head of all artisans, 'the great artificer' of a 'dignified craft',[2] and it is appropriate that he should be responsible for the external manifestation of the most important component of society. The basic structure of the house is a framework of wooden posts, with a varying amount of solid wall between them, and a roof which, for farmers, was traditionally thatched, but which is now usually made of tiles.[3] Houses are of course of various sizes and of various degrees of adornment, and the most modern Japanese houses differ in several ways from the traditional ones. The oldest houses have the least solid wall, rooms usually being divided by rather thin, removable sliding doors, whose upper part is often paper-covered lattice work, and much of the outer walls being composed of similar, stronger sliding doors. Thus the whole house can be opened up for cleaning, airing and for formal occasions, or closed to form rooms. These rooms often afford little privacy, however, and indeed traditionally families were not expected to provide 'personal space' for their members.[4] In contrast, newer houses frequently have more solid wall and some rooms which can be completely closed off, although they usually also retain some of the traditional features, especially an area which can be opened up for formal occasions. Several households in Kurotsuchi built on a first floor and a tiled roof instead of rethatching the last time this became necessary, and thus, like others who have rebuilt completely, have been able to provide a separate room for the young couple, or perhaps for older children. This would appear to illustrate a post-war demand for some individuality within family life. Most houses need rebuilding in the lifetime of a single inhabitant, and recent affluence has allowed more families than usual to adapt themselves to new houses. In Kurotsuchi, no less than 18 houses had been completely rebuilt and 10 extensively modernised in the ten years preceding the original investigation. By 1979, there were 5 more new houses, 8 others to which some addition had been made or a work-shed rebuilt, and 2 relatively new ones in the process of major reconstruction.

Modern houses frequently include an area with Western furniture, but none in Kurotsuchi has completely dispensed with the Japanese *tatami* woven-rush matting areas, where formal gatherings are held.

This matting is also used for sleeping on in most houses, and the bedding is folded away into large cupboards during the daytime. Typically, such rooms have little furniture, and visitors are received kneeling on the matting, a table and cushions being brought out if refreshments are to be served. Different rooms traditionally represent different degrees of formality rather than different functions, and they are named accordingly. Plan 1 shows the most traditional type of house found in the village, with notes illustrating how even the most modern house varies only slightly. Others usually retain in some way the chief components illustrated here, even if they must compress them into a smaller space, or also provide 'personal' rooms. The lay-out also varies, but in this plan the left-hand side of the house is family space, and the right-hand side formal space for visitors. The *butsudan* (household Buddhist altar) was traditionally kept in a special room, where the oldest member of the family would sleep, and one such person explained it was comforting to be near the memory of his dead wife. However, most houses now have it in the *zashiki*,[5] the formal reception room, and here a visitor might expect to sleep, although this would depend on the degree of intimacy he or she had with the family. The wooden-floored room next to the kitchen is usually a family room, where everyday meals are served, and often where the television is kept, although some houses have this in a more comfortable *tatami* room. Old houses have earth-floored kitchens, which used to be smokey places with wood-fired stoves, but modern propane equipment has made it possible for new kitchens to have wooden floors, and then these often become the chief family room.

Informal visitors are received in the *tatami* room by the entrance hall, or sometimes now in a Western room, but an intimate visitor might soon be allowed into the inner, family room, especially if a good television programme was in progress. More formal visits are held in the *zashiki*, and the whole right-hand area of the house can be opened up for large receptions. The *zashiki* is distinguishable from other rooms by the presence of an alcove with a polished raised base, set into one wall, where a scroll or painting hangs, and flowers and other beautiful objects are displayed. This is the *tokonoma*, supposed anciently to have been what it means literally, 'a bed-space', but later having religious significance as a 'seat of *kami*', 'a shrine to Amaterasu', and a Buddhist priest's room.[6] Ceremonial equipment is displayed here before use, and seats of guests and ceremonial participants are determined in relation to it, the highest or most important seats being directly in front of it, from right or left depending on its own position.

Plan 1: A Traditional Family House (not to scale)

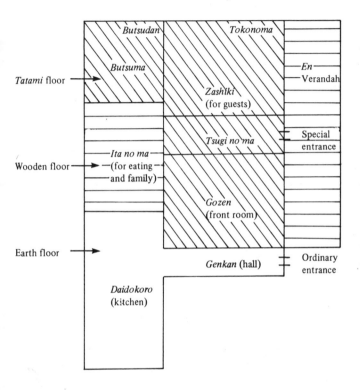

Two of the most recently constructed houses in 1979 had adopted a plan remarkably similar to this. The chief differences were the inclusion of a Western room in the space to the left of the entrance, the addition of a second floor with accommodation for the young married couple, and the presence of the *butsudan* in the *zashiki* rather than in a room of its own.

Only a few houses have the *tsugi no ma* (literally, next room), which is said to provide a special entrance for important visitors through to the *zashiki*, and also to prevent less distinguished visitors waiting in the *gozen* from overhearing conversation in the *zashiki*. This facility traditionally distinguished an affluent or influential house from its neighbours, and modern houses are rather more varied in design. Poorer houses are necessarily smaller, and the distinction between formal and informal areas becomes less clear-cut; the poorest house in Kurotsuchi has only one room to serve every occasion.

The *butsudan* is present in every house which has deceased members to remember, including those in which perhaps only a baby has died, so that only very new households are without one. It is usually a box or a cupboard with doors which close, and of a more or less ornate appearance, depending on the economic resources and the Buddhist sect of the household concerned. Such altars are made in Yame, and, for good ones, the work is so intricate that seven specialists contribute to their construction.[7] Prices range from about £200 to over £2,000, but they last for a hundred years or more. A family without sufficient money could manage by placing a few items of ceremonial equipment on a shelf or in a plain black wooden box. Most important are the *ihai*, which are wooden tablets on which the posthumous Buddhist names of the dead are inscribed, with the date of death and secular names on the back. There is usually also a Buddhist image. Receptacles for offerings of flowers, food and water are kept freshly filled, and candles and incense are available for devotional rites. Photographs of the dead are often displayed in or above the *butsudan*, and sometimes an old person who is still living will have their photograph up beside a dead spouse. Such people commented that it was comforting to know they would be remembered.

In almost every house in Kurotsuchi,[8] including those with no need for a *butsudan*, there is a *kamidana* (god-shelf), which is associated with Shinto worship, particularly of the Imperial ancestress, Amaterasu Ōmikami, though a number of other talismans and amulets purchased at various Shinto shrines are kept there too. In particular there is usually one from Izumo, where the deity is celebrated for his ability to cement marital alliances, and these are sold locally, since the shrine is too far away for an easy visit. There is no particular location for this shelf, though it is usually high up in the corner of a room, since it is said to be disrespectful to be able to look down on it. It has a little wooden shrine at the back, which is much cheaper to buy than the ornate *butsudan*, and also usually has fresh offerings of rice, water and branches of a tree called *sakaki* (*Cleyera ochnacea*), traditionally used at any form of Shinto worship.

Some households have shelves where other deities are remembered, and some keep other Buddhist images, but there is one pair of jovial faces, raised on a surface which hangs like a picture, found in nearly every house. These are Daikoku and Ebisu, said to bring good fortune, prosperity and safety to the household, though many informants laughed them off as superstition. They are found in different parts of Japan, sometimes associated especially with fishermen, agriculture, shopkeepers or general wealth.[9] Ideas about the orientation of houses according to rules of geomancy will be discussed in Chapter 6, pp. 216-17.

The People

The most common form of household in Kurotsuchi is one with three generations living together, and each of these follows the *ie* ideology of having only one married successor remaining in the family home. Some other households have followed this principle but at present have only two generations alive, so to distinguish them from newly created nuclear families, I follow Koyama's terminology of 'succeeded' and 'created' households which gives Kurotsuchi 45 of the former and 8 of the latter.[10] The eight 'created' nuclear families all have one member who was born and brought up in one of the older households, so that a description of the operations of a three-generation household will not be in any way unrepresentative.

When all the possible positions in such a household are filled, the members are as shown below, which gives terms used by and in front of children.

Reference	Polite	Familiar	
ojii	ojiisan	jichan[11]	grandfather
obā	obāsan	bāchan	grandmother
oyaji/chichi	otōsan	tochan[11]	father
ofukuro/haha	okāsan	kachan[11]	mother
ani	oniisan	niichan	elder brother
ane	onēsan	nēchan	elder sister
oji	ojisan		uncle
oba	obasan		aunt

The polite forms may also be used by outsiders in place of a personal name or pronoun, especially within a household context, and a young married man may be called *tōsan* even before he has any children, because this is the position into which he is expected to move. Reference terms are humble forms, used to deprecate oneself and one's own family when showing respect for the person to whom one is speaking. *Oyaji* (father) is also used by women to refer to their husbands, just as *tochan* might be used within the family. A man of the household may also be addressed as *taishō*, which means 'general' or 'admiral' in military terminology, but colloquially used here to mean 'chief' or 'boss'. A woman may be politely addressed by an outsider as *okusan* (wife), but older members of the household still refer to a young wife as the *yome*, which can mean 'wife' or 'daughter-in-law', 'woman of the house'. The first child of each sex is addressed using the terms for elder brother and elder sister quite frequently even if there are only two children, and any older brother or sister should be addressed thus by a younger sibling. The reference words for younger brother and sister (*otōto* and *imōto*) are not used to address children; a proper name would be used. Even twins are distinguished in this way, and it is said that the child born last is the older, for it must have been conceived first. As a general principle, members of the family address their elders with a kin term, and are addressed by them with a personal name, and this rule applies among children, so that each is constantly made aware of his or her relative position. Unmarried siblings of the older generations who were born in the household have a right to remain there (i.e. uncle and aunt), but there are few of these. In Kurotsuchi there are two single women over 30 living in their natal homes, one of whom claims to be frail and the other who says she was ill at the time she should have married. There is one unmarried man, who may be a little simple, but he is only 34 and still hopes to take a wife eventually.

Older people in the village often had many siblings. In their young days infant mortality was common and large families were a precaution to ensure an heir and a practice encouraged by the government during Japan's years of Imperial expansion.[12] During the 1940s women were needed as labourers and were discouraged from having so many children, but after the war there was a sudden and sharp increase in the birth rate. This coincided with a decline in the death rate and a return of people from abroad, so that a government programme was soon under way to disseminate information about abortions and contraception.[13] It appears that for a while the former was more widely practised than the latter, but contraceptive information was distributed widely during the 1950s, and was included in much detail in a manual about marriage published then.[14] Baber reported a preference for three children as an ideal among young people in 1958 and, indeed, by this time there had been a spectacular drop in the birth rate.[15] This is illustrated well in the figures from Kurotsuchi families. No couples who started their families since 1960 have had more than three children, and even those with three often had two of the same sex first, or their mothers commented that they had one too many. Of 21 families started between 1945 and 1960 no less than 13 have three children, which seems to have been the most popular number. Four families had more, the most numerous being six, and four had less. Previously the range was much greater, and there are several examples in the village of families with every number between two and seven, single cases having had as many as 10 and 13.

With regard to sex, men commonly claim to prefer boys, to be sure of a successor, while women, although they recognise this need, usually express the desire to have girls to help with the housework.

Household Activities

Work and Authority

In the past, every member of the family worked for the household, but even now, when some have members working outside, there is still frequently a household purse. Within the household, women are always responsible for cooking, washing and cleaning, and men are rarely to be found in the kitchen. Women are usually also employed in some other way, and in households with a grandmother, she often takes care of young children, while the mother works in the fields, or perhaps at sewing. Domestic tasks are then shared, although the less pleasant ones like rising first traditionally fall to the young wife. In farm work, men and women work together, but a modern division of labour is illustrated in the way men usually operate machines while the women are left to do manual tasks like planting and harvesting the corners the machine cannot reach. However, some women do manage all farm work alone, particularly if they are widowed or have husbands who work elsewhere. Women are also able to substitute if necessary for men at meetings of the Agricultural Co-operative, though few men would claim to be able to order domestic supplies at the Women's Branch of the Co-operative. Girls begin to help with housework from about middle-school age, and boys too may help with farm work during busy periods from the same age. School work is not to be neglected, however, and may take priority.

Decisions about work are frequently said to be made after discussion (*hanashiai*) involving the whole family, but further inquiry sometimes elicited a division of large and small decisions between men and women, and most people said that men had the last word.[16] Where two men work together in the same family there does not seem to be a clear point at which the younger man takes over the authority from the older, despite the 'return to dependence' ceremony at 61 (Chapter 6, pp. 208-9). Informants described the process as gradual. Meetings of the flower growers' union were attended by predominantly younger men, but the older men remain active and busy as long as they possibly can, and land is usually registered in the name of the oldest male until he dies. Before the war, the family register listed one of the men in a household as the house head, and it was usual for an older man eventually to register retirement (*inkyo*) and make way for his successor. In some places this involved the elder couple moving into a separate room or residence, but elsewhere the older man seems to have retained a good deal of tacit authority.[17] Since Kurotsuchi records include examples of a retired house head taking back his official authority, it seems likely that the latter was the case here too. Although there is no longer a category of house head in the official register, the local policeman keeps a list of residents in his area, each in relation to the head of their household, and this has only one Kurotsuchi house listed in which the head is not the oldest male. In practice, however, the position of the person with greatest influence varies from house to house, and an expression frequently used to emphasise the importance of the role of the younger man is to call him the *daikoku bashira* (the principal post in the house construction).

The charge of the family purse is another matter which varies from one household to another, but of 49 households asked, only 5 said that each member was responsible for their own money. Twenty-eight families said that a female member controlled the purse, though some added that big financial transactions were made by men.[18] There appeared to be no correlation between farming or three-generation families and male or female control. People who are employed outside the home either turn over their salaries to the purse-keeper and receive an allowance for their needs, or pay in a fixed amount and retain the rest, sometimes, especially for young single people, paying another fixed amount into a savings account. Only a few children receive regular pocket-money, and most ask for a sum when they need it.

This applies also to sons and daughters working on the family farm, though a son who helps his father in business receives a salary and, indeed, in this family, each member including the wife and student daughter receive a monthly sum.

Leisure

Farming families in particular expressed an unwillingness to leave the house entirely unoccupied, so that three-generation families would rarely all go out together. In general, people tend to go out or away with peers, and activities of age-mate groups provide a good deal of social life. Trips are often made with members of the same sex, and young married couples laughed at the idea that they might go out or take a holiday without the children. However, older people sometimes go away in groups of married couples, three age-mate groups meet as couples and, recently, newly-weds are to be seen going out together. This last idea is still a cause for some gossip, but Kurotsuchi practices seem less strict than elsewhere, since traditionally men and women are said to seek entertainment separately, even in cities.[19] Even so, women with young children have little opportunity to go out, except occasionally to visit their own families, as was illustrated by the age-mate group which could find no time to have their cookery classes. Men are much freer to go off and meet friends, and one man explained that this was why women were better than men at looking after the family purse. Young wives have little time to themselves at all in three-generation families, and even wives in nuclear families seemed to spend most of their time at home, although some complained about their husbands' outside activities. Children are occasionally taken out by both parents, typically to a shrine, shopping or perhaps to the zoo, and when children grow up, they may occasionally take their parents out, especially if they learn to drive. During free time from school, children are often to be seen playing within the village.

Bathing

One of the often mentioned privileges of the head of the traditional household was that he would bathe first,[20] but in Kurotsuchi, where there were few family baths, it was not possible to see if this prevailed. Informants were aware of the idea, however, and reported that all men used to bathe before women, just as men's clothes would be washed separately some two generations ago. This practice concerned the avoidance of pollution, and women still refrain from using the public bath for a month after childbirth, and some also during menstruation.

In houses where there were private baths, the oldest man was said to have the option of going first, except in one case, where the widowed grandmother had this perogative, but others often preceded them for convenience. The pattern at the village bath seemed to be for grandmothers, who could leave preparation of the evening meal to younger women, to go down early when it was quiet, followed by older men as they finished work. The men's side would apparently remain in constant use throughout the evening, but there was a peak period in the women's side about the time supper would have been cleared away.

Eating

Hierarchy in the traditional household is said to have been observed at mealtimes, too, when the head would receive preferential treatment,[21] but there seems to have been a good deal of publicity about the 'feudal'[22] nature of such a practice, and direct questions would frequently meet with assurances that the whole family ate together. In practice, everyday meals I was able to observe or share varied from house to house, but were usually served by the younger wife, who attended to men in order of age, though a grandmother was sometimes served before her son. The women sit with the men on a normal day, but if an occasion is in any way formal, they often eat separately. When I was fairly new in the village I would sometimes be afforded formal treatment which involved the serving of a refreshment to myself and to the man or men of the house at the table, while the women, though often present, would sit at some distance from the table and either refrain from eating or do so rather surreptitiously at one side. Sometimes, on such an occasion, the man concerned called his wife to see me out when I was ready to leave, and made his farewell in the *zashiki*.[23] At a large formal gathering, the women sit below the men where both are entertained together, but often men take the formal seats while their wives serve or remain helping in the kitchen. If a woman is seated in a position of honour in mixed company, it may well be that she is representing a man, or at least an honoured household for that specific occasion. Small children are often allowed to run in and out of the most solemn affairs with apparent unconcern on the part of the participants, and if they are hungry or noisy they may also be fed before adults at everyday meals.

Ritual Activity

Rites and ceremonies for specific occasions will be described in subsequent chapters, but ancestors and deities are by no means forgotten in daily life. Attentions vary from house to house, and older people are more likely to practise regular devotion than younger ones, but offerings of water and the first helping of the day's rice are usually made every day, and flowers or *sakaki* branches changed frequently. Many people also pay their respects to the *butsudan* and the *kamidana* night and morning, and a few old people set aside time each day to chant sutras. Gifts received by members of the household are offered to the ancestors before they are opened, and visitors may well make an offering at the *butsudan* before they greet living members of the family, particularly if they are descendants who have moved away. It is to the ancestors that the bride makes her final farewell when she leaves home to be married, and when she enters her husband's home she must pay her respects to the new ancestors before she acknowledges anyone else present.

The *butsudan* is opened for any special occasion, so that the ancestors may be included, but the intensity of daily attention probably depends on whether anyone has recently died in the family. Even children are encouraged to share their joys and sorrows with an individual they remember, now referred to as *hotokesama* (literally buddha).[24] The physical remains of the dead are stored in the *nōkotsudō*, as was mentioned in the previous chapter, and a spiritual part of the dead is thought to reside with these remains, for visits are made to this resting place, and once a year at the Bon summer festival these souls (*tamashii* or *rei*) are said to return to the house for three days.[25] There is also a certain spiritual presence in the *butsudan*, however, and especially after a recent death, this is identified particularly with the individual lost. Gradually this individual merges with his or her predecessors, and eventually joins the more general category of *senzo* (forbears or ancestors).[26] In some places the individual's *ihai* is destroyed after fifty years or so, and his or her name added to a common tablet,[27] but in Kurotsuchi there are individual tablets (*ihai*) dating back almost two hundred years, though individual memorial ceremonies have long since ceased (see Chapter 6, p. 213).

Various rites are observed annually for the benefit of the household, the most important being at New Year and at Bon, both of which will be considered in detail in Chapter 6, pp. 213-16, since they are also concerned with relations between households. On 3 February, which is called *setsubun* and officially marks the end of winter, beans are thrown out of the house to symbolise the expulsion of devils, and the cry '*Fuku wa uchi, oni wa soto*' ('Fortune in, devils out') accompanies this. This custom is widespread, and has been observed, sometimes with variations, by earlier writers.[28] Another rite, said to be for the purification of the house and protection against sickness, has not been described elsewhere. This involves going to a shrine in Kurume to collect a little holy water, which is offered first to the village shrine, then to the *kamidana*, and finally consumed by members of the family. It takes place on 1 September, which is known as Hassaku, an ancient holiday still also celebrated in a neighbouring village where a procession is held to pray for a good harvest. In Kurotsuchi it is a work day, but many villagers rise early to collect the water from Kurume at daybreak, and thus discharge this small obligation to the welfare of the household. In the feudal period, it is said, people would walk the 12 km. to Kurume to perform this rite.

Intra-familial Relations

It is already evident that rules of behaviour within the household vary considerably from one household to another, and intra-familial relations depend to some extent on these rules and on the characters of the individuals concerned. However, certain collective ideas about specific relationships exist, and deviations from usual expectations are still subject to sanctions such as gossip and even open comment. This section will be confined to relationships for which attitudes are well defined.

Parents-Children

This relationship is traditionally said to be the first and foremost in Japanese society, and one modern informant remarked that at least the love (*aijō*) between parent and child must be the same the world over. The terms *aijō* and *jōai* (affection) are now often used to describe the relationship between parent and child, but in the traditional view it was rather a matter of honour and respect.

The care parents gave their children incurred in the latter a debt known as *on*, which bound them not only to care for their parents for the rest of their lives, but also to afford their own children the same attentions they had received. By law, children were to give unconditional obedience to their parents, who had no reciprocal duties, but rather a far-reaching power over their child.[29] A proverb which illustrates these expectations is 'Fubo no on wa yama yori takai (takaku umi yori mo fukai')' ('Your parents' grace is higher than the mountain (and deeper than the ocean')').[30] Informants said that *on*, here translated 'grace', is a term now rarely used in connection with this relationship, and indeed it has been adversely associated with 'feudalism',[31] but the concepts of obligation and debt to one's parents have certainly not been abandoned. It seems possible that the use of the word *aijō* in this context is perhaps a recent substitute born of Western influence.[32] The extent of the debt of children to their parents is emphasised in the country, where many householders owe all their land and livelihood to their position as successor. One informant pointed out that he (as a carpenter) and his elder brother, who had inherited the main house and land, were less well off then their neighbours because their father had died before his children were well established in life, so the family had had to struggle and sell land to bring up the children.

The importance of the traditional relationship between parents and children is illustrated in the way it has been used as a model for many other relationships in society (*oyabun-kobun*), so that similar obligations of aid and indebtedness are created between master and pupil, employer and employee, landowner and tenant, as well as in patron-client links of business, politics and even underworld activities. Finally, the extent of its importance even now was illustrated in a discussion with a group of young people about marriage, when I asked how they thought of the relationship between their own parents. Except for one girl, who knew that her parents had had a love match, all agreed that they had never really thought about the link, always relating to each separate parent through the vertical bond. This would seem to confirm the suggestion of Suzuki Takao that

> for the Japanese, marriage is not a dynamic, direct, contractual relationship, which the persons concerned must maintain by constant confirmation of their love for one another. For them, it is rather a natural, noncontractual relationship, based on the static and unchangeable parent-child relationship.[33]

Husband-Wife and Other Male-Female Relations

Questions about the nature of the relationship between husbands and wives met, in general, with little clear response. Even if *ren'ai* (love)[34] had been the reason for marriage, informants explained that couples with children would be unlikely to describe their relationship as such, since the element of 'impulse' or 'urge' (*shōdō*) involved made it a term more often associated with extra-marital affairs and unrequited love. Some people mentioned *aijō*, but with clear reservations, and more commonly it was said to be a relation of 'sympathy' or 'fellow feeling' (*dōjō*), or even just 'endurance' or 'tolerance' (*gaman*).

There is traditionally much less expected emotionally of a marital relationship in Japan than in the West. It has already been mentioned that couples do not often seek recreation in each other's company, and it would appear to be enough if they can work together (for farmers), and are sexually sufficiently compatible to produce children. Two grandfathers explained independently that an element of *ren'ai* was necessary even in their youth, but other long-married people preceded any remarks about *ren'ai* with a statement that they had never experienced it. However a husband and wife treat each other in private, it is not uncommon for a man to order his wife around in public,[35] and call her from other business to attend to his needs. Once when I was in conversation with a man who wanted to show me a picture which was out of reach, he called his wife from the other end of the house rather than get up and look for it himself. The wife's role in this respect is not merely one of physical service, and a man never hesitates to consult his wife if he thinks she might be better informed than he. In this way, the wife is often to her husband as a bureaucrat is to a politician, an idea which is reinforced on ceremonial occasions when men take the official seats while women may well advise from the kitchen on the order of proceedings.

In general, men like to be fussed over by women, and in towns, most bars have hostesses to top up the customers' drinks and light their cigarettes, as well as to listen to their conversation. In the home, mothers wait on their sons, and encourage their daughters to do the same. Girls are also encouraged to prepare for marriage rather than to develop any individual talents, so that a high-school girl who had represented her school, city and prefecture in athletics was said by her mother to have limited scope for such activities after she left school, merely because she was a girl rather than a boy. Kyūshū has been found to rate low in attitudes to sexual equality,[36] and informants readily pointed out the greater freedom enjoyed by men, but it was quite interesting to find that only young, usually unmarried women wished they had been born otherwise. These envied the way boys could choose a career and go out and enjoy themselves, but married women frequently said that they preferred the role which lacked the burden of responsibility which fell to men, and pointed to the satisfaction to be found in rearing children. Women in Kurotsuchi work harder than men do, for after a full day's work, they must turn to household tasks. However since women are usually at least theoretically able to support themselves economically, men are actually more dependent for their daily needs on women than vice versa, and a household without women (of which there were none) would be more at a loss than one without men (of which there were two). Women are also usually able to wield a good deal of influence within the home, although the extent of this depends on individual abilities.[37]

Sibling Relationships

Relationships between siblings of different sexes follow the patterns described in the previous section, and, especially where brothers are older, sisters will cook, wash and run errands for them. Boys enjoy this attention, and girls say they like to have brothers because they will sometimes take them to places they could not go alone; but both boys and girls usually add that they have a closer relationship with a sibling of the same sex. Even this is usually marred by an age discrepancy, however, since the expectation of a certain degree of respect for older siblings, reinforced by the clear classification of schoolfellows into seniors, juniors or contemporaries, seems to inhibit the establishment of much intimacy. Older sisters sometimes say that though they would listen to a younger one, they would prefer to confide in a friend, and schoolgirls frequently have a close confidante of their own age (*shin'yū*). Boys also seem to prefer the company of age-mates of their own sex, and two separate informants said that brothers know each other so well that they have no need for conversation. The expectation of respect for an older sibling is illustrated in the way children are encouraged to suffix the names of older children with *nēsan* or *niisan*, precisely as a term of deference. Since all but one member of a group of siblings usually move out of the household, relations between adult siblings become relations between households, and these will be considered later.

In-law Relationships

Within the household, the relationship between a man's wife and his mother is that which is said to be subjected to most strain. These women must co-operate and work together if the household is to run smoothly, and many writers describe how, especially before the war, women were very harsh with their daughters-in-law, often as a kind of asymmetric retaliation for treatment they had received from their own mothers-in-law.[38] If things became intolerable, the daughter-in-law would be sent home, even if her husband were fond of her, but these days the young couple may well move out and set up a separate home.[39] This was the case with the only family totally unrelated to others, which moved into Kurotsuchi some eight years before the investigation.

The older man had started married life as eldest son living with his parents in the Kawasaki school zone, but, when his children were small, relations between his wife and his mother became so bad that they moved out and tried to establish a small business in a neighbouring village. They managed to struggle on for fifteen years, but eventually the business failed, and they were forced to move again, this time to Kurotsuchi. They rent their present house, and both the older man and his son are employed, as is the son's young wife. The daughter-in-law has now become a mother-in-law, and she takes care of the young couple's baby, often walking it up and down outside their house, but the family has its own bath, its members rarely take part in village affairs, and they belong to few village organisations. They are in an anomalous position in this village of old, often related families, and it seems consistent that their circumstances stem from a breakdown in the family system.

The break between this family and the older man's original household was too long ago and too far away to excite much comment these days, but a similar break occurred in an Inobu family much more recently. It was a well-known family, and the first young wife had died tragically, leaving two small daughters. Her replacement was over 30 when she married, had already had a career of her own in Tokyo, but nevertheless expressed a desire to live with and learn from her mother-in-law. She soon gave birth to a son, but disputes over the care of the child brought so much trouble that eventually her husband decided that they would move out. The situation has upset the inheritance plans for the family business, and disapproval is expressed in this and neighbouring villages of the wife who could not live at peace with her husband's mother.

In Kurotsuchi itself, there are apparently no examples of relations breaking down completely, and it is a common sight in the bath of an evening to see a mother and her daughter-in-law soaking side by side or scrubbing one another's backs. Different households obviously have different problems, and some young women had nothing but good to say of their mothers-in-law, with whom they share domestic tasks, and from whom they can seek advice and aid in the care of children. Others were more reserved. However, it is said that older women treat their daughters-in-law much less harshly these days, indeed, that they need to in order to keep them.[40] It has also been suggested that the whole problem was the recent result of a period of considerable social upheaval.[41]

Developmental Cycle of the Household

Succession and Inheritance

Despite clear changes in the laws of inheritance, evidence from Kurot-suchi would suggest that practice corresponded exactly to neither pre-war nor post-war legislation, but has continued relatively unchanged. Before the war, the law stipulated that all household property and authority (*katoku*) should pass to the eldest son, but post-war legislation gives all sons and daughters equal rights to inherit. As has been found elsewhere (p. 28), a successor is still chosen who inherits most of the land, as well as the responsibility to care for his parents and the ancestral tablets, while other siblings waive their rights.[42] The other siblings are by no means forgotten, however, since daughters are sent off in marriage with a large, expensive trousseau (see Chapter 5, pp. 165-9), which they regard as their share of the inheritance, while other sons may well receive help with education, house purchase or possibly a small amount of land so that they can set up a branch house in the village. Informants reported that such practices had been going on where possible since long before the war,[43] and, conversely, where brothers have left a household which subsequently has difficulties, they may well send money, or return to help at a time of crisis.

There is no doubt, however, that one person is regarded as the successor (*kōkeisha* or *atotsugi*) in any one household, and, even if no child wishes to follow the family occupation, parents express the hope that one of them will remain in the house to take care of them in their old age. This was the case even with 'created' families, whose members admitted that they enjoyed their own freedom from parental presence. Nineteen out of 22 possible farming households do have a son farming,[44] and where sons have done so well at school, and perhaps at university, that they have taken up outside employment, parents are often torn between being proud of such achievements and lamenting the recent idea of encouraging individual success over the demands of the household. In the past, too, well-established households did move away, and records reveal that eight complete Kurotsuchi families, with three generations or more in the register, have moved away since 1888. There was also a case where a successor ran off to America at the turn of the century, but fortunately the family was able to adopt a sister's husband to succeed, so that the household continued.

Primogeniture was institutionalised in the Meiji period, although previously other types of succession had also been customary and in some regions of Kyūshū ultimogeniture was practised.[45] In Kurotsuchi, informants stated that the ideal was for the eldest son to inherit, but that, in practice, sometimes another would do so. Details were available in the family register of pre-war succession to the headship, and these are given in Table 7, where they are compared with post-war cases, including those where the older generation is still alive, but the successor already decided, about which oral information was collected.

Table 7: Succession to the Headship of Kurotsuchi Houses

Pre-war and up to 1947				Post-New Constitution			
Eldest Son	Other	*Yōshi*	Women	Eldest Son	Other	*Yōshi*	Women
56	2S(7)	eDH(7)	W(2)	39	2S(3)	eDH(4)	eD(1)
	3S(1)	yBeS(2)	D(3)		3S(3)	2DH(2)	W (1)
	4S(1)	yBDH(1)	gM(1)		yB(3)	½BS(1)	
	yB(1)	W→HyB(1)	M(1)			W→HyB(1)	
	yBeS(1)	distant				non-	
	DeS(2)	relative(1)				relative(1)	
		unknown(1)					
Sub-total							
56	13	13	7	39	9	7 (+ 1)	2
Percentage of Total							
62.9	14.6	14.6	7.9	67.2	15.5	13.8	3.1

Information for 89 cases recorded up to 1947 in the family register, and 58 cases reported by informants since that time, including projected successors where head is alive.

It can be seen that the proportion of other brothers and adopted sons inheriting is little changed, but that the eldest son inherits in a majority of cases. Women were only registered if there was no male in the direct line, before the war, and even a baby boy would be registered head, with a guardian, before a wife or mother would. A wife would precede a brother, however, and the few cases where a younger brother of a previous head did inherit indicate that the first successor died childless and usually young, in two cases killed in active service during the war. The women shown in the table were usually only in the position of head until they could find a man to adopt in their place, and, since the head is no longer registered anyway, a similar situation after the war would not be recorded. Thus there is no significance in a comparison of the figures for women. Nowadays, a woman would assume the position of head if there were no adult male, usually until a son was married.[46]

In practice, now, an eldest son is in a position to choose whether or not he wants to succeed, so that if he decides to take up a career elsewhere the choice passes to the next son. There are four pre-war cases, at least, where an eldest son did not inherit the main house even though he was registered as having done so. In each case, the descendants of the eldest son concerned report that they are a branch of a household descended from another son – in other words, the other house has the ancestral tablets, perhaps because the eldest son left the village for a while, or died young and left his children in the care of a younger brother.[47] The oldest records give no indication of what became of non-inheriting sons, so that a few of the older cases of other-son inheritance may also have been because the original successor died young. There are also cases where the eldest son of a branch house has been adopted back into the house from which his own had split, because the latter had no heirs, and this would leave only a younger son to inherit the branch house. The most important thing is and was that someone stay in the household to continue the family line, and if the eldest son proved difficult in some way, or was required elsewhere, there was certainly no customary rule against another son being chosen or preferred by the parents, whatever the legal niceties were.

Marriage, Adoption and Divorce

The other requirement for the continuation of a household is a wife for the heir, or if there are no sons, a husband who is free to inherit for a daughter. The word most commonly used for wife is still *yome*, which, with the meaning implied in its Chinese character of 'woman of the house', aptly describes the way a woman traditionally married not only her husband but his whole household. The adopted son-in-law is a *muko-yōshi* (*muko* is husband or son-in-law, *yōshi*, adopted child), and in many ways the position of such a man parallels that of the wife who marries in.[48] In both cases, the family concerned is said to be 'receiving a *yome/yōshi*', both take the surname of the family into which they marry, and both bring a trousseau of some sort, their own family receiving betrothal gifts (see Chapter 5). The relationship set up between the two families is in both cases one of *engumi*, where *en* is a notion of karmic destiny or fate, especially for a relation, and *gumi* the noun formed from the verb *kumu* to join, unite or co-operate.[49] Both *yome* and *yōshi* are strangers at first among people who know each other well, and they must adapt to ways new to them but well-established to the others, often while being assigned the least attractive tasks. The bride's first period in her new home has frequently been described as trying and lonely, 'the bitter-moon' rather than the honeymoon,[50] and traditionally she was only allowed to visit her old home at certain fixed times.[51] The *mukoyōshi* is in a similarly inferior position, at least at first, and there is a certain aversion on the part of men to fill such a role, against which even a proverb advises.[52] Both *yome* and *yōshi* were traditionally expected to prove their worth, and frequently marriages were not registered legally until the family was satisfied, usually just prior to the birth of a child, according to the records (see p. 54). Otherwise the *yome* or *yoshi* could be sent home without legal recourse or record of the wedding.[53]

Once a child was born, however, the place of the mother was much more secure.[54] As one writer put it, 'child-birth pain is the purgatory out of which the young wife rises to be received with deeper love by the whole family.'[55] Informants quoted the proverb: 'ko wa kasugai' ('a child is a clamp') to summarise the effect of the birth of a child on marriage, explained further to mean that the child provides a bridge between the family and the previous outsider. Parents, children and siblings are automatically related through blood, a connection of *nikushin* (flesh-relation), one informant elaborated. The *yome* or *yōshi* at first establishes only a relation of *giri* (in-law or duty), but when a child is born, the *nikushin* relation is established with the child, and through it, with the husband and his parents.

Today, too, young wives report that they only began to feel at home after their first child was born, even though efforts are made to make life easier for the bride. As more younger sons were able to move away to the cities and set up their own homes, girls began to express a preference for this freer life.[56] Farming families found it correspond-ingly more difficult to find wives for their sons, which seems to have led to better treatment for the *yome* once found.[57] One family in Kurotsuchi bought a kitten for their new *yome*, another allowed their son to take his wife to visit her parents two or three times a week at first. Most marriages are now registered within a few weeks of the ceremony, and, although there were no recent cases of infertility to provide a test, informants claimed that a child would be adopted rather than a wife returned if a couple proved barren nowadays.

This is another type of adoption, and although the term *yōshi* is still used technically, an adopted child is more frequently referred to as a *moraigo* (received child). Preferably, it is said, the barren couple seeks a blood relation; the child of a sibling of one of the partners is especially favoured.[58] One barren couple in Kurotsuchi adopted the five-year-old son of a husband's brother, who had nine children, and later married the boy to the daughter of the wife's brother, so that blood from both sides of the family was passed on to the heirs. In another case, a woman's second *yōshi* husband, who had no children, asked as a dying wish that the successor through her first marriage be married to a girl from his family so that the union would bring an injection into the household of his family's blood. The wish was fulfilled and there are now two healthy sons to link the families and continue the line. Thus the blood link is sought where possible, though the continuation of the household is sometimes necessarily made through an unrelated child, and the 40-year-old wife at the rice-polishing shop was adopted at the age of five by barren parents who were unrelated to her own, and later her husband was received as an unrelated *yōshi* as well.

Despite the practice of delay in the registration of marriage, family records reveal a number of cases of divorce over the years in Kurotsuchi (see Table 8). Legal divorce, as legal marriage, simply requires that both husband and wife stamp an official form in the presence of two witnesses. Only one of the total number of 29 divorces involving Kurotsuchi residents was disputed and taken to court, which suggests that a family wishing to return a *yome* or *yōshi* was usually able to persuade them to agree. As elsewhere, the usual explanation of the family is that the *yome* or *yōshi* was unable to adjust to the 'ways of the house' (*kafū*). There have been no recent divorces in Kurotsuchi, and the figures in Table 8 would suggest a significant decrease since the war. This is no doubt related to the difficulties experienced by farming families in finding a *yome* and the consequent better treatment they receive. Also, as was noted in the section on relations between mother and daughter-in-law, the young couple would be more likely to move out today if insurmountable problems arose, rather than the wife being sent home.

The one reason that still seems to be generally considered sufficient ground for divorce is if a wife falls ill and can no longer work. Unless her children were old enough to take care of themselves and the house, such a woman would probably be returned to her own natal household, it was reported. In 1941 a woman of 33 returned to Kurotsuchi for this reason and lived with her brother's family until she died in 1969. Thus

Table 8: Marriage and Divorce Figures into, out of and within Kurotsuchi from 1886 to May 1979

Years	Marriages (including *yōshi* — numbers of these in brackets)			Divorces			Remarriages
	In	Out	Within	In	Out	Within	
1886-90	12(3)	7(2)	2	5*(1)	1		5
1891-95	9(1)	5(1)	1	1			1
1896-1900	9	5(1)	1(1)	1	2(1)		3
1901-5	2	6(2)	3				
1906-10	4(1)	7	3	3(2)*	1	1	5
1911-15	7	4	1				
1916-20	6(1)	3	1		1	1	2
1921-5	10(2)	8	4	1			1
1926-30	2	6	2(1)	1			1
1931-5	9	10(1)	3(1)	1	1		
1936-40	5	9(1)					
1941-5	7(3)	7	2	1	2		3
1946-50	12(1)	18(4)	2(1)	2	1		3
1951-5	9(1)	16(2)	1	1			
1956-60	8	17(2)		1	1		2
1961-5	8	11(1)	1				
1966-70	5(1)	15					
1971-5	9	17(2)			1		
1976-9	8(2)	12					

Totals

Pre-1945	82(11)	77(8)	23(3)	12(2)	8(1)	2	
1946-79	59(5)	106(11)	4(1)	4	3	0	
1886-1945	14.6%	10.4%	8.7%	Divorces as percentage			
1946-75	7.8%	3.2%	–	of marriages			

Total no. of pre-1945 marriages: 182, divorces: 22, % div./marr. 12.1%
Total no. of post-1945 marriages: 149, divorces: 7, % div./marr. 4.7%
Ditto, discounting most recent 10
years to allow time lapse for div.: 103, divorces: 6, % div./marr. 5.8%
(The marriages which took place between 1975 and 1979 were investigated fully
and are therefore included. I did not hear of any divorces, but was unable to
examine the family registers and am therefore not absolutely sure that none
took place. so the div./marr. rates are based on 1975 figures.)

Note: * indicates divorce of one remarriage so not included for comparison with
marriage figures at left.
* on right of bracket indicates a *yōshi* divorce of remarriage.

a household is always ultimately responsible for its original members and, although healthy women were often soon married again, divorcees usually returned to their old home at first. The children, however, belonged to their house of birth, the father's household except in the case of a *yōshi*, who would also be returned in the same circumstances. The parent left in the main household with the children would be married again as soon as possible, as in the case of bereavement, and remarriage might well take place the following year.

The *yome* who is left bereaved in her husband's home is in a difficult position, unless she has not yet had any children, when she would be free to return to her own *ie*. If there are children, however, she is related to the family by blood through them and they would probably expect her to stay and work for the continuation of this household, that of her children. Two cases in Kurotsuchi illustrate such a situation. The second was resolved, apparently quite happily. In 1977, a young man was killed in an accident, leaving his wife and three small children living in the home of his parents. He was a farmer and the couple had always seemed hard-working during my study, so the family was no doubt left with a large number of problems. By 1979, just before I returned in early May, the widow had married again a pleasant young man who had moved into the house as a *yōshi* and taken over his predecessor's work. He was the younger brother of his new wife's elder sister's husband, and such an arrangement was praised throughout the area. An earlier case had not ended so well. During the summer of 1975 another young man had died suddenly leaving a similar family, again farmers with a good acreage of land and a large, recently reconstructed house. This time I was able to witness the reactions of other farmers. Their first concern was always for the *ie* and the loss of its *daikoku bashira*, rather than compassion for the individual losses of son, husband and father. They lamented the fact that the children were too young to start work, that the eldest daughter was not old enough to receive a *yōshi*, and that the parents were getting past heavy work. The wife was unable to eat or sleep for some time, growing so thin that her father-in-law complained that soon she too would die and desert him. She repeatedly expressed regret that she had not died in her husband's place, because he could have remarried whereas she could not. During the rest of that year she worked on for the family, and her father-in-law talked of hopes to work on until the eldest daughter could be found a husband to adopt as a *yōshi*. However, in 1976, the wife left her husband's family home, taking the three children with her, and she has not been seen there since. She left many of their belongings which she has apparently not tried to reclaim, although the children now visit sometimes on Sundays. The family lives somewhere not too far distant, apparently supported by the mother, and I did not hear harsh words condemning her. Several people expressed sorrow at the plight of the abandoned grandparents, and were pleased when I stayed with them on my return visit, but one or two noted that they were strict members of an old school, which must have made it hard for the widow.

Family records reveal numerous crises such as these over the years, and in many cases a widow appears to have soldiered on unmarried to enable her son, or daughter's husband, to have a house to inherit when they came of age.[59] Today it is evidently possible for a wife to escape such an onerous duty if she has the courage and can find no other way.

Branch Households

Many sons who are either ineligible or unwilling to inherit their own household move away to work elsewhere, usually in cities. They may receive aid and introductions from a relative already in the city, but nowadays job opportunities also arise through educational qualifications. Table 9 gives the numbers of boys leaving in this way. Such people are regarded as members of their own *ie* until they marry, and many return home to look for a wife, but once married they usually set up their own household elsewhere. After this, they may well return quite frequently at Bon and New Year to pay respects to their ancestors, but such visits will probably decrease over the years, perhaps dwindling eventually to important ceremonies, and subsequent generations will visit even less often, if at all.[60]

Some non-inheriting sons are able to remain in the village, however (see Tables 9 and 10 for proportions), and the households they form usually on or around the time of marriage are known as *bunke* (branch house) of their original *ie*, which are called their *honke* (main house). Between such households special relations of mutual aid, participation in life crisis ceremonies, and visits at Bon and New Year usually persist for about three generations, though they may be curtailed in case of dispute,[61] or extended if one of the households concerned lacks other similar connections. After this time, some groups of households still meet for an annual 'ancestor festival' (*senzo matsuri*), and in Kurotsuchi this is observed by two separate groups. One of these includes the ten households with the name Shibata, plus one other household which claims common ancestry, but which reports that one of their ancestors left the village as a *yōshi*, thereby changing his name,

Table 9: Adult Destination of Sons Born in Kurotsuchi from 1881 to 1950

Year of Birth	Total[b]	Inherited	*Bunke*	*Yōshi*	Left Village	Died
1881-90	26	8	2	5	3	8
1891-1900	32	14	5	1	3	9
1901-10	34	5	6	3	7	13
1911-20	24	7	1	2	2	12
1921-30	39	14	4	5	6	10
1931-40	46	14	0	4	18	10
1941-50	42	10	2	2	25	3
1951-60[a]	19	12	–	–	5	2
	+12 undecided yet					
	31					

Notes: a. Boys of the 1951-60 group have not yet reached marriageable age, thus the *bunke* and *yōshi* columns would be unlikely to have entries in them.
b. The 'total' column is almost certainly incomplete, since some families left in the past without leaving records, so older figures would have been slightly larger, as would those of boys who left the village. There are no recorded figures of the total number of births, or even of population of Kurotsuchi until 1965.

Table 10: Criteria of Membership of Household of All Married Members of Kurotsuchi

	Men		Women
Successor	50	Came as *yome*	71
Yōshi	11	Received *yōshi*	9
Bunke	7	Adopted as child	1
Moved in	3	Built house by B	2
	71		83

but subsequently returned with his family. These families know roughly how they are related to one another, and they used also to share a common graveyard. The other group has only three households, though it is said that a larger group with the same surname – Kawaguchi – used to celebrate a *senzo matsuri*, but gave up because numbers were too great. There are no less than 31 households with the name Kawaguchi, but they do not claim all to be related, and they even have two distinct family crests[62] among them. Informants seemed not to know why so many families shared the same name.[63] It is a phenomenon found in many regions of Japan, which has been associated with the ancient clan system.[64] However, farmers were not allowed to use surnames during the Tokugawa period, and apparently when this changed in early Meiji, many chose to be named after a place or an influential person in the district, and it was as acceptable for everyone working a certain area of land to share one name as for people related consanguinially.[65]

Several families with other surnames in the village are actually related to the Kawaguchis or the Shibatas, four households being those of daughters of Kawaguchi families who were given a small plot of household land on which to make a home with their husbands. This illustrates the way children other than the successor may be helped, even though not an official *bunke*. The Shibata *yōshi* relative has also been mentioned, and there is a Kawaguchi family which has taken the surname of a female ancestor because her original household was otherwise destined to die out, and this household had a *bunke* to continue the name. There is one totally unrelated household, but the other five are related to each other, three sharing one surname, two another.

In this part of the country, *honke-bunke* links are much weaker than in north Japan, and interactions with affinally and geographically related households may be as frequent. Detailed descriptions of life crisis ceremonies in subsequent chapters will illustrate the way neighbours participate as well as relatives, and certainly little distinction is made in everyday affairs. On a formal occasion, the person representing a household's *honke* may be distinguished by being introduced as *honke no oji* (uncle from the main house), but otherwise all bilateral kindred are known as *shinseki* for about three generations, *oba* (aunt) and *oji* (uncle) referring to the same people as do the English terms.[66] After that time, *shinseki* are usually referred to as *mukashi no shinseki* (distant relatives). Interactions between affinally related households usually decrease more rapidly than *honke-bunke* ones after the death of the generation which formed the original link. This is perhaps related to the fact that most marriages are village exogamous (see next chapter), and the intensity of relations between households outside the village must depend to some extent on the distance between them. Most relations between households are initiated by marriage, either because this creates direct affinal ties, or because it gives the individuals setting up their new household the status of adults and householders. It is appropriate at this point, then, to turn to the ways in which marriages are made. The following chapter will be concerned with matchmaking, the subsequent one with the ceremonies involved. Chapter 6 will provide a wider consideration of the expression of these relationships between households.

Notes

1. *Kazoku* is a nineteenth-century Japanese word devised to translate the English 'family' (R.K. Beardsley *et al.*, *Village Japan*, Phoenix edn (University of Chicago Press, Chicago, 1969), p. 217). It means literally 'people of the *ie*' or '*ie* group'.

2. Jukichi Inouye, *Home Life in Tokyo* (Tokyo, 1910), p. 37. 'Great artificer' is a literal translation of the Chinese characters used to write 'carpenter', namely *daiku* (大工).

3. In pre-Meiji times only samurai houses were permitted to have tiled roofs or more than one floor (cf. Kunio Yanagida, *Japanese Manners and Customs in the Meiji Era*, (trans. and adapted by Charles S. Terry, Obunsha, Tokyo, 1957), p. 59). A detailed description of traditional Japanese houses as observed and sketched during the Meiji period is to be found in Edward S. Morse, *Japanese Homes and their Surroundings* (Boston, 1886).

4. Cf. David W. Plath, *The After Hours* (University of California Press, Berkeley, 1964), p. 175. Several amusing descriptions of the consequences of this lack of privacy in Japanese houses are given in Mrs Bishop's account of her travels in rural Japan only ten years after the Meiji Restoration: *Unbeaten Tracks in Japan* (John Murray, London, 1900).

5. *Zashiki* literally means 'cushion-spreading', as this is where cushions are spread for guests (Yanagida, *Manners and Customs*, p. 59).

6. Morse, *Japanese Homes*, p. 133; Yanagida, *About Our Ancestors*, trans. Fanny Mayer and Yasuyo Ishiwara (Japanese National Commission for UNESCO, Tokyo, 1970), p. 125; Edward Norbeck, *Takashima* (University of Utah Press, Salt Lake City, 1954), p. 62; John B. Cornell, 'Matsunagi' in J.B. Cornell and R.J. Smith (eds.), *Two Japanese Villages* (Greenwood Press, New York, 1969), p. 171; Tsutomu Ema, *Kekkon no Rekishi (History of Marriage)* (Yūzan-kaku, Tokyo, 1971), p. 73.

7. Specialists are required to do the following parts: *soto no kiji* (outside box), *kanagu* (metal fittings), *chōkoku* (carving), *kindei* (carved wooden roofing work), *nurishi* (varnishing), *busshi* (sculpting of Buddhist image) and *makie* (gold lacquer work).

8. The Sōka Gakkai houses are an exception to this because they take no part in Shinto worship.

9. Cornell, 'Matsunagi', p. 171; Bishop, *Unbeaten Tracks*, p. 180; J.F. Embree, *Suye Mura* (University of Chicago Press, Chicago, 1939), pp. 240-1; Norbeck, *Takashima*, p. 123; Tokutarō Sakurai, 'The Major Features and Characteristics of Japanese Folk Beliefs' in Kiyomi Morioka and William Newell (eds.), *The Sociology of Japanese Religion* (Brill, Leiden, 1968), p. 17; Yanagida, *Manners and Customs*, p. 265.

10. Takashi Koyama, 'The Significance of Relatives at the Turning Point of the Family System in Japan' in Paul Halmos (ed.), *Japanese Sociological Studies* (The Sociological Review, Monograph 10, University of Keele, 1966), p. 104. Using this classification Kurotsuchi has 85 per cent succeeded houses, which differs by only 1 per cent from Koyama's findings in Yamanashi prefecture. However, both are much greater than Koyama's urban sample, which was around

30 per cent (ibid., p. 105).

11. The *ji*, *to* and *ka* are pronounced with a short vowel in the local dialect, although in standard Japanese they would have a macron.

12. Cf. R.P. Dore, 'Japanese Rural Fertility', *Population Studies*, vol. 7 (1953), p. 73; Joy Paulson, 'Evolution of the Feminine Ideal', p. 19, and Gail Bernstein, 'Women in Rural Japan', p. 29 in Joyce Lebra *et al.* (eds.), *Women in Changing Japan* (Westview Press, Boulder, Colorado, 1976).

13. A.N. Mehra, 'Fertility Decline in Japan', *Eastern Economist*, vol. 51 (1968), p. 102; Harumi Befu, *Japan: An Anthropological Introduction* (Chandler, San Francisco, 1971), pp. 46-7; Fumiko Amano, 'Family Planning Movement in Japan', *Contemporary Japan*, vol. 23 (1955), pp. 755-7. A recent study suggests that family planning is no new phenomenon in Japan. It would appear that during the eighteenth century infanticide may well have been practised as an efficient, if morally condemned, means of sex-selective fertility control (Thomas C. Smith *et al.*, *Nakahara* (Stanford University Press, Stanford, 1977).

14. Amano, 'Family Planning Movement', pp. 761-3; C. Bartlett, 'Planning Japan's Families', *Far Eastern Economic Review*, vol. 54, no. 11 (1966), p. 556; R.J. Smith, 'Kurusu: a Japanese Agricultural Community' in Cornell and Smith (eds.), *Two Japanese Villages*, p. 69; Ryōhei Minami, *Konrei-shiki to Kekkon no Kokoroe (On Marriage and the Marriage Ceremony)* (Taibunkan, Tokyo, 1953), pp. 117-26.

15. R.E. Baber, *Youth Looks at Marriage and the Family* (International Christian University, Tokyo, 1958), p. 47; Bartlett, 'Planning Japan's Families', p. 555; Mehra, 'Fertility Decline', p. 102; cf. *Statistical Handbook of Japan* (Bureau of Statistics, Tokyo, 1977), p. 25.

16. Of 46 families asked about decision-making, 21 reported that decisions followed *hanashiai*, though a few added that men have the last word, 20 named one or both of the men, 3 said that men made large decisions and women small ones, and 2 named women, both in households where there were males over 20, but unmarried.

17. Chie Nakane, *Kinship and Economic Organization in Rural Japan* (University of London, The Athlone Press, London, 1967), pp. 11-16; Kenne Chang, 'The *Inkyo* System in Southwestern Japan', *Ethnology*, vol. 9 (1970), p. 342; Geoffrey Bownas, *Japanese Rainmaking and Other Folk Practices* (Allen and Unwin, London, 1963), p. 168; Tokuzō Omachi, '*Ashiire-kon*' in Richard M. Dorson (ed.), *Studies in Japanese Folklore* (Kennikat Press, Port Washington, New York, London, 1973), pp. 255-6; Cornell, 'Matsunagi', p. 159; Norbeck, *Takashima*, p. 49.

18. Of 49 households asked about who has charge of the purse, 11 named the older man, 2 the younger, 3 the only man, 6 the older woman, 6 the younger and 15 the only woman. The remaining household provided the answer that while in principle the younger man held the purse, in practice the children sought money from his wife because she had ready cash in the fish-shop till. It seems often to be women who control the purse in urban families too (R.P. Dore, *City Life in Japan* (University of California Press, Berkeley, Los Angeles and London, 1971), p. 173.)

19. Takeyoshi Kawashima, *Kekkon (Marriage)* (Iwanami Shoten, Tokyo, 1954), p. 56; Joyce Lebra, 'Women in Service Industries' in Lebra *et al.* (eds.), *Women in Changing Japan*, p. 118; Ezra F. Vogel, *Japan's New Middle Class* (University of California Press, Berkeley, Los Angeles and London, 1963), p. 102.

20. Nakane, *Rural Japan*, p. 19; T. Fukutake, *Japanese Rural Society*, trans. R.P. Dore (Cornell University Press, London, 1972), p. 47; Embree, *Suye Mura*, p. 80.

21. Nakane, *Rural Japan*, p. 19; Embree, *Suye Mura*, p. 80.

22. Traditional practices are sometimes described as 'feudal' in a derogatory sense to contrast them with post-war 'democratic' ones; for example, see Befu, *Anthropological Introduction*, p. 166; Ronald Dore, *Shinohata* (Allen Lane, London, 1978), pp. 294, 311; Edward Norbeck, *Changing Japan* (Holt, Rinehart and Winston, New York, 1965), p. 13.

23. Later, when people had grown more used to my continual presence in the village, I was usually able to join a family more informally in the room where they watch television. In fact I frequently found conversation had to proceed alongside professional wrestling or some other popular programme.

24. Sir Charles Eliot (*Japanese Buddhism* (Edwin Arnold, London, 1935), p. 185) suggested that the use of the word for Buddhas for all departed spirits was in imitation of the Shinto idea that all dead eventually become *kami*. Yanagida, *About Our Ancestors*, p. 107, put forward another theory that this use of *hotoke* comes from a word for vessel called a *hotoki* in which food offerings were made. Whatever its origin, Dore, *City Life*, pp. 313, 457fn., found in Shitayama ward in Tokyo that some people recognised a difference between spirits of the dead, which he terms *hotoke*, and Buddhas, which he refers to as *Hotoke*, and some did not.

25. Explanations of the afterlife are varied (cf. Carmen Blacker, *The Catalpa Bow* (Allen and Unwin, London, 1975), pp. 69-70; Robert J. Smith, *Ancestor Worship in Contemporary Japan* (Stanford University Press, Stanford, 1974), pp. 51, 63-8), and even include reference to *tengoku*, which is a translation of the Christian heaven. There is some idea that one's behaviour during life may be relevant too and that a character named Enma will make judgement after death, and enter in a big book (*Enmacho*, used also to refer to a teacher's bad book) the length of time to be spent in hell (*jigoku*) as punishment for sins (cf. William Erskine, *Japanese Festivals and Calendar Lore* (Kyo Bun Kwan, Tokyo, 1933), p. 94). The Buddhist ideal is said to be rebirth in the paradise of *gokuraku* where a *hotokesama* sits in a lotus flower and meditates (cf. Mock Jōya, *Japanese Customs and Manners* (The Sakurai Shoten, Tokyo, 1955), pp. 119-20) and a soul unable to reach this paradise becomes a ghost or an evil spirit who may cause trouble among the living. It is to prevent such a disaster occurring to one's own family that Buddhist rites as described in Chapter 6 are held (cf. Smith, *Ancestor Worship*, pp. 69-70), but oddly enough a Shinto priest may be called to deal with a bothersome evil spirit (cf. Narimitsu Matsudaira, 'The Concept of Tamashii in Japan' in Dorson (ed.), *Studies in Japanese Folklore*, pp. 185-6). According to Shinto doctrine, spirits of the dead eventually merge into a single category of *kami* of their ancestors. Thus explanations of individuals, even in one community, are by no means consistent, except in reference to the ways in which the living may interact with the dead, discussed here and in Chapter 6.

26. This term also includes collaterals who died in the house in previous generations.

27. David W. Plath, 'Where the Family of God is the Family', *American Anthropologist*, vol. 66 (1964), pp. 302-3.

28. Erskine, *Japanese Festivals*, p. 38; Ernest Clement, 'Calendar (Japanese)', in James Hastings (ed.), *Encyclopaedia of Religion and Ethics*, Vol. 3 (Edinburgh, 1910), p. 116; B.H. Chamberlain, *Things Japanese* (John Murray, London, 1902), p. 159; cf. Norbeck, *Takashima*, p. 159; Smith, 'Kurusu', p. 95; Hitoshi Miyake, 'Folk Religion' in I. Hori *et al.* (eds.), *Japanese Religion*, trans. Yoshiya Abe and David Reid (Kodansha International, Tokyo and Palo Alta, 1972), p. 127; Vogel, *Middle Class*, p. 208.

29. Yozo Watanabe, 'The Family and the Law' in A.T. von Mehren (ed.), *Law in Japan* (Harvard University Press, Cambridge, Mass., 1963), p. 368.

30. Lillian Hino, 'Twenty Japanese Proverbs', *Journal of American Folklore*,

vol. 66 (1953), p. 18.

31. Befu, *Anthropological Introduction*, p. 166.

32. Cf. Yoshida *et al*., quoted in T.S. Lebra and W.P. Lebra (eds.), *Japanese Culture and Behaviour* (University of Hawaii, Hawaii, 1974), p. 204; Vogel, *Middle Class*, p. 180.

33. Takao Suzuki, *Japanese and the Japanese*, trans. Akira Miura (Kodansha International, Tokyo, New York and San Francisco, 1978), pp. 137-8.

34. The terms for 'love' are discussed in more detail in Chapter 4, p. 116-17).

35. Vogel, *Middle Class*, pp. 194-5, reported that informants in Tokyo 'jokingly comment that even husbands who give orders to their wives in public now apologise to their wives when they return home'.

36. Baber, *Youth Looks at Marriage and the Family*, p. 107.

37. An example of the way in which a woman might get her own way was provided when I was delivering some photographs I had taken at a wedding to the groom's mother when the father was present. She had asked for three copies of a photograph on which she later noticed that four friends were depicted, and since she wanted to give copies to the people concerned, she mentioned that another copy would be required. Her husband scorned the idea, commenting that it was a very ordinary photograph and not worth copying, though he could see that three copies had already been made. His wife agreed with him immediately, saying clearly that they would not need that one. Further discussion ensued about who would like copies of which photograph, and as a final list began to emerge, the wife picked out the three copies previously rejected and set them on one side, commenting loudly that they would not be required since it had been decided not to give those three away. This time her husband looked up and said, 'Why not? Now they are there we might as well give them.' A further copy was quickly added to the list. The woman had got her way, and had also avoided crossing her husband, though it is impossible to say whether she manipulated the situation consciously or unconsciously (cf. Vogel, *Middle Class*, pp. 200-3, a section entitled 'The Art of Husband Management').

38. Takie Sugiyama Lebra, 'Reciprocity and the Asymmetric Principle' in Lebra and Lebra, (eds.), *Japanese Culture and Behaviour*, p. 197; Bernstein, 'Women in Rural Japan', pp. 29-31; D. Sladen and N. Lorimer, *More Queer Things About Japan* (Anthony Treherne, London, 1904), p. 412; Naomi Tamura, *The Japanese Bride* (Harper and Bros., New York and London, 1904), p. 68; Kawashima, *Kekkon*, pp. 76-138.

39. Cf. Dore, *City Life*, pp. 126-7.

40. Cf. Dore, *Shinohata*, pp. 160-2; Bernstein, 'Women in Rural Japan', p. 39; Smith, 'Kurusu', p. 81; and a later section of this chapter.

41. Jirō Kamishima, *Nihonjin no Kekkonkan* (*The Japanese View of Marriage*) (Chikuma Sōsho, Tokyo, 1969), pp. 153-7; Yanagida, *Manners and Customs*, pp. 169, 241-4. Previously there were various institutionalised ways of avoiding the problem, it seems. Women had greater authority in their own spheres and there was a formal transfer of this from older to younger, which provided a limit to the young bride's inferior position (Yanagida, *Manners and Customs*, p. 118). There was also a system of duolocal residence practised in some areas when the groom would merely visit his bride until the time came for her to take his mother's place (e.g. Befu, *Anthropological Introduction*, p. 49; Ichiro Kurata, 'Rural Marriage Customs in Japan', *Contemporary Japan*, vol. 10 (1941), pp. 366-9). The moving out of the older couple at this time has already been mentioned. A modern version of this separation of living quarters of senior and junior couples is found as a new phenomenon in Kurusu (Robert J. Smith, *Kurusu* (Dawson, Folkestone, 1978), p. 139).

42. As far as I could determine, there was only one case of possible conflict

over the inheritance of one successor in Kurotsuchi. This man was farming land that was still registered in the name of his father, who had died seven years previously, because he feared the demands of an estranged brother who is legally entitled to press for the value in money of his share of the land. Otherwise, most households seemed so sure that their previous members would sign away their rights for the good of the *ie* that no one bothered to take the precaution of making a will, which would have settled the matter legally.

43. Cf. Embree, *Suye Mura*, p. 88.

44. A few sons went off for a few months to try out other employment, perhaps to exercise the individuality they learn is so important, only to return and settle down to farming (cf. Dore, *Shinohata*, p. 151). Shogo Koyano's 'Changing Family Behaviour in Four Japanese Communities', *Journal of Marriage and the Family*, vol. 26, no. 2 (1964), p. 154, shows a greater expectation of elder son succession to occupation in rural areas.

45. Kanji Naito, 'Inheritance Patterns on a Catholic Island', *Social Compass*, vol. 17 (1970), pp. 21-36.

46. At least two households in Kurotsuchi were registered in the local office under the names of women for the address list, and when I was working there, I overheard the employees clarifying that this was correct even though there were adult males resident. One woman had a 28-year-old son, and when she enquired whether his name should be used, she was told that she should wait until he marries. The other woman's husband was suffering from tuberculosis, and spent most of his time in hospital, and I just happened to overhear her name being supplied to an inquirer as head of the household.

47. Takashi Maeda, *Summary of Ane Katoku* (Kansai University Press, Osaka, 1976), pp. 31-2 has pointed out that family registers were often falsified to make it appear that an eldest son inherited, whereas reality may have different. Possibly the family entered on the registry form what they thought would be most acceptable to the authorities.

48. Cf. Arnold Van Gennep, *The Rites of Passage* (Routledge and Kegan Paul, London and Henley, 1977), p. 141.

49. Cf. Nakane, *Rural Japan*, p. 152. Further information about the concept of *en* is to be found in the Japanese index, which also gives page references to other usages.

50. Tamura, *The Japanese Bride*, p. 56; E. and S. Vogel 'Family Security, Personal Immaturity and Emotional Health in a Japanese Sample', *Marriage and Family Living*, vol. 23 (1961), p. 165; Sladen and Lorimer, *More Queer Things about Japan*, p. 326; Kawashima, *Kekkon*, pp. 89-90.

51. Usually at the three traditional annual holidays of Bon, New Year and Sekku (see Chapter 6), and after rice transplanting and harvesting (cf. Toshimi Takeuchi, 'Satogaeri' ('Homecomings') in *Nihon Shakai Minzoku Jiten* (1954), pp. 502-3; Kunio Yanagida and T. Omachi, *Kon'in Shūzoku Goi (Popular Terms associated with Marriage)* (Minkan Denshō no Kai, Tokyo, 1937), pp. 213-21). These visits were institutionalised and will be discussed again in Chapter 5.

52. *Kome nuka sango areba, yōshi ni wa ikunazo* (If you have three measures of rice bran, don't go as a *yōshi*) is also quoted with minor variations by several other writers.

53. Watanabe, 'The Family and the Law', p. 365. This intervening period was like a trial which one informant termed *ashiire* (foot-in) marriage, but this term has also been applied by scholars to more specific practices, often involving a period of matrilocal residence. See, for example, T. Omachi, 'Izu Toshima no Ashiire-kon' ('A Form of Bi-local Marriage on the Island of Toshima, Izu Province'), *Minzokugaku Kenkyū*, vol. 14, no. 3 (1950), pp. 76-81; 'Ashiire-kon', pp. 251-66; Takeuchi, 'Satogaeri', p. 503; Kunio Yanagida, *Minzokugaku Jiten*

(*Dictionary of Folklore*) (Minzokugaku Kenkyūjo, Tokyo, 1953), p. 4; Yanagida and Omachi, *Kon'in Shūzoku Goi*, pp. 242-3.

54. Cf. Norbeck, *Takashima*, p. 167; Kawashima, *Kekkon*, p. 106; Tamura, *The Japanese Bride*, pp. 79-80; Smith, 'Kurusu', p. 81; William Erskine, *Japanese Customs* (Kyo Bun Kwan, Tokyo, 1925), p. 2; Toshio Fueto, 'The Discrepancy between Marriage Laws and Mores in Japan', *American Journal of Comparative Law*, vol. 5 (1956), pp. 264-5.

55. Inouye, *Home Life in Tokyo*, p. 202.

56. Kawashima, *Kekkon*, p. 136; Bernstein, 'Women in Rural Japan', pp. 44-5; Itsue Takamure, *Nihon Kon'in Shi (A History of Marriage in Japan)* (Nihon Rekishi Shinsho, Tokyo, 1963), pp. 261-2.

57. Plath, *The After Hours*, p. 149; Fukutake, *Japanese Rural Society*, p. 56.

58. Cf. Embree, *Suye Mura*, p. 82; Smith, 'Kurusu', p. 65; Cornell, 'Matsunagi', p. 160. Strict Confucian norms prohibit non-agnatic adoption, and there was a long intellectual controversy during the Tokugawa period about whether this rule should be enforced in Japan, but conflicting indigenous practices proved too well ingrained to be dislodged (I.J. McMullen, 'Non-agnatic Adoption', *Harvard Journal of Asian Studies*, vol. 35 (1975), pp. 133-89; cf. Sōkichi Tsuda, *An Inquiry into the Japanese Mind as Mirrored in Literature*, trans. Fukumatsu Matsuda (Japan Society for the Promotion of Science, Tokyo, 1970), pp. 196-7). In some areas adoption seems to have been practised more freely than just to provide heirs, for example for extra labour. A poor family could thus enable a child to be better brought up by giving it to a rich one (Maeda, *Summary of Ane Katoku*, pp. 10-12; Yanagida, *Manners and Customs*, p. 120-1).

59. One informant did report, however, that widows were sometimes re-married to their first husband's younger brother, especially during the war. This practice of levirate marriage was not illustrated in Kurotsuchi, but was apparently fairly common in Kyūshū among war widows (Michio Aoyama, 'Gyakuenkon' ('Levirate Marriage') in Itsuo Emori (ed.), *Nihon no Kon'in* (Gendai no Esupuri, no. 104, Tokyo, 1976), pp. 192-8), and previously (Embree, *Suye Mura*, p. 89). It is an institution of ancient Japan which was prohibited during part of the Tokugawa period (Einosuke Yamanaka, 'Meiji no Gyakuenkon' ('The Levirate Marriage of the Meiji Era'), *Hōseishi Kenkyū*, vol. 7 (1957), pp. 112-30; Tarō Nakayama, *Nihon Kon'in Shi (A History of Marriage in Japan)* (Shunyō-dō, Tokyo, 1928), pp. 255-60, 946-7).

60. Cf. Dore, *City Life*, p. 149. According to Vogel, people who have moved away to cities often find requests for help from country relatives so troublesome that they are reluctant to return to their village of origin, even for the annual ancestral memorials (*Middle Class*, pp. 134-5).

61. One Kurotsuchi man was reluctant to refer to his first cousin as a relative (*shinseki*), explaining that he had not been asked to help with his house-building (see Chapter 6, p. 216), so the mutual obligation would seem to be a requisite for the relationship to be recognised. The other party had disclaimed close connection.

62. This is a motif, displayed on formal garments and sometimes above the door or elsewhere in the house, which is passed from *honke* to *bunke*. Although some unrelated families share a motif, it would be unusual for related families to have different ones.

63. Cf. Norbeck, *Takashima*, p. 10; Embree, *Suye Mura*, p. 86.

64. E.g. Nobushige Hozumi, *Ancestor Worship and Japanese Law* (Maruzen, Tokyo, 1913), pp. 53-4.

65. Yanagida, *Manners and Customs*, pp. 106-7; Beardsley et al., *Village Japan*, p. 264. People sharing a certain area of land are regarded as related by *chi'en* (land-relation, a common destiny through land), which Varner has called a 'territorial consciousness' ('The Organized Peasant', *Monumenta Nipponica*,

vol. 32 (1977), p. 461). He discusses the term together with *ketsu'en*, a blood-relation or common destiny through consanguinity.

66. Dore, *City Life*, pp. 152-4, found in his Tokyo sample that nuclear families apparently had as much contact, if not more, with their matrilineal relatives as with patrilineal ones, so perhaps this lack of patrilineal emphasis is quite widespread.

4 THE MECHANICS OF MAKING A MATCH

In Kurotsuchi there were only three adults over the age of thirty who had not married, and each of them had, or had had, some problems with his or her health. In general, it is regarded as most unusual for people to remain single, and young people of both sexes appear to regard marriage as inevitable.[1] In this chapter, the evidently efficient means by which marriages are initially created will be considered, emphasis again being placed on changes which have taken place during the lifetime of the oldest inhabitants. In Chapter 1, the post-war legal changes with regard to marriage were indicated, and the new Constitution quoted which makes marriage an affair only of the man and woman concerned. It was also suggested that practice has not yet caught up with these legal ideals, and the case of Kurotsuchi provides further evidence that this is so. In the previous chapter, the importance of marriage to the *ie* was explained, and some evidence presented of the way marriage is still very much an involvement with the whole household. In case of dispute, a couple may choose to preserve their marriage rather than the *ie* to which they belong, but this action is still subject to social censure. However, modifications have certainly been made to previous practices, and the attitudes of young people often reflect their post-war education.

The start of the chapter gives an idea of the way young people approaching marriageable age regard the institution of marriage based on the various consciously expressed purposes they ascribe to it. After this, the various mechanisms whereby partners meet each other are described, and Kurotsuchi marriages are classified according to these criteria. Then follows a detailed examination of the factors which are considered in the selection of a spouse, the methods by which information about possible candidates is determined, and the recourses used if it is necessary to turn down a proposal. The go-between, who still plays an important part in these matters, is the subject of the subsequent section. Finally, in the light of this information the attitudes of people to the initiation of their own and their children's marriages are discussed, and some concluding remarks are made.

The Purpose of Marriage

Views of members of Kurotsuchi on the subject of marriage were wide-ranging and various, but the answers to questions about its purpose (*igi, mokuteki*) illustrated well the changes through which the institution is passing. The following discussion is confined to the views of young people approaching marriageable age. Of 27 people asked, several found the question very difficult, and 7 girls and 2 boys were entirely unable to answer. A common reply was that everybody married and it was expected of one. 'If you don't, after a certain age, people begin to ask,' was one answer. Some inheriting sons gave a traditional answer concerned with the household: the eldest son must bring a wife into the home to produce descendants (*shison*) and help with the housework. One added that children were required to take care of one in one's old age. The most common answer in general was concerned with having descendants, though this was not always couched in terms of the household, one girl adding that otherwise she herself would just end, leaving nothing in the world.[2] A boy said that one of the reasons for marriage was to be seen as an adult (cf. Chapter 6, p. 206-7), and another, who was a non-inheriting son expecting to move out of the family home on marriage, said his reason for marriage would be to settle down. A few answers were more concerned with the relationship to be established. One boy said marriage was to provide spiritual peace of mind, another, to enjoy life with someone else rather than alone, and a third said that a wife should be the person closest to one's heart. Another gave a more down-to-earth reason: that he would need someone to attend to his needs when he returned home from work. Yet another said a wife was to help one with things one can't do alone. Finally, one pointed out that a wife provided an outlet for sexual desire.

This list of reasons emphasises different aspects of marriage for different people. A clear distinction is evident between the position of boys remaining in the household and those expecting to move out, and their views usually, but not always, reflected this. For all of them, a recognition of adulthood would follow marriage, but for those setting up their own home, there would be a greater sudden increase in responsibility. They would also be expected to have a more intense relationship with their wives than inheriting sons, who would share interaction with their parents, and in these cases, the husband-wife relationship was usually of more concern than matters of the household. It is interesting that some of the inheriting sons still think of marriage in terms of the continuity of the *ie*. The difficulty experienced by girls in answering the question illustrates perhaps the total commitment involved by marriage for them. It is simply the life of a woman. A purpose is superfluous.

Meeting

There is a tendency in Japan to classify marriages into two types: the modern *ren'ai* union, which reflects the spirit of the post-war Constitution, and the *miai* marriage, which is associated with traditional aspects of the family system. These words are usually translated 'love' and 'arranged', but there is more than one question involved. Not least is whether the individuals chose each other without aid, or whether an introductory meeting (*miai*) was arranged by a prospective go-between. It is thus difficult strictly to classify marriages in this way. Some couples claim that their unions, though initiated through a *miai*, later developed into *ren'ai*, while others deny that their relationship is one of *ren'ai*, though the meeting was informal and the decision to marry largely their own. Sometimes parents think of the marriage of their son or daughter as a *miai* union, whereas he or she may well describe it as *ren'ai*. It can be seen that the distinction is far from clear-cut. Nevertheless, the distinction remains part of the language, so that an inquiry about whether a person's marriage was *ren'ai* might well produce the answer 'No, *miai*', though the couple had never actually experienced a *miai*, perhaps having known each other from childhood. In Kurotsuchi, questions about marriage produced a variety of explanations of how the couple had met, but most people were quite definite about whether or not their marriage was *ren'ai*. It is appropriate, therefore, to define more clearly the meaning of this word, and explain some of its connotations. Then the other possibilities will be considered.

Ren'ai

The concept of 'love' is difficult to define in the English language,[3] and it is therefore not surprising that there is no word in Japanese which exactly corresponds to it. Two words are commonly used to translate 'love' in different contexts, *ren'ai* and *aijō*, which share the common component *ai*. This is the nearest concept to 'love' in the wide sense, including that between parent and child, friends, a human and an animal, even love for a certain food. According to Benedict, *ai* was originally used for the love of a superior for his dependants, but Christian missionaries chose the concept to translate the love of God for man, and also the love of man for God, and it is now also used to describe a love between equals.[4] *Aijō* merely means 'the sentiment or feeling of *ai*', but the characters for *ren'ai* include the element *ren*, which can also be pronounced *koi*, a concept with definite sexual connotations. It is specifically the love between a man and a woman, the feeling of attraction that each might experience, a word applied to lovers in the physical sense. This element tends to predominate in the meaning of *ren'ai*, according to the explanations of informants, and the word is used of sweethearts, recently married couples and extra-marital affairs. There seems to be no doubt about whether an experience can be described as *ren'ai*, and one informant explained: 'I should know if I was in love (*ren'ai*), for I should feel my temperature rise, I should feel the fever.' A lack of such passion, even if a marriage were initiated entirely by the individuals concerned, would preclude the epithet *ren'ai* from being applied.[5]

To many young people in Japan, a *ren'ai* marriage sounds attractive because it implies the freedom of the individual to decide for him or herself and because it involves the charm and romance of novels, poetry and pop songs, which seem particularly to appeal to girls.[6] However, *ren'ai* involves few of the Christian ideals which support the Western concept of love, and its strong association with sexual attraction above all else probably explains why many older people are still sceptical about the idea of founding marriages only on this basis. Manuals on marriage are also reserved on the topic of love as a sole foundation for marriage.[7] Thus some young couples who have decided they are in love and want to marry say nothing to their parents directly, but approach first a sympathetic third party to act as a go-between. If they judge their parents to be too old-fashioned even to entertain the possibility of a love match, they may enact a charade of meeting for the first time in the presence of family to convince their parents that all is proceeding in a traditional fashion. If the family still fails to approve, there are various possibilities: the couple may try waiting, in the hope that time will bring them round, they can elope and set up home together, making their union a *fait accompli*, or they can resign themselves to separation, and succumb to the parents' veto.

In Kurotsuchi, there are cases to illustrate both the eventual success and marriage of love matches, and also of the separation of couples who had hoped to marry. The latter seem mostly to take place when the boy is in line to inherit and must therefore take his wife to live with his parents. Two cases in which parents reversed their disapproval both involved girls who were at first said to be too young to marry. There is a word in Japanese for the appropriate time for marriage (*tekireiki*);[8] at present, in Kurotsuchi this is 22-23 for a girl and 26-27 for a boy, though the latter is said to be affected by economic circumstances. As two corollaries of this, it is also thought appropriate for siblings of the same sex to marry in order of age, and for the boy to be older than his wife. The last preference is said also to aid the husband's position of authority, and two informants whose position was reversed said that this was less important for a *ren'ai* match. Indeed, by their very nature, *ren'ai* marriages are concerned with other factors, and they thus frequently upset these preferences, which gives another explanation of why parents and other relatives may sometimes be reserved about giving their approval. Table 11 shows the number of Kurotsuchi marriages which took place at particular ages, divided by sex and into age groups. It illustrates the cluster of marriages around the *tekireiki*, but also rather suggests that this phenomenon has only recently become marked, since the older groups have a wider variation in ages at marriage than the younger ones. Many *ren'ai* marriages have fallen within the central cluster on the table, but a few seem to coincide with early marriages for men, and late ones for women. These are marked 'R'. Table 12 shows how many husbands are older than wives, and vice versa, and it can be seen that *ren'ai* marriages account for three of the five cases in which the wife is older.

Of a total of 90 marriages in Kurotsuchi, including those of widows and widowers,[9] only 17 couples claimed that their marriages were based on *ren'ai*. Three of these were pre-war marriages and will be discussed shortly. The other 14 took place between 1951 and 1979 and are distributed fairly evenly throughout that period (see Table 13, p. 127 for details). Only six cases were farming households, and each of these had unusual circumstances. One, which took place shortly after the war, involved a Kurotsuchi woman whose parents died before she was married, leaving no son to continue the household. A neighbouring family arranged for her to receive a *yōshi*, but this marriage broke up six months later. The three daughters of the family were very vulnerable, this woman explained, and they received many visitors since there were no men in the house to protect them. One of the regular callers moved in with her on an informal basis, and after a son was born to them, they registered themselves married. No formal ceremony was held, but in 1975 this was the only union in the village not so sanctioned.[10] However, in 1979, there was one household in which the 19-year-old inheriting son had a girlfriend living and working with

Table 11: Age at Marriage Ceremony of Members of Kurotsuchi (divided by sex and by period of birth)

Men	18	19	20	21	22	23	24	25	26	27	28	29	30	31	32
Before 1905				1^R			3	1	1	1			1		
1906-15	1	1^R			1			1	1	1	1		1		
1916-25				2		1	1	2	5	2	1		1		
1926-35			1				2^{RR}	3	1	5	5				
1936-45					1^R		1	1^R	4	2	4				
1946-55						2^{RR}		1	5	3	2	1			2
	1	1	1	3	2	5	5	8	17	14	14	1		3	2

Women	15	16	17	18	19	20	21	22	23	24	25	26	27	28	29	30	31	32	33
Before 1905		1	1	1	1	1		2	1	1				1					
1906-15		1		1	1^R	1	2	1	1			1	3						
1916-25	1		1			2			1	3		1^2		$1^{R(2)}$	1			1^2	
1926-35					2	4	6	1	2	2	2								1^R
1936-45					1	2	2	4	1	3	2								
1946-55					1^R	3	1	5	1	3	2^R	1				1^2			
	1	2	2	2	2	8	11	12	13	8	8	8	4	1	1	1	1		2

Notes: R = *ren'ai* marriage; X^2 = second marriage; however, not all such marriages are so marked, merely those which fall outside the central cluster.

Age at marriage ceremony is not documented officially, so depends on informants' reports. Some older people claimed to be unsure, so their ages must be regarded as approximate.

Table 12: Numbers of Cases in Kurotsuchi of Differences in Age between Spouses

Husband older by	1	2	3	4	5	6	7	8	years
	11	9	11	7	14	5	3	1	cases
Wife older by	1	2	3	4	5	6	7	8	
	1^R	2^R	1					1^R	

Husband and wife born in the same year: 8 cases.

Notes: as for Table 11.

him. His father had had a *ren'ai* marriage, a second case in a farming family, and he had married a girl whose parents were dead, the friend of his brother's wife. The brothers were sons of one of the pre-war *ren'ai* marriages. A third case involved a family with a daughter in mental hospital, a definite disadvantage when marriages are to be arranged, as will be discussed in the next section. The wife in this case is eight years her husband's senior. The fourth case in a farming family is a couple who were contemporaries at school, and the problem at the time they wished to marry was that an older brother was still unwed. However, the latter had chosen to work elsewhere, and the second son was to remain on the farm. The younger brother's sweetheart was willing to do farm work, and she had passed the *tekireiki* at 25, so the marriage took place. The parents seemed a little embarrassed about it, and while I was working at the registry office I overheard a telephone conversation in which an employee there commented on the fact that the second son was to inherit and had married before his elder brother. However, the elder brother did marry within a year of the first wedding, his union initiated by a *miai*, so it seems that the parents did their duty by him as soon as they could. The fifth and sixth cases were described as *ren'ai* by the couples concerned, but *miai* had also taken place and the parents described the marriages as such.

Of the eight non-farming households with a *ren'ai* marriage, five are three-generational, but in two of these the older generation described the marriage of the younger one as *miai*. In one case, *ren'ai* was said to have developed after the *miai* meeting; the other was probably similar, but the descriptions of premarital relations were various and not always consistent. A third case involved a couple who met at their mutual place of work, the fourth the daughter of a woman who married out of Kurotsuchi, who had frequently met her husband-to-be while visiting the village, and the fifth a couple of middle-school sweethearts. One of the three 'created' households with a *ren'ai* marriage involved no opposition from the family, but the other two are the cases mentioned earlier where the daughters were at first said to be too young to marry. One involved another couple who had known each other since schooldays. They reported that they wanted to marry after a six-year romance, when the man was only 19 or 20 and had no regular employment. The girl is 18 months older, and her parents were also worried about whether this man would be able to support her. Eventually, the couple set up home together, and, after three months, the girl's parents relented and the wedding was arranged. Later they must have been totally reconciled, for the couple was given a plot of the wife's family land on which to build a house. The other case involved a girl of 19, whose parents suggested that she wait a few years, but the couple decided that they would elope to Hokkaido. The husband explained that the plan had been to make her parents worry so that, when they were eventually found, relief at their safety would lead to agreement. Before they had time to carry out their plan, however, a relative intervened and managed to persuade the girl's parents to co-operate.

Had their plan been put into effect, this might have provided a modern example of an old practice known as *yome-nusumi* (bride-stealing), which was said by one informant in his seventies to have been quite common in the past in this part of the country.[11] This particular informant was the husband involved in one of the pre-war *ren'ai* marriages, again a couple who had been contemporaries at school, where they had made a secret agreement to marry. Later they asked a sympathetic third party to make the formal arrangements between the families, he explained. He claimed that such agreements were not infrequent in his day — they married in 1924 — and it was in cases where the parents refused consent that the boy would sometimes 'steal' his sweetheart and take her either away or to his own house if his parents approved. He added that the girl's parents might then disown their daughter, or break off relations, but, eventually — perhaps after a child was born — the marriage would take place with the blessing of both families.

Many of this informant's contemporaries reported that their marriages had been arranged by parents, and this was the case even for the other pre-war *ren'ai* marriages. One was described as *ren'ai* in a jocular but convincing manner as a saving grace for a union arranged, largely for economic reasons, when the man was only 19. There is considerable evidence that young people had some opportunity to grow fond of each other before marriage, at least up to about fifty years ago. As already mentioned, there seems not to have been a residential youth group concerned with arranging marriages, but several older informants reported the practice of *yobai* (see p. 24) in the area. Typically a boy confined his visits to one sweetheart, they explained, but they claimed not to know whether the parents had been aware of their presence, though they suspected that nothing would have been said as long as they approved of the boy. The men who described such nocturnal visits also claimed that their marriages were more respectable, and that such activities ceased after marriage, but one widowed grandmother was not ashamed to admit that her marriage had started in this way. In her case, she had come to the village to make paper, and she explained that girls were often left in the paper-shed to finish the work alone in the evenings, which made them rather vulnerable. She had become pregnant and her marriage was arranged forthwith. Not all premarital pregnancies resulted in marriage, however, and family records include a few illegitimate children at about that time. They were usually brought up in the mother's home, even if the mother later married.[12]

The way the word *yobai* has taken on a derogatory meaning in recent times was mentioned in Chapter 1. In ancient literature it referred to a legitimate proposal of marriage, and it seems in various forms to have been sanctioned as a type of courtship leading to marriage in many areas until the Meiji period.[13] It is likely that it was more institutionalised here too, but that pre-war propaganda, advocating segregation of the sexes before marriage, effectively eradicated the practice. Illegitimate births in the family register petered out during the Taishō period, and there were few recent cases of pregnancy leading to marriage. Even nowadays, despite opportunities at school and in the youth group for young people to get to know members of the opposite sex, there is relatively little courtship in the Western tradition. Several recent *ren'ai* marriages have features such as secrecy which rather resemble traditional practices.

Miai

The more common approach to betrothal involves the whole family to some extent.[14] As a son or daughter begins to draw near the *tekireiki*, members of the family initiate discreet inquiries, among their friends and relatives, to see whether a suitable partner might not be known to one of them. Usually for a girl this goes no further than insinuating the occasional *onegai shimasu*[15] into any conversation which touches on the daughter's age and expectations of marriage, with the implied request to introduce any eligible young men to the family. A boy's family, or that of a girl hoping to receive a *yōshi*, may be more active in looking for a suitable partner, perhaps approaching directly someone who knows well a boy or girl they have heard about. Anyone who decides to take seriously the marriage prospects of a young person of their acquaintance may well ask for some photographs of the candidate and a brief personal history (*rirekisho*) to show to interested families. Similarly, families which experience difficulties in finding a suitable partner for their son or daughter may well deposit such information with someone who has a reputation for making matches.

A prospective go-between often takes a boy to catch a glimpse of a girl he thinks likely before any approach is made directly. This is called a *kagemi* (hidden look),[16] because the girl is usually unaware of it. Summer *matsuri*, which bring many visitors to local shrines, are said to be good occasions for boys to assess girls in other villages. Another method is for the boy to wait with the prospective go-between for the girl to pass on a habitual route, perhaps sitting in a car as the girl passes on her way home from work. The practice is usually justified as a means to avoid loss of face on the part of the girl, who would not then knowingly be turned down for her looks. If this is successful, the prospective go-between may seek permission to call with the candidate at the girl's home so that the couple, and possibly also their parents, may be introduced.

This is the *miai* itself, the form of which varies from place to place, and indeed over the years. A Kurotsuchi couple married in 1947 explained that in those days the boy would make an excuse to visit the girl's home with his father, and they would ask to be shown the daughter of the house. A door would be opened to reveal the girl, perhaps sitting at the far side of the room, and this was supposed to be sufficient to enable the visitors to make up their minds. They said that where the eldest daughter was not good-looking, a younger sister would sometimes be shown, but the oldest taken to the wedding. The style of the bridal head-dress was such that the deception would not be realised until the couple were wed. However, they gave no examples of unions thus initiated.[17] In their own case, the visit was expected, and the family made arrangements for the daughter to be sitting in a soft light while the visitors would be clearly illuminated in the hall, so that the girl would also have a chance to assess her possible spouse.

More recent *miai* were reported to be longer, with an opportunity for conversation, and, for about twenty years, the couple has been given a chance to speak to each other alone for a while. In the last few years, the initial introduction has been followed by one or more 'dates' (*odēto* is the Japanese rendering of the American word), after which a decision is made. Several informants described such an outing as a visit together to a beautiful place, and it seemed typically to involve a drive to a scenic spot, or a meal in an expensive restaurant.[18]

It seems to be customary in Kurotsuchi and other rural places for prospective candidates to visit a girl's home, but, in Fukushima, *miai* also take place in restaurants or cafés, and some people prefer neutral ground for the introduction. An article on Japanese etiquette, published in 1885, mentioned as a suitable place for a *miai* a Shinto shrine, where the boy sat at an agreed time, and the girl walked by, casting a glance at her prospective husband, so that each could assess the other.[19] Several writers mention parks, theatres and restaurants as favoured places for city *miai*, some describing how members of the two families arrange through the go-between to meet there as if by accident.[20] In the past, the initial *miai* may have been attended by several members of each family as well as the candidates for marriage and the go-between.[21] One Kurotsuchi informant, who had received visits from several hopeful candidates, said that usually the boy and his father are brought by the prospective go-between, and she and her parents receive them. Her brothers, of which there were two still living at home, were definitely excluded, she added. A man in Yame, who had arranged 37 marriages successfully, always introduces the couple first before arranging the formal visit involving other members of the family.

Marriages Arranged without Ren'ai or Miai

No less than 25 of Kurotsuchi's 88 marriages fall into neither of the two categories *ren'ai* and *miai*. Within this third group, however, there are three main different reasons for their non-conformity. First of all, the *miai* was introduced into this area during the lifetime of some of the older people in the village, some of whom describe meeting their spouses for the first time on their wedding day. When they were young, they explained, marriages were matters to be arranged by their elders, and they sometimes expressed relief that they were not asked to shoulder the responsibility of choosing their own spouses.

A second group of marriages required no *miai* because the young people were related to one another and had usually known each other since childhood. Consanguineous marriages[22] used to be quite common in Japan, particularly in Kyūshū, although they have diminished with recent publicity about the possible adverse effects on children.[23] Persons to the third degree of kin, which includes parent/child, siblings, uncle/niece and aunt/nephew, are prohibited,[24] and recently first-cousin marriages have been discouraged.[25] Such discouragement has been so effective in Kurotsuchi that there have been no first-cousin marriages since 1952, although they were quite common before the war. There are 15 examples of marriages between cousins of some sort, and 9 of these are between first cousins. No preference is stated for any particular cousin, the language making no distinction between parallel or cross, paternal or maternal cousins, though one informant told me that no adverse effect would result from the marriage of the children of sisters, whereas it might if a man were involved. This informant's wife was his mother's sister's daughter, but the other 8 cases are marriages of men with their mother's brother's daughters, in all cases with the child of the man's mother's original household. In Niiike, a similar predominance of cross-cousin marriages was reported, as well as an absence of marriages between patrilineal parallel cousins, which Beardsley regards as to be expected in a 'society emphasizing descent through males'.[26] However, in Suye Mura, Embree found that marriages between the children of brothers were more common than other types.[27] There are also two such cases in the Kurotsuchi family records, but the guiding principle was perhaps rather one of reinforcing existing links between two households. Informants explained that cousin marriages are 'convenient for everyone', for the family of a cousin is well known, likely to be of an appropriate social status, and easier for a bride to adjust to then an unrelated household.

If affinal relations between two households have proved satisfactory in one generation, than it is reasonably safe to assume that they will continue to do so in the next, it seems. It was mentioned in the previous chapter that relations between affinally and *honke-bunke* (usually agnatically) related households are similar, but there are certain differences. One of these is the way interactions between the former are said to diminish more quickly than those between the latter after the generation which created the link has died. Thus two affinally related households would have more need to marry a new generation in order to ensure the continuation of strong relations. The mention of the importance of *honke-bunke* links is conspicuous by its absence in Embree's account, which makes little distinction between different types of relatives. Possibly this is connected with the greater number of marriages between the children of brothers. Elsewhere there may be a stronger incentive to preserve the conceptual distinction between affinal and agnatic relatives.

Connected with the more rapid decrease in interaction between affinally related households is the fact that these are usually physically more distant than *honke* and their *bunke*. Village exogamy is usually practised here (see Maps 6-9, pp. 129-32), as elsewhere,[28] and, indeed, marriages within the village are said to be avoided because one can know too much about the other family. There are, however, seven couples which represent endogamous unions and one widow of such a union, and these form the third group of marriages which required no *miai*, although one of them is the 1924 *ren'ai* marriage. The others are classified as being arranged by parents, but they often also seem to be special cases of some kind, which adds further weight to the usual rule of exogamy.[29] For example, three of these marriages took place shortly after the war, which was a time of considerable upheaval and uncertainty with regard to traditional practices. Another is said to have involved a household with a notoriously difficult mother-in-law, and yet another was the case where two families, which were previously united by a barren marriage, had agreed to the dying husband's wish to try for children in another union between the families.

Table 13 classifies the 90 Kurotsuchi marriages into those where *ren'ai* was claimed to be present, those where a *miai* took place, with a column between these two for *ren'ai* which followed or accompanied a *miai*, and those arranged chiefly by parents or other elders, with sub-classification indicating consanguinity and endogamy within the village. However, this gives no indication of how much part the individuals played in the selection of their own spouses. Early *miai*, for example, usually involved only a glimpse of the prospective partner, and sometimes they were described as more like a *kagemi*. On the other hand, some marriages between cousins were described by informants as similar to *miai* marriages in that the individual's opinion was also sought, even though no *miai* was required. Nevertheless, the table does illustrate a transfer of numbers of marriages over the years from the 'elders' column to the *'miai'* column, until the former appears, together with cousin marriages, to have petered out altogether. It also shows how the *ren'ai* marriages have remained a fairly constant minority since quite soon after the war, although they seem to represent quite a large percentage of the total in the 1961-5 and 1971-5 groups. In general, the *ren'ai* marriages involved the eventual co-operation of parents and a go-between, and the *miai* ones have come more and more to allow the individuals concerned to assess each other and play a part in the final decision.

The problems of classification were well illustrated in a marriage which took place during the investigation in 1975. The couple had known each other for some years through agricultural college and farming connections, and, at a friend's wedding, the go-between suggested casually to the boy that this girl might make a good match for him. Before agreeing, the boy approached the girl privately to propose marriage, and, when this had proved successful, the go-between arranged a formal *miai* at which the two sets of parents were able to meet. The boy described the marriage as 'between *miai* and *ren'ai*', but the go-between was in no doubt about the fact that it was a *miai* marriage. The boy was careful to play down his own initiative since a

Table 13: Classification of Kurotsuchi Marriages according to Presence or Absence of *Ren'ai*, *Miai*, Consanguinity and Village Endogamy

Year of Marriage	Arrangement of Elders		Cousins		Endog.		*Miai*	*Miai* + *Ren'ai*	*Ren'ai*
1911-15	1	1*	1		1				
1916-20		1	1				2		1
1921-5		1	1			1	2		1
1926-30	1	1			1		3		
1931-5	3	2	1	2	1		1		1
1936-40	1	2	2				2		
1941-5		2	2				3		
1946-50		6	3		3		4		
1951-5	1	1	1				5		2
1956-60							7	1	1
1961-5		1*	1		1		4		4
1966-70							5		
1971-5							4	3	2
1976-9							6		1
Totals	25		15		8		48	4 + 13 = 17	

Note: Numbers on the left-hand side of the first vertical column refer to marriages arranged by elders with no further qualification. Those on the right hand side of the same column are further classified as 'Cousin' or 'Endogamous', and they appear again at the left-hand side of the appropriate column. Those marked with an asterisk appear in both. Figures on the right-hand side of the 'Cousins' and 'Endog.' columns appear again in the *Miai* or *Ren'ai* columns.

previous friendship with a girl had been brought to an abrupt end when his parents disapproved of her.

So far, figures have been given only for marriages of people who remained resident in Kurotsuchi. I did also investigate marriages out of the village and some families reported the marriages of their daughters, or non-inheriting sons, as *ren'ai*, *miai* and so forth. However, many of these relatives now lived far from the village, and, although some were interviewed when they returned to visit, it was not possible to build up a complete and accurate picture of these patterns merely from second-hand evidence. There seemed to be a greater proportion of *ren'ai* marriages than in the village sample and this was borne out for the period between 1976 and 1979 for which I was able to get a fairly accurate picture of all the marriages that took place involving villagers. The proportion of *miai* to *ren'ai* marriages for people remaining in the village was 6 to 1, as shown in Table 13. Of 12 marriages out of the village, no less than 5 were *ren'ai*. However, these figures cover only three and a half years and it would be dangerous to draw too many conclusions from them.

A much longer-term picture was available about where people had married to, however, and in general the marriage sphere for spouses leaving the community was rather wider than that for villagers seeking to bring spouses in. This is illustrated in Maps 6 and 7. Brides leaving the village sometimes went to families similar to their own, but for several there was the opportunity to marry non-inheriting sons leaving the area. In some cases, a villager would establish himself in a city elsewhere, only to return when he was ready to marry to seek a wife from his own district. Such a wedding took place during the investigation, involving a younger son of the village head, who now works in Kyoto, and a girl from his sister's village by marriage, whom he met at a *miai* which he flew home to attend. Occasionally, girls leave the village to spend some time working elsewhere, and one *ren'ai* match in Kurotsuchi involved a girl who met her husband in Osaka. This is an example of another means by which the outgoing marriage sphere is enlarged.

Maps 8 and 9 indicate the extent to which the marriage sphere has enlarged since the war. It had been enlarging gradually with increased ease of travel and subsequent connections further afield since the end of the Taishō period. It was at about that time that a Kurotsuchi youth returned from a period in Tokyo, bringing with him a wife, who represented the first marriage link with the main island of Japan. More usually, even now, marriages with people from so far afield are of people who have moved out of the village. Maps 8 and 9 also show that the number of matches made within the old *mura* of Tadami, i.e. the present school zone, have decreased in proportion to the total, as have those made within the village.[30] It seems that here, as Beardsley suggests also for Niiike, people marry from as far away as can easily be visited as possible, which is considerably further now that people have cars than it was in the past.[31]

Map 6: Sources of Spouses from outside Kurotsuchi

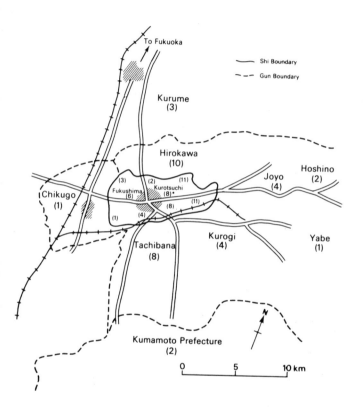

Other Fukuoka prefecture (3)
Elsewhere in Kyūshū (2)
Elsewhere in Japan (1)

KEY TO CENTRAL AREA

Number of couples from within Kurotsuchi	8
Number of spouses from within Tadami school zone: Muta 3; Tadami 5; Hon 1; Tachiyama 1; Ogumori 1	11
Number of spouses from within Yame-*shi*: Kawasaki 11; Kōzuma 8; Fukushima 6; Sango 4; Okayama 3; Yahata 1; Nagamine 2	35
Plus Yame-*gun* 30; Fukuoka-*ken* 6; Kyūshū 4; elsewhere 1	41
Total	95

Map 7: Destinations of Spouses Marrying out of Kurotsuchi

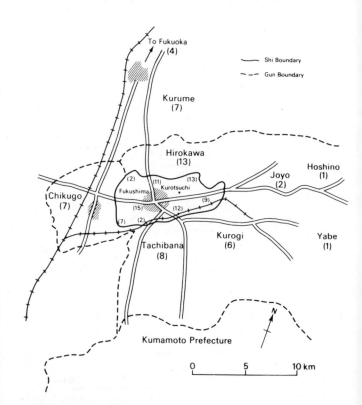

Other Fukuoka prefecture (6)
Elsewhere in Kyūshū   (10)
Elsewhere in Japan   (15)

KEY TO CENTRAL AREA

Number of spouses to Tadami school zone: Hon 4; Tadami 7; Ogumori 2	13
Number of spouses to Yame-*shi*: Kawasaki 9; Kōzuma 12; Fukushima 15; Sango 2; Okayama 7; Yahata 2; Nagamine 11	58
Number of spouses to Yame-*gun* (including Chikugo-*shi*)	38
Number of spouses to Fukuoka prefecture	17
Plus, as above, Kyūshū 10; elsewhere in Japan 15	25
Total	151

Map 8: Sources and Destinations of Post-1945 Kurotsuchi Spouses

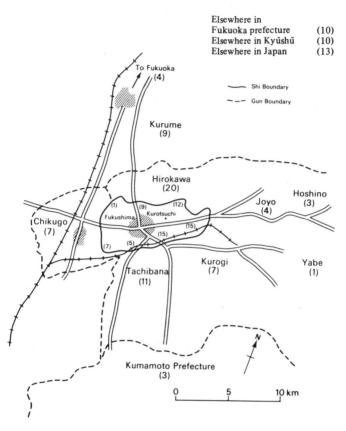

Elsewhere in
Fukuoka prefecture   (10)
Elsewhere in Kyūshū   (10)
Elsewhere in Japan   (13)

To Fukuoka
(4)

——— Shi Boundary
– – – Gun Boundary

Kurume
(9)

Hirokawa
(20)

Hoshino
(3)

(1)   (9) Kurotsuchi   (12)
Fukushima   •
Chikugo
(7)

Joyo
(4)

(15)

(15)

(7)   (5)

Yabe
(1)

Kurogi
(7)

Tachibana
(11)

N

Kumamoto Prefecture
(3)

0   5   10 km

KEY TO CENTRAL AREA

Within Tadami school zone: Tadami 6; Muta 1; Hon 1; Tachiyama 1; Ogumori 3;	12	6.7%
Within Yame-*shi*: Tadami 12; Kawasaki 15; Kōzuma 15; (clockwise on map) Fukushima 13; Sango 5; Okayama 7; Yahata 1; Nagamine 9	77	43%
Within Yame-*gun* (including Yame-*shi* and Chikugo-*shi*)	130	72.6%
Within Fukuoka prefecture	153	85.5%
Plus elsewhere in Kyūshū 13; in Japan 13 Total	179	
(6.1%) (6.7%)		

Endogamous marriages within Kurotsuchi   4 couples = 2.2% of 181

Map 9: Sources and Destinations of Pre-1945 Kurotsuchi Spouses Included in Family Register since 1888

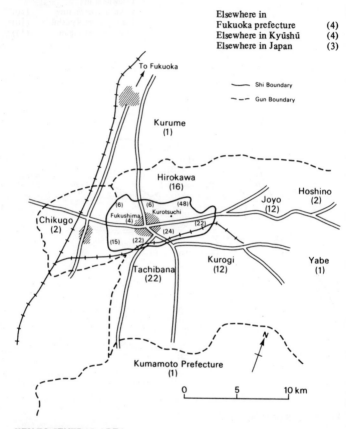

Elsewhere in
Fukuoka prefecture   (4)
Elsewhere in Kyūshū   (4)
Elsewhere in Japan   (3)

KEY TO CENTRAL AREA

Within Tadami school zone: Tadami 24; Muta 1; Hon 19; Ogumori 3; Inobu 1	48	21.0%
Within Yame-*shi*: Tadami 48; Kawasaki 22; Kōzuma 24; Fukushima 4; Sango 22; Okayama 15; Yahata 6; Nagamine 6	147	64.0%
Within Yame-*gun* (including Yame-*shi* and Chikugo-*shi*)	214	93.5%
Within Fukuoka prefecture	221	96.5%
Plus elsewhere in Kyūshū 5; in Japan 3 Total	229	
(2.18%) (1.32%)		
Endogamous marriages within Kurotsuchi 20 couples = 8.05% of 249		

The Investigation and Matters of Concern

However the possibility of marriage originated, unless the other party is well known, considerable investigation usually precedes the final agreement of the family. The go-between will provide as much information as possible, but in the enthusiasm to make a match anyone may emphasise good points and perhaps forget entirely to mention bad ones.[32] In cities, some families hire detectives for this purpose, but in the country a common practice is personally to visit the home village of the household concerned, and ask about the family at shops and neighbours' houses. This is known as the *kuchikiki* (literally, inquiry of mouth), or sometimes *kikiawase* (inquire variously and compare).[33] It is particularly useful if the inquirer has a relative or acquaintance in the village concerned, and several Kurotsuchi housewives told me where they came to ask about their husbands' families, sometimes describing a twilight walk past their present home, in order to observe it inconspicuously. If no one is known, however, it seems to be quite in order to stop passers-by, knock at doors, and wait for a free moment in shops to put questions about the family. The two shopkeepers in Kurotsuchi confirmed that this happened, and complained that they were sometimes put in a difficult situation by it. One claimed that she said everyone was fine, but the other pointed out that if too rosy a picture is painted and the marriage takes place but fails, blame may return to the shopkeeper's praise. There is, however, an advantage to the shopkeeper, for those families with a son or daughter approaching marriageable age are aware of the possibility of such inquiries, and probably make an effort to maintain favour with the shopkeepers by keeping their custom in the village. Indeed, this practice is a sanction for good relations to be maintained as much as possible with neighbours and other villagers, for it is precisely whether the family is pleasant and friendly that the strangers will want to know.

Investigation may well proceed further than this, especially into delicate matters not easily discussed, and until recently, the local registry office apparently used constantly to be besieged with requests for copies of family records. This has now been prohibited, and it is difficult to obtain permission to see any family records but one's own.[34] The reasons for this prohibition were for some time given to me in most nebulous terms, such as *mibun no koto* (a matter of birth, station or social position), or 'for the sake of "privacy" ', using the English word. The family register does of course include details of previous divorces in the family, of illegitimacy and early death, and a tendency to infertility might also be evident in some cases. However, the reason why the register has been banned from public inspection is rather to be connected with a recent determined effort to eradicate the discrimination which still persists against the previous outcaste class, the *burakumin*.[35] In the early registers, the social classes *shizoku* (ex-samurai), *heimin* (commoner) and *shinheimin* (new commoner, i.e. former outcaste) were apparently added after the name in an entry. Although this practice has ceased, and at various times since the war the qualifications have been more and more firmly erased, it is in order to be quite sure that they cannot be read that inspection of the old records is prohibited. The same restriction applies to older records which are kept at some Buddhist temples.

There is, however, still a good deal of prejudice expressed against the formerly outcaste groups. The most tolerant people in other ways express disgust for them, or claim that they have no objection to them, as long as reasonable distance is maintained. Informants explained that such people are traditionally associated with certain trades such as shoe-mending and butchery, both of which are less than pleasant, since shoes are too dirty to be taken into the house, and meat was in the past forbidden by the Buddhist faith. A number of opportunities for other employment have opened up for the *burakumin* in recent years, but most of them still live in certain parts of the city, known to others, and it is difficult for them to escape their own background. Other people were sometimes reluctant to talk about the problem, preceding their remarks by a declaration that one was not supposed to mention *burakumin* these days, and, indeed, some young people claimed to have reached their early teens without having heard of them. However, films and school classes designed to benefit the outcastes serve to arouse curiosity, and when these young people speak to their elders about the problem some of the prejudice is likely to be passed on.

In particular, marriage with *burakumin* is especially to be avoided. The problem seemed not to have arisen in Kurotsuchi, but elsewhere such mixed marraiges lead to a total break in relations between the non-*burakumin* and their family, and, in one case, the father of a girl who married a *burakumin* with a police record committed suicide.[36] Marriage involves the uniting of *kettō* (blood or stock), and the *kettō* of the other family is one of the first things mentioned when a family is asked about what they are concerned to check before a decision is made to marry. The many-times-go-between, mentioned in the *miai* section, commented that today this is basically a concern that the other party is not *burakumin*. He receives many requests for matchmaking, including some from outcastes, whom he claims to be able to distinguish by their surname and place of origin. To be sure, however, he asks everyone to bring him a copy of their family records, and those who fail to comply he concludes must be *burakumin*. For the most part, these people must be content with endogamy.

The *burakumin* are not the only people thought to contaminate the *kettō*, and foreigners were also mentioned by informants in this context. In some parts of Shikoku, certain families are said to own the spirits of foxes, snakes or dogs, a condition which would affect adversely any other family with which they married.[37] The Ainu, the indigenous people of Hokkaido, are also avoided by others for marriage, as are the members of several other small groups throughout the country.[38] A relatively recent pariah group is made up of the descendants of people who were exposed to the radiation of the atom bomb attacks on Nagasaki and Hiroshima, justified by tales of the possibility of deformity in children, and susceptibility to rare disease.[39]

An important concern everywhere is that the *kettō* should not be contaminated with disease. This was a greater issue when less was known about heredity, and diseases such as leprosy were more prevalent and feared hereditary.[40] Epilepsy, neurosis and other mental illness are still especially feared,[41] and a law in Japan makes sterilisation and abortion legal for people with a history of mental defects or other hereditary diseases (Eugenic Protection Law — Law No. 156 of 1948). Relatives with a criminal record are also likely to prejudice the chances of a person's marriage. It is considered important that the proposed partner and his or her family be as healthy as possible, at least as healthy as one's own. Shiotsuki holds a clean bill of health to be worth more than any number of betrothal gifts, including a diamond ring, and she itemises what such a document should include: details of height and weight, results of a chest X-ray, blood test, urine examination, and an indication of blood pressure and eyesight, etc.[42] A talk given by a doctor to the *seinen daigaku* (p. 58) on the subject of *ren'ai* and marriage included a good deal of advice about how to ascertain tactfully whether one's sweetheart had had mumps or German measles, and whether there was any hereditary disease in the family. Some people apparently call at the school or place of work of the proposed partner to see how often they were registered as off sick, and perhaps also to gain a reference on general qualities of character, and from the school, a scholastic record.

There is also a concern that the two families to be united in marriage be of an approximately equivalent social standing, especially if the wife is to live with her in-laws. A saying, applied to a marriage between unsuited households, likens them to a kimono which doesn't fit.[43] Nowadays, evidence of wealth and income are playing more and more of a part in determining the social status of a household, but in the country, where families have lived in the same spot for generations, historical factors are still important.[44] For example, the single daughter of a respectable Kurotsuchi farming family was greatly sought in marriage, probably because apart from being attractive, she was actively and visibly engaged in farm work. One of her suitors was the son of a previous rich landowner, who had become a city councillor after much of his property was removed during the post-war land reform, and who was also the prime instigator of the *pairotto* tea field project in the hills behind Kurotsuchi. He was a contemporary of the girl's father at school, but although both the young people said independently that they would be happy to marry each other, the girl's father refused because the other family was too far above his own in social status. The other side had not given up entirely, however, intending to wait until the family feared their daughter might pass marriageable age without betrothal. This is quite common practice where a girl's family proves difficult, it seems, and, unless a more suitable offer is received, repeated requests sometimes bring success. The girl's father explained that he was reluctant to be related to a family with whom he would feel obliged to use deferential behaviour,[45] but the establishment of such affinal ties may also bring increased status to the household. As Nakane has pointed out, families which have gained wealth and a certain amount of prestige can only gain social recognition of their increased status by creating an affinal alliance with a previously superior household.[46]

Among farmers, property is still an important consideration, and some poorer families, when describing the customs of their own household, would sometimes add that things would be done differently in a house with property. One girl approaching marriageable age in 1975 said that although she would like to experience *ren'ai*, marriage was too serious for this, since factors such as property had to be considered. She is the eldest daughter of a family with no sons, but which owns a good deal of land, so that it was expected that she would receive a *yōshi*, and, indeed, by 1979 she had done so. Other informants said that property was less important than it used to be, however, and one woman turned down a prospective marriage partner because his farm had too much land and she did not want to do farm work. This is not an exceptional case, and the number of girls unwilling to do farm work and live with their parents-in-law is said to be so large that families with property are unable to be as selective as they once were. However, Kurotsuchi families are well enough off to avoid the situation, described by Bernstein, where many poorer farming families in Shikoku have to rely for wives on 'bridal banks' run by officials of the local Agricultural Co-operative.[47] Moreover, of 27 girls in Kurotsuchi between middle-school age and marriage, asked whether they would prefer to live in the country or a city, 21 said they would rather live in the country, usually a place similar to Kurotsuchi, and only 6 expressed a desire to marry someone who would take them to live in a more urban place. Within the village, farming households tended to be better off than those of employees, and some girls actually stated a preference for a farming family, especially those who had attended the agricultural high school in Yame. Perhaps this is a recent result of factors such as the new affluence of farming families, and the better treatment that daughters-in-law are now said to receive. Some other girls were not averse to the idea of living with their parents-in-law, but sometimes had another skill, such as sewing, which they hoped to use commercially after marriage. As a rule, however, girls must wait for offers of marriage to be brought to their families, and, as mentioned above, the *tekireiki* poses a limit on the time it is advisable to hold out against offers which are less than ideal. Almost all men express an aversion to marrying a girl older than 24.

Religion is also sometimes important, for though many of the Buddhist sects are so similar in practice that intermarriage poses no problems, Sōka Gakkai is quite different, and its adherents seek either another member of the movement, or someone willing to be converted, one informant explained. She was acting as go-between for two Gakkai families of her acquaintance.[48] The activities of this and other new religions often provide a venue for young people of like interests to meet, and perhaps to find their own suitable partners for marriage, and such an example existed in Kurotsuchi. Similarly, the married daughter of another family had met and fallen in love with her spouse at a Christian church. Where the sect does differ, women or *yōshi* are expected to change their sect to that of their new family.

Almost everyone seems to marry eventually, so that even those with the worst 'faults' may be accepted by someone. A family with an impediment will have to accept another. Two crippled men in Kurotsuchi were married, one to a woman with a rather unattractive squint, although they seemed to have three normal children, and the other's wife was over thirty when they married. A person marrying for the second time cannot expect a partner as perfect as the first might have been, and as a girl's age increases, the quality of her suitors may well decrease. There is a saying in Japanese which Inouye translates into English: 'For the cracked pot a rotten lid', when he used this analogy for men and women. However cracked and imperfect the pot, there is always a lid to match, he explains, likewise, with the help of a go-between, men and women with defects can be brought together.[49]

The *Kotowari* (Excuse, Apology or Refusal)

In the Meiji period, and in some country areas until more recently, the *miai* was little more than a formal introduction of the two parties after the investigation was complete and the marriage had been virtually settled, so that the rupture of negotiations at that stage would reflect very badly on the household responsible.[50] Nowadays, however, the *miai* has a more experimental aspect, and it is not unusual for an individual to experience several such meetings before a successful match is made. The eligible girl mentioned in the previous section had had more *miai* than she would number, and one marriage which took place in Kurotsuchi during the study represented a union established at a fourth *miai* for the boy and the third for a girl. This was probably about the average for Kurotsuchi, but people were reluctant to be exact about such details. An acquaintance in Tokyo had had no less than 33 *miai* without finding a wife.

Once a *miai* has taken place, it is the business of the go-between to maintain contact with the two parties, and to establish and communicate their reactions. Where these are favourable, the task is a pleasant one, mainly a matter of co-ordinating future events; where either is unfavourable, a good deal of tact is required. There are, however, certain institutionalised ways of turning down an offer with relatively little loss of face on the part of the party refused, and these will now be considered.

The go-between usually consults first the initiating party, the boy's side, except in the case of a *yōshi*, and here the answer is frequently favourable, because a *kagemi* as well as a good deal of investigation probably preceded a direct approach. He must then make a series of visits to the girl's house, for, even if they are well impressed with the suitor, the family will rarely make an immediate reply.[51] One man, who had matched half a dozen couples successfully, related his method of assessing their attitude. He takes along a bottle of *sake*, and if the girl's family opens it, he is likely to be successful. If they put it on one side and open a bottle of their own, he must expect bad news. This is not standard procedure, however, and different people have different methods of approach, it seems.

At first, the girl's family may protest that she is still too young to marry, that she has not yet mastered the arts of cooking and house-keeping. Persistence on the part of the go-between may break down such resistance, and a more definite refusal would probably involve the phrase: 'go-en ni narimasen deshita'.[52] Since many excuses after a first impression are based on a fairly irrational feeling of aversion, or lack of attraction, this would seem to be a sufficiently vague reason to give. However, it probably sounds a little weak to a go-between who has tried hard to bring about a match, and further reasons are usually put forward. Such a reason may be found by consulting a calendar, for certain birth signs are traditionally said to be incompatible, and a number of other factors can be drawn upon to cast the match in an inauspicious light.[53] It would be thought that this could have been established before the couple ever met, and a calendar may well have been consulted, but, if all else is favourable, the calendar is scorned as superstition.

A specialist may also be consulted on this matter. Usually this is a diviner or shaman, known in this area as an *ogamiyasan*, and two or three were visited by different members of Kurotsuchi at such a time. One claimed to be able to ascertain the compatibility of a couple just by watching the way they poured tea out of a pot, but he added that people mistrust such assertions, and he usually chants a prayer at his altar before announcing his opinion. His aim is to establish whether a couple will be happy together, he claimed, and if his answer were totally negative, this could very well be used as a legitimate excuse. The quality he seeks is called *aishō* (affinity or compatibility), and this is quite different from *en*, the notion of karmic destiny. If *en* is present, the couple will marry and may or may not be happy; if *aishō* is present, no marriage will take place unless there is also *en*. This consultation is a good recourse in case of indecision, perhaps after two or more similar offers have been received, and it can be turned to good effect even if omens are at first inauspicious. Two girls who married in 1975 changed their first names slightly on the advice of an *ogamiyasan* in order to achieve better *aishō* with their husbands. In one case, this involved a change of character with no change in pronounciation, in the other a dropping of the last syllable.[54] The second case also involved an inauspicious combination of ages, and this problem was solved by the performance of a short marriage ceremony within the household before *setsubun*, the official celebration still taking place on the previously arranged day. This is a not uncommon occurrence, it seems, and several couples reported that their actual marriage was held in advance of the official celebration (see Chapter 5, pp. 172-6).

The Go-between (*Nakōdo*)

The use of a go-between in Japanese society is quite common, both to avoid potential embarrassment or difficulties, and to provide an introduction for people entering a new situation. Embree has noted that the intermediary present at the three great events of a man's life — midwife at birth, go-between at the wedding, and priest at death — is always given pride of place at the associated party for relatives.[55] Despite Vogel's suggestion in 1961 that most Japanese were ideologically opposed to the marriage go-between,[56] such a person — the *nakōdo* — still seems to be a necessary part of nearly every wedding, including those based on a pure love match.

Moreover, a number of distinct roles can be identified when the complete process of matchmaking and marriage is considered.[57] First, where an introduction is made, there is the bridging role (*hashikake*)[58] and this is of course unnecessary between two families which are related or mutually acquainted. Secondly, there is the liaison between the two families. This is to avoid direct confrontation and possible differences of opinion between the two households to be linked. The go-between, or sometimes two (one appointed by each side), must travel back and forth until all the details of the union and its ceremonies are ironed out. This part of the procedure is usually the most arduous, and certain phrases used of the go-between illustrate the hard work involved: for example, 'nakadachi sakadachi' ('a go-between stands on his head'), 'nakōdo wa waraji senzoku' ('a go-between needs a thousand pairs of sandals'). For these two roles, the go-between may be a man or a woman, but at the marriage ceremony itself, a married couple is usually required so that each of the individuals to be married may receive the attentions of a representative of his or her own sex. The man is also expected to make an important speech (details of the marriage ceremony will appear in the next chapter), even if his wife made all the previous arrangements. This ceremonial role is sometimes completely distinct from the previous ones, it may have a separate name, and it is quite common for a couple to ask some prestigious person of their acquaintance, who has done no previous negotiation, to play this part. This involves a certain prestige for both sides, and may involve more concrete advantages for people such as politicians. There is an idea also that a successful person might in some way bring success to the couple.[59] The relationship thus formed resembles that between patron and client, and it is often an *oyabun-kobun* relation of the type mentioned in the previous chapter.[60]

Finally, there is the role of guarantor. The same go-between who brought the couple together must mediate in case of dispute, and if the matter becomes serious enough, arrange a divorce and negotiate the return of betrothal gifts and trousseau. The couple usually visits their go-between for a few years after marriage, especially at Bon and New Year, and they also invite the go-between couple to the celebration following the birth of their first child.

The go-between in this form is a relatively modern phenomenon. The concept was introduced to Japan from China in the Nara period, but was little used until it was adopted by *samurai* families in the Tokugawa period as a means of matching their social status over long distances.[61] Such mediators began to be used widely among the general population during the Meiji period. Before that the intermediary roles described were filled in other ways, and these varied in different districts, the youth lodge being one example. According to Omachi, a senior relative of the bridegroom used to go and ask for the bride in several areas,[62] and the details given in the following paragraph would suggest that this may also have been the case in Kurotsuchi.

Of the marriages of 80 couples, 46 involved as go-between a relative, 11 of these related to both sides. Twenty-six of the remaining 35 were relatives of the husband's side, and of the other nine, two were families where a daughter's husband was being received as *yōshi*. Some relationships were quite distant, but they ranged from the sibling of one partner to one case where the connection was HFeZDHyBWF, whose grandfather was a cousin of the grandfather of the wife (see Table 14). Typically the relative would be someone living in the same village as the wife's family, and in this way marriages between two specific villages tend to persist. Nakane suggested that these avenues of inter-village marriage relationships were created originally by the fact that prosperous households needed to look outside their own village for another household of equal status, and the links they established then extended the area of possibility for other villagers.[63]

A number of other Kurotsuchi marriages were arranged by a neighbour of one or other of the parties, and certain villagers have been

Table 14: Relationship of Go-between, where Known, in Kurotsuchi

Husband's Relative:		HFeB	Adopted gMeBS	
	HeB x 2	HFyB	H's cousin	26
	HeBWeB	HFyZ	HM's cousin x 2	
	HeBWF	HFeBS	H relative	
			Distant relative	
	HeZ	HMyB x 3		
	HeZH	HMZ x 2		
	HeZHeZ	HMyZHeB		
		HMFyB		
		HMMZS		
		HMeZD		
Wife's Relative:	WeZHF	WFBD + H (yōshi)	W's uncle	
	WeBWgF	WFMBS	W's F's relative	
			(yōshi)	
		WMeZ + H	Distant relative	
		WMZHB		9

		HFF = WMF	
Relative of Both:	HMZ = WMZ	HFMHBS = WFB	
	HMZ = WFZ	HFZDHBWF = W's 3rd cousin	
	HMBZ = WeZ	F's cousin = WM's cousin	
	H's adopted MyZ = WFeZ		
	HM's cousin = WF's cousin	Aunt of both	
		Distant of both	11

	46

Unrelated Kurotsuchi neighbour[a]	10
Unrelated neighbour[a] of wife's family	7
Other friend or acquaintance	10
Business connection	3
Teacher (carpentry master)	1
Saleswoman	2
Bank connection	1
	80

Note: a. 'Neighbour' here merely indicates that the go-between lives in the same village.

responsible for three or four such unions. The saying was often quoted to me that anyone with a happy marriage should try, in return to society, to arrange three more. In reality, many people never match-make, while others seem to have a flair for it and exceed their three by far. Nor are people whose own marriages were *ren'ai* excluded, for two such people in Kurotsuchi had each arranged several *miai* marriages. Just as there are various roles involved, there are various degrees of involvement and various different types of go-between. The only basic qualification seems to be that the go-between should be married. Sometimes a couple explained that their parents had decided their match directly — particularly if they were cousins or both from Kurot-suchi — and had then asked a go-between to officiate at the wedding. This is similar to the procedure for an approved love match. In these cases, a prestigious person such as a village official or a company superior would be appropriate, and an example of where the latter was asked was a couple who met at work.

A company superior might also be asked to carry out the bridging role. An employee at the City Hall in Yame related such a case when he explained how he had been introduced to his wife, previously a librarian at a school which he used to visit. He had admired the girl, but was unwilling to approach her directly, so he sought the aid of his superior at the City Hall. He, in turn, spoke to the head of the education depart-ment, who contacted the head of the school concerned, and a formal *miai* was arranged. There are also examples in Kurotsuchi of connec-tions through business. In one case a company friend made the intro-duction whereas a relative was asked to make further negotiations and preside at the wedding; in another, a relative arranged the *miai*, and the wife's boss became the official go-between at the wedding. Where a boy goes as an apprentice to live in the house of his master, the latter seems to be an appropriate person to concern himself with his pupil's marriage, and there are examples in Kurotsuchi of both a couple whose marriage was arranged by a carpentry master, and another master who arranged his apprentice's match. There is also a case in Kurotsuchi of a man's banker becoming his *nakōdo*, his wife being the cousin of a colleague from the bank. There are also two cases where a regular visiting cosmetics saleswoman has fulfilled this function, select-ing a match from her other clients. Here one can see how business may be enhanced by responsible matchmaking activities, for households linked successfully by such a person will surely continue to make their cosmetic purchases from their benefactor. It is said also that insurance salespeople are good matchmakers, since lengthy conversations with their clients are an integral part of their sales technique, so that a relationship of trust can be built up.

For families lacking an appropriate introduction from relatives and neighbours, a photograph and a brief life history may be taken to someone known to be a matchmaker, and one example in Yame is a woman who runs a shop selling bridal wear. The information she requires is: name, date of birth, address, father's occupation and that of siblings, details of family composition, with marriages and children of siblings, and scholastic and employment record of the individual concerned, as well as information about the type of partner sought. The people who lodge requests with this shopkeeper are usually girls and their families, she said, and she speaks to her other clients and contacts about them until a possible partner turns up. A *miai* may be arranged in the shop, and if this is successful, further arrangements are usually made by someone closer to one of the parties. Again, this service probably brings trade to the shop, for successful brides will no doubt return to fit themselves out for the wedding.

The previously mentioned many-times-go-between has not arranged any Kurotsuchi marriages, but is an interesting example of someone who has made the art of matchmaking a full-time hobby. In eight years, he has successfully completed negotiations for 37 marriages, and, at 42, he has set himself a lifetime target of 500. He talks of his work as a 'study' (*nakōdogaku*), and claims to spend any time he is walking in the street noticing the kinds of faces that go together so that he can introduce appropriate people. It seems as though this study, together with the expertise developed through experience, may have proved fruitful, for whereas at first he might make one success in 30 *miai*, he has now reduced this proportion to one in three. His usual routine procedure is to take the boy for a *kagemi* first, then to introduce the young couple in a coffee house or restaurant, and if all is well, he then approaches the parents. He does much of the investigation himself, and emphasises the importance of introducing all impediments and problems at the earliest moment, so that any subsequent investigation can bring only good news. He has now gained something of a reputation, it seems, for he is approached frequently and has collected a large file of requests from which to select his matches. In 90 per cent of cases, he sees the marriage through to the wedding, and takes responsibility for mistakes, claiming to do the whole thing as a hobby rather than as a business. In fact he does receive remuneration, as does any go-between, but the sum depends on the people concerned, and many laugh this off as barely covering the travel expenses during

1. A view of Kurotsuchi taken from the rice fields just after harvesting.

2. The village shopkeeper, still wearing his market union cap, shows off his visiting grandson to a group of schoolgirls.

3. Age-mates drink a toast while preparing *sukiyaki* at their first meeting of the new year.

4. The first and eponymous part of the *honja* betrothal gifts — the packets of tea. To their left is the stand which features Takasago, the old man and woman.

5. Three Japanese garments for the most expensive part of the betrothal gifts. They are seen here with, from left, bottles of sake and tables of *tai, surume,* and *konbu.*

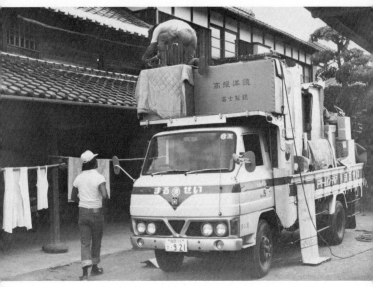

6. Part of a bride's trousseau is delivered to her new home in Kurotsuchi a few days before the wedding.

7. The farewell party for a bride may be quite a jovial occasion.

8. Before leaving for the wedding ceremony, a Kurotsuchi bride and her family share a farewell breakfast. The bride is seated between the go-between and his wife; her parents are to her left and some of her uncles to her right. The betrothal gifts are on display in the rear. (Photograph by Alan Smith)

9. The bridegroom takes one of his sips of sake at a *karishūgen*. To his right sit the bride, the go-between's wife, and the bride's father. (The go-between has moved from his seat beside the groom to act as master of ceremonies.) In the foreground are the three serving girls. This ceremony took place in the groom's home in front of the *butsudan* and the *tokonoma*.

10. A Kurotsuchi bride, with her new husband, after she has changed into a different kimono at the wedding reception. (Photograph courtesy of Alan Smith)

11. A Kurotsuchi bride and her mother-in-law visit the village shrine to pay respects to the *ujigami-san* during the course of the wedding day.

12. Boys and girls in their finery leave the shrine after the 7-5-3 ceremony on November 15.

negotiations. He gave an average estimate in the region of 30-50,000 *yen* (£50-£80 at the 1975 rate of exchange) for the whole procedure, usually divided in the ratio 2:1 or 3:2 boy's family to girl's. However, he does not demand payment, and in 2 of his 37 cases he received nothing. Other go-betweens mentioned a similar sum.[64]

There are also professional marriage bureaux in cities, the first having been opened in Kyoto in 1881, according to Yanagida,[65] but I heard of no marriages arranged in this way. In modern Japan, television is not without its intermediary function, and an extremely popular programme is one which matches and brings together young people seeking partners with a view to further dates and marriage. Each is described to the other by a pair of compères, who communicate through the window with a curtain separating them, and comparisons are made with expectations. After a good deal of banter to and fro, the curtain is raised, and the two are allowed a minute's televised conversation before deciding whether they want to meet again. There is no subtlety in the communication of impressions here, for the participants are then given a yes/no switch, and at the count of three, they make their decision. The result appears behind them in a mass of flashing lights to the accompaniment of a prolonged roll of drums and a clash of cymbals.

It seems, then, that the bridging role of the go-between has a good deal of flexibility. Rather than diminishing, as Kawashima suggested,[66] it has recently become more varied. Even a love match usually involved a third party who formally introduced the two people, though this individual may play no further part. Such an introduction certainly seems to lend an air of respectability to a love match, and one informant added very quickly after stating that her marriage was *ren'ai* that a proper introduction had been made. The following chapter includes details about some of the ceremonial activities of the go-between, once a match has been made.

Attitudes

In general, attitudes about *ren'ai* and *miai* vary enormously, and could well be quite different in theory from what they might be if an actual situation arose in the family. Some informants answered that they were in favour of *ren'ai* for young people, perhaps because they thought this an appropriate answer to give to a Western investigator, for later these same people spontaneously expressed an aversion to too great a degree of freedom on the part of their children. In one case, a third party told me that such a person had forbidden his own daughter to marry someone with whom she had fallen in love. There are, however, a number of families whose daughters have successfully completed marriages based on *ren'ai*, and though these are often said to have caused problems at the time, the parents are not ashamed to report them as examples of *ren'ai* matches. Many informants with children said they were not against *ren'ai* for their own sons and daughters, but that a decision to co-operate or not would depend on the other party concerned. Young people also gave this answer frequently when asked if their parents would approve of a love match for them. Some parents even said that they would prefer their children to fall in love with a suitable person because this might lead to greater understanding in a marriage, but others emphasised the advantages of security and knowledge gained if a *miai* and subsequent investigation are carried out. One or two people pointed out that a *ren'ai* marriage saves the parents and go-between a lot of trouble, but more frequently parents said they would not feel happy about a match until full investigation was complete. One informant said that families with property are more concerned to make *miai* marriages for their children, and this does seem to be consistent with the figures, although there are exceptions. Similarly, some members of property-owning families gave quite liberal views, but it was members of this group who gave the most conservative ones too. One grandfather said flatly that he did not approve of *ren'ai* because 'he was old-fashioned'; another head of such a family said that one can only achieve a well-matched marriage with a *miai* arrangement, and added a totally unsupported assertion that divorce is more frequent among *ren'ai* marriages; a third said that a *miai* is more suitable for an arrangement to last a lifetime; finally, a slightly more tolerant farmer's wife said she would not mind her son having a love match as long as she liked the girl too.

In general, it seemed that young people could achieve a marriage based on love if the partner were a person who would be appropriate anyway by the usual standards applied when investigating a partner proposed by a go-between. A child moving out of the home may experience greater lenience than an inheriting son, for the spouse of the latter must also appeal to the parents with whom she will co-habit. Young people seemed concerned not to upset their parents by making a rebellious marriage. I discussed personal aspirations to marriage with 27 young people between school-leaving age and marriage, whom I shall call *seinen*, and with 18 school pupils, 15 from high school and three from middle school. I broached the subject with more pupils than this, but three high-school boys, and the other middle-school students (three boys and a girl) said they had not formulated any views on the subject, and some were unwilling to talk about the opposite sex at all. The three middle-school students with opinions were all girls, and they were unanimously in favour of *ren'ai* marriages, as were six out of six high-school boys and seven out of nine high-school girls. One of the other two girls said she would prefer *ren'ai*, but if she couldn't manage it she would have a *miai*, and only one said she would prefer a *miai* so that she could turn to her parents and the go-between if things went wrong. The replies from the *seinen* group were much more varied, and usually better thought out than those of the students, particularly as they approached the age at which they would be expected to marry. Only one member of this group (male) answered that *ren'ai* is better, without qualification, although three girls and two boys said they would not even attempt a decision, as they were sure they would not find *ren'ai* for themselves. Nine boys and four girls answered that they would not mind either *ren'ai* or *miai*, four boys and three girls adding that a *miai* leading to *ren'ai* would be ideal, one boy and one girl that they would need to feel right about the person, another boy saying that if he was unable to find a partner himself, he would have to have a *miai*, and two boys, expecting to inherit, adding that the girl would have to get on with their parents too. One member of the group said that he had no opinion, and the other seven favoured *miai* over *ren'ai*. Of these, one girl said she would like to experience *ren'ai*, but that a *miai* was more appropriate for marriage; another said she had already experienced *ren'ai*, but would rather be in a position to discuss things with a go-between and her parents for marriage; another girl gave an unqualified preference for *miai*; one boy and one girl said *miai* is better because sufficient is then known about the other family; a boy expecting to inherit opted for *miai* as best for the *ie*, his parents, and to avoid gossip, commenting that his sister's *ren'ai* marriage had caused a good deal of trouble; and, finally, one boy used an old argument, that a *miai* is better because *ren'ai* emotions may well cloud his judgement. Boys expecting to inherit, as well as girls whose families hoped they would receive a *yōshi*, usually noted that the opinions of their parents would need to be favourable before a final decision could be made, though some expressed the hope that they might also achieve a *ren'ai* match with such a suitable person.

On the whole, then, young people seem to have been sufficiently impressed with what they have seen of Western love to seek this where possible with a marital partner, though as they draw closer to marriageable age, practical considerations grow more and more important too.[67] Few institutionalised modes of courtship seem to have developed, except for the 'dating' practices following a *miai*, and with a definite view to mutual assessment for marriage. A few young people claimed to have boyfriends or girlfriends:[68] three girls and two boys of the 15 high school students, but only four boys of the 27 *seinen*, though three girls said they had friends who might become boyfriends, given time. By 1979, one of these had, indeed, achieved a love marriage. Boys appeared to spend much of their free time in the company of their own sex, and girls were on the whole less free to go out, except within the village. Youth Group activities are the exception, in both cases, so that the opportunities for boys and girls to meet were present, and the one case mentioned had developed in this way. However, many young people commented that villagers were too familiar to be considered for marriage and although other youth activities are also plentiful in the Yame area, they always seem to involve groups, rather than couples, and this fact even seems to be a requisite for attendance. Several girls also commented that their parents would disapprove of them going out regularly with one boyfriend. If a *ren'ai* match is to develop, it probably needs to do so in a fairly surreptitious manner in this kind of face-to-face community. One boy, who had a girlfriend in Fukuoka, where he worked, said that he could not possibly bring her home to meet his parents because of the gossip it would arouse. The only *ren'ai* marriage which took place during the first period of study was that of the girl who had been working in Osaka where she had met her husband. She was back in the village for several months before her marriage, but news of it only began to leak out of the immediate family a few weeks before the wedding. Several informants did comment that there is more freedom of social intercourse between young boys and girls in urban areas, but Befu wrote in 1971 about Japan in general, that 'a more or less serious, "steady" relationship between an unmarried man and woman with no definite intention of marriage is still frowned upon as improper. Yet, having dates with several persons one after another is considered "loose".'[69] Rohlen has also described how romantic pairings within office groups of the bank community he studied are viewed as disruptive, so that superiors may warn against them with threats of transfer. Dating itself is not encouraged, and Rohlen writes, 'marriage itself has a definite place in the total scheme of social affairs, a place dating does not'.[70]

The ideal situation seems to be for a young person to fall in love with someone also suited in socially defined ways so that the rest of the family will be satisfied too. This conclusion is similar to that found by Blood and Vogel in the Tokyo area over ten years ago: that the best form of marriage was '*miai* plus *ren'ai*',[71] and also that of another writer, Theodore Brameld, who wrote of an unspecified fishing village:

A synthesis of both practices recognizes the need of young couples to approve of their own marriage by sufficient opportunity to know each other well beforehand, and an equal need to be guided by the greater experience and perspicacity of elders in judging the qualifications of prospective mates.[72]

This kind of compromise was also suggested in the manual on marriage by Minami, as early as 1953.[73] However, the number of such marriages still remains quite small, although it appears that young people are more and more able to take part in the decision about whom they should marry. In cases of conflict, sometimes one side wins, sometimes the other, but as a rule an inheriting child will defer to the household, a tendency probably reflected in the small number of *ren'ai* marriages found in farming households. A traditional-modern compromise has almost been reached, but where the *ie* remains strong, the older generation still seems to have the final word.

Notes

1. Cf. John F. Embree, *Suye Mura* (University of Chicago Press, Chicago, 1939), p. 89; Jean Stoetzel, *Without the Chrysanthemum and the Sword* (Unesco, Paris, 1955), p. 181. As Ronald Dore, *Shinohata* (Allen Lane, London, 1978), p. 152, writes of Shinohata girls, 'not to marry would be a mark of failure to make the grade as a person.'

2. Of course, it is unnecessary to marry to have descendants (cf. P.G. Riviere, 'Marriage: a Reassessment' in Rodney Needham (ed.), *Rethinking Kinship and Marriage* (Tavistock, London, 1971), pp. 58, 60), but the number of informants who gave this kind of answer illustrates the extent to which having them is regarded as part and parcel of marriage.

3. E.g. William J. Goode, 'The Theoretical Importance of Love', *American Sociological Review*, vol. 24 (1959), p. 41.

4. Ruth Benedict, *The Chrysanthemum and the Sword* (Secker and Warburg, London, 1947), pp. 103-4.

5. Cf. Robert O. Blood, *Love Match and Arranged Marriage* (The Free Press, New York, Collier-Macmillan, London, 1967), pp. 29-32.

6. Cf. Jirō Kamishima, *Nihonjin no Kekkonkan* (*The Japanese View of Marriage*) (Chikuma Sōsho, Tokyo, 1969), p. 92.

7. Ryōhei Minami, *Konrei-shiki to Kekkon no Kokoroe (On Marriage and the Marriage Ceremony)* (Taibunkan, Tokyo, 1953), pp. 14-16; Yaeko Shiotsuki, *Kankonsōsai Nyūmon (An Introduction to Ceremonial)* (Kōbunsha, Tokyo, 1970), p. 10.

8. *Tekireiki* literally means 'time of appropriate age'; *tekirei* (appropriate age) was also used in reference to conscription age, but the phrase used without qualification is usually in reference to marriageable age (see, for example, Minami, *Konrei-shiki*, pp. 127-9; Hiroshi Fujisaki, *Kankonsōsai Jiten (Dictionary of Ceremonial)* (Tsuru Shobo, Tokyo, 1957), p. 24.

9. No discrepancy was found in the classification of marriages by a husband and wife separately, and although this might conceivably occur in the case of *ren'ai*, there was only one such example among widows and widowers.

10. There were no casual unions of the type described by R.P. Dore in *City Life in Japan* (University of California Press, Berkeley, 1971), pp. 165-7, for Tokyo, although one cousin of a Kurotsuchi man, who returned to the village after an unsuccessful marriage, did live for many years with a man to whom she was not married, it was said.

11. This practice has been described by several Japanese scholars, particularly in reference to Kyūshū, and these include Kunio Yanagida, *Kon'in no Hanashi (On Marriage)* (Iwanami Shoten, Tokyo, 1948), pp. 125-58; and *Minzokugaku Jiten (Dictionary of Folklore)* (Minzokugaku Kenkyūjo, Tokyo, 1953), pp. 664-5; Yanagida and T. Omachi, *Kon'in Shūzoku Goi (Popular Terms associated with Marriage)* (Minkan Denshō no Kai, Tokyo, 1937), pp. 246-56; T. Omachi, 'Kon'in' ('Marriage'), p. 200-1, and 'Konrei' ('Marriage Ceremony'), p. 271, in T. Omachi *et al.* (eds.), *Nihon Minzokugaku Taikei (An Outline of Japanese Folklore* (Heibonsha, Tokyo, 1962); Tarō Nakayama, *Nihon Kon'in Shi (A History of Marriage in Japan)*, (Shunyō-dō, Tokyo, 1928), pp. 173-214. A description of an example of *yome-nusumi* from the Taishō period is to be found in Kigai Izumimoto, 'Yomenusumi' ('Bride-stealing') in Itsuo Emori (ed.), *Nihon no Kon'in* (Gendai no Esupuri no. 104, Tokyo, 1976), pp. 176-87. Also of the practice as found in Yamaguchi prefecture in Toshio Fueto, 'Nōgyōson ni okeru Kon'in mae no Danjo Kōsai no Kanshu' ('Customary Premarital Relations between the Sexes in Farming Villages'), *Hōshakaigaku*, vol. 4 (1953), p. 108.

12. In two cases the illegitimate son became the heir, for his mother's generation consisted only of women, and in both these families a *yōshi* was later received by the mother. It is possible that the first father was married by ceremony, but that before the marriage was registered, a dispute caused his departure.

13. Fueto, 'Danjo Kōsai'; Kamishima, *Nihonjin no Kekkonkan*, pp. 146-7; Kizaemon Ariga, *Nihon Kon'in Shiron (A Study of the History of Marriage in Japan)* (Nikko Shoin, Tokyo, 1948), pp. 5-10; Kunio Yanagida, *Japanese Manners and Customs in the Meiji Era*, trans. and adapted by Charles S. Terry (Obunsha, Tokyo, 1957), pp. 164-6; Yanagida and Omachi, *Kon'in Shūzoku Goi*, pp. 271-9.

14. It is reported that in Miyage prefecture a medium may even be asked to consult the family ancestors about arranging a marriage (Carmen Blacker, *The Catalpa Bow* (Allen and Unwin, London, 1975), p. 155).

15. *Onegai shimasu* is literally 'I make the request,' usually after asking a favour.

16. This may also be called a *shitamiai*, according to Shiotsuki, *Kankonsōsai Nyūmon*, p. 16, who recommends the practice to avoid hurting the other party after a *miai* (cf. Minami, *Konrei-shiki*, p. 20).

17. An example of the reverse situation, where a younger brother of the man to be married was taken to visit the prospective spouse, who did indeed marry the older, ugly brother, is described in Dore, *Shinohata*, pp. 134-5.

18. One girl in Kurotsuchi, who was very eligible for marriage because she

did farm work, had had a number of such 'dates' of which her contemporaries were openly envious, and it seems that several boys' families were being kept in suspense about the decision. However, this kind of practice seems to be relatively recent in this area, cf. Takeyoshi Kawashima, *Kekkon (Marriage)* (Iwanami Shoten, Tokyo, 1954), p. 43; Edward Norbeck, *Changing Japan* (Holt, Rinehart and Winston, New York, 1965), p. 72; Joyce Lebra, 'Women in Service Industries' in J. Lebra *et al.* (eds.), *Women in Changing Japan* (Westview Press, Boulder, Colorado, 1976), p. 116.

19. J.M. Dixon, 'Japanese Etiquette', *Transactions of the Asiatic Society of Japan*, vol. 13 (1885), p. 14.

20. Fujisaki, *Kankonsōsai Jiten*, p. 42; Tsutomu Ema, *Kekkon no Rekishi (History of Marriage)* (Yūzan-kaku, Tokyo, 1971), p. 134; Naomi Tamura, *The Japanese Bride* (Harper and Bros., New York and London, 1904), pp. 27-8; Yanagida, *Manners and Customs*, p. 174; Jukichi Inouye, *Home Life in Tokyo* (Tokyo, 1910), p. 179.

21. Fujisaki, *Kankonsōsai Jiten*, p. 43; Shiotsuki, *Kankonsōsai Nyūmon*, p. 18. However, Shiotsuki recommends that not more than one or at most two members of each family accompany the person to be married. She suggests that the father be the one to accompany a girl, and the mother a boy, so that the other party will not be reminded of how the young person will probably age. She adds also that it is not a good idea for a sister of the prospective bride, nor a brother of the groom to be present, since they might detract from the main person involved (ibid.).

22. These date back at least to the Heian period (Ivan Morris, 'Marriage in the World of Genji', *Asia*, vol. 11 (1968), p. 60; William H. McCullough, 'Japanese Marital Institutions in the Heian period', *Harvard Journal of Asian Studies*, vol. 27 (1967), p. 136).

23. W.J. Schull and J.V. Neel, *The Effects of Inbreeding on Japanese Children* (Harper and Row, New York, 1965); James V. Neel *et al.*, 'The Incidence of Consanguineous Matings in Japan', *The American Journal of Human Genetics*, vol. 1 (1949), pp. 156-78.

24. Fujisaki, *Kankonsōsai Jiten*, pp. 23-4, also gives details of step-relatives who are prohibited.

25. E.g. Minami, *Konrei-shiki*, pp. 34-5.

26. Richard K. Beardsley *et al.*, *Village Japan*, Phoenix edn (University of Chicago Press, Chicago, 1969), pp. 323-4. Marriages between persons bearing the same surname, who were considered agnatically related, were condemned in Confucian thought (James Legge (trans.), *Li Chi Book of Rites*, edited by Ch'u Chai and Winberg Chai, Vol. 1 (University Books, New York, 1967), p. 78) and prohibited in traditional Chinese law (see T'ang Code in Masaaki Ishihara *et al.* (eds.), 'Ritsu Itsubun' in Katsumi Kuroita (ed.), *Shintei Zōho: Kokushi Taikei*, Vol. 22 (Yoshikawa Kōbunkan, 1929), p. 117). It is not known whether the eighth-century Japanese codes, which were closely based on the codes of T'ang China, prohibited such marriages, since the regulations concerning households are no longer extant. Condemnation of marriages between those of the same surname is, however, fairly widespread in the writings of Japanese Confucians and other sources during the Tokugawa period, including the widely read *Legacy in One Hundred Clauses (Goyuijō hyakkajō)* attributed to Tokugawa Ieyasu (Seiichi Takimoto, *Nihon Keizai Taiten* (Tokyo, 1928), p. 785).

27. Embree, *Suye Mura*, p. 88.

28. Ibid., pp. 72-3; Beardsley *et al.*, *Village Japan*, p. 318; John B. Cornell, 'Matsunagi' p. 212, and Robert J. Smith, 'Kurusu', pp. 65-7, in J.B. Cornell and R.J. Smith, *Two Japanese Villages* (Greenwood Press, New York, 1969); Teigo Yoshida, 'Cultural Integration and Change in Japanese Villages', *American*

Anthropologist, vol. 65 (1963), p. 105.

29. Cf. Embree, *Suye Mura*, p. 72.

30. Morimitsu Ushijima, *Henbō suru Suemura (Suye Mura in Transition)* (Minerva Shobo, Kyoto, 1971), pp. 219-20, reports similar findings in Suye Mura.

31. Beardsley *et al.*, *Village Japan*, pp. 320-1.

32. The expression 'nakōdoguchi' ('go-between mouth') is used of people skilled in sales talk and persuasion, although go-betweens are said to be much more honest and straightforward these days than they have been (Fujisaki, *Kankonsōsai Jiten*, p. 30, cf. Shiotsuki, *Kankonsōsai Nyūmon*, p. 15; Inouye, *Home Life in Tokyo*, p. 179.)

33. Cf. Edward Norbeck, *Takashima* (University of Utah Press, Salt Lake City, 1954), p. 176; Beardsley *et al.*, *Village Japan*, p. 316; Ema, *Kekkon no Rekishi*, p. 171.

34. In order to obtain permission to see the family records for the purposes of this study, I had to apply formally to the Ministry of Legal Affairs (Hōmushō), include a letter of recommendation from a Japanese professor, attend several interviews, and sign an undertaking not to publish any of the material obtained without disguising names. The general permission took over a month to come through, and I still had to request the agreement of every family involved and gain their official stamp as proof for the registry office. Fortunately, no one refused.

35. A comprehensive 1966 source of information about *burakumin* and studies of them is George Devos and Hiroshi Wagatsuma, *Japan's Invisible Race* (University of California Press, Berkeley, Los Angeles and London, 1966). More recent works include John D. Donoghue, *Pariah Persistence in Changing Japan* (University Press of America, Washington, DC, 1977) and Roger Yoshino and Sueo Murakoshi, *The Invisible Visible Minority* (Buraku Kaiho Kenkyusho, Osaka, 1977).

36. Theodore Brameld, *Japan: Culture, Education and Change in Two Communities* (Holt, Rinehart and Winston, New York, 1968), pp. 96, 140. See also Harumi Befu, *Japan: an Anthropological Introduction* (Chandler, San Francisco, 1971), p. 124; Cornell, 'Matsunagi', p. 189; John D. Donoghue, 'An Eta Community in Japan', *American Anthropologist*, vol. 59 (1957), p. 1,000.

37. Blacker, *The Catalpa Bow*, p. 56; Teigo Yoshida, 'Mystical Retribution, Spirit Possession and Social Structure in a Japanese Village', *Ethnology*, vol. 6 (1967), pp. 244-7.

38. For details of these, see Edward Norbeck, 'Little-Known Minority Groups of Japan' in Devos and Wagatsuma, *Japan's Invisible Race*, pp. 183-99. Norbeck, *Takashima*, p. 166, has also suggested that twins or triplets keep the fact a secret if at all possible at the time of marriage.

39. Befu, *Anthropological Introduction*, pp. 124-5.

40. Minami, *Konrei-shiki*, p. 9. Brameld, *Japan*, p. 222, tells of a graduate of Tokyo University who made the explicit comparison between *burakumin* and lepers in saying that he could no more imagine his daughter marrying the former than the latter.

41. The difficulties experienced by a Kurotsuchi family with a member in mental hospital have already been mentioned. The extraordinary fear of mental illness is illustrated forcibly in Junichirō Tanizaki's novel *The Makioka Sisters*, trans. Edward Seidensticker (Grosset and Dunlap, New York, 1966), p. 59, in which what appears to be an ideal match between a man of forty and a girl well past the approved marrying age is abruptly called off when a detective reports that the prospective groom's mother, in the distant village from which he came, was held by local tradesmen to be mentally unbalanced.

42. Shiotsuki, *Kankonsōsai Nyūmon*, p. 27; cf. Minami, *Konrei-shiki*, pp. 94-5.

43. 'Obi ni mijikashi, tasuki ni nagashi' ('too short at the waist, too long in the arms').

44. Details of some historical class differences are given in, for example, Befu, *Anthropological Introduction*, pp. 121-34; R.P. Dore, *Land Reform in Japan* (Oxford University Press, Oxford, 1959), Part IV; Tadashi Fukutake, *Japanese Rural Society*, trans. R.P. Dore (Cornell University Press, London, 1972), pp. 138-45; Thomas C. Smith, 'The Japanese Village in the 17th century' in John W. Hall and Marius B. Jansen (eds.), *Studies in the Institutional History of Early Modern Japan* (Princeton University Press, Princeton, New Jersey, 1968).

45. This man may well have been guided by recent experience in making this decision, because one of his sons had gone, only just over a year previously, as a *yōshi* to another branch of the same family as the girl's suitor's.

46. Chie Nakane, *Kinship and Economic Organization in Rural Japan* (University of London, The Athlone Press, London, 1967), p. 158.

47. Gail Bernstein, 'Women in Rural Japan' in Lebra *et al.* (eds.), *Women in Changing Japan*, p. 45.

48. Another example of a Buddhist sect which appears to prefer endogamy is a group of Shin Amidists in the Noto Peninsula, described by Kiyomi Morioka in 'Préférence pour le mariage non-mixte parmi les Amidistes "Shin" du bouddhisme japonais', *Social Compass*, vol. 17 (1970), pp. 9-20.

49. Inouye, *Home Life in Tokyo*, p. 191.

50. Fujisaki, *Kankonsōsai Jiten*, pp. 27-30; Kawashima, *Kekkon*, p. 42; Yanagida, *Manners and Customs*, p. 174.

51. This has been described as a Kyūshū custom (Yanagida and Omachi, *Kon'in Shūzoku Goi*, p. 108).

52. 'It was not fated that they should marry,' 'the necessary karmic relation was not achieved.' *Go* is an honorific term, *en* the relation of karmic destiny, *ni narimasen deshita* is a polite phrase for 'was not achieved' or 'did not become so'. The idea that marriages are divinely determined is partly an indigenous one (see pp. 18-19), despite this use of the Buddhist concept of karma.

53. E.g. Fujisaki, *Kankonsōsai Jiten*, pp. 32-41; Dore, *City Life*, p. 167; William Erskine, *Japanese Festivals and Calendar Lore* (Kyo Bun Kwan, Tokyo, 1933), pp. 181-5; see appendix.

54. Norbeck, *Takashima*, p. 138, reported that in Takashima a geomancer may advise a name change in cases of illness or misfortune too.

55. Embree, *Suye Mura*, p. 219.

56. Ezra F. Vogel, 'The Go-Between in a Developing Society', *Human Organization*, vol. 20 (1961), p. 114.

57. This analysis of the roles of the go-between draws on the comments of several writers, among them Kawashima, *Kekkon*, pp. 37-52; Kamishima, *Nihonjin no Kekkonkan*, pp. 86-7; Omachi, 'Konrei' pp. 253-5; Yanagida, *Manners and Customs*, pp. 171-3; Nakayama, *Nihon Kon'in Shi*, p. 906; Itsue Takamure, *Nihon Kon'in Shi (A History of Marriage in Japan)* (Nihon Rekishi Shinsho, Tokyo, 1963), pp. 226-7.

58. Tamura, *The Japanese Bride*, p. 27, reports that some early *miai* actually took place on a bridge, which reflects the title and nature of this role.

59. Ema, *Kekkon no Rekishi*, p. 189.

60. Cf. Dore, *Shinohata*, p. 290; Kawashima, *Kekkon*, pp. 48-52; Yanagida, *Manners and Customs*, pp. 172-3; Seiichi Kitano, 'Dōzoku and Kindred in a Japanese Rural Society' in Reuben Hill and René König (eds.), *Families in East and West* (Mouton, Paris and The Hague, 1970), p. 258. Chamberlain likened this role to that of 'a sort of godfather to the young couple' (*Things Japanese* (John Murray, London, 1902), p. 308); cf. Dore, *City Life*, pp. 165, 169.

61. Ema, *Kekkon no Rekishi*, p. 23; Takamure, *Nihon Kon'in Shi*, p. 226;

Nakayama, *Nihon Kon'in Shi*, p. 906; Kamishima, *Nihonjin no Kekkonkan*, pp. 81-2.

62. Omachi, *'Konrei'*, p. 255. In Okinawa the bridegroom himself would go and propose to the bride's parents (Ichiro Kurata, 'Rural Marriage Customs in Japan', *Contemporary Japan* (Tokyo), vol. 10 (1941), p. 372.

63. Nakane, *Rural Japan*, p. 160. Other factors, such as similarity of economic activity, are also important as Cornell, 'Matsunagi', p. 212, noted.

64. Shiotsuki, *Kankonsōsai Nyūmon*, p. 88, suggests that the gift to the go-between be 20 or 30 per cent of the amount spent on the betrothal gifts, which will be described in the next chapter, but Fujisaki, *Kankonsōsai Jiten*, pp. 128-9, writing in 1957, said the usual figure was 10 per cent, sometimes 10 per cent from each family. He emphasised, however, that this is an expression of gratitude for the work done, rather than a fixed fee (ibid.).

65. Yanagida, *Manners and Customs*, p. 173.

66. Kawashima, *Kekkon*, p. 71.

67. Cf. Thomas P. Rohlen, *For Harmony and Strength* (University of California Press, Berkeley, Los Angeles and London, 1974), pp. 238-9.

68. There is no Japanese terminology exclusively for 'boyfriend' and 'girlfriend'. The English words are sometimes used, or words which also mean 'he' (*kare*) and 'she' (*kanojo*), used with a meaningful emphasis.

69. Befu, *Anthropological Introduction*, p. 51; cf. Dore, *City Life*, p. 170; Ezra F. Vogel, *Japan's New Middle Class* (University of California Press, Berkeley, Los Angeles and London, 1963), pp. 217-19.

70. Rohlen, *For Harmony and Strength*, p. 238.

71. Blood, *Love Match and Arranged Marriage*, pp. 89-91; Vogel, *Middle Class*, p. 176.

72. Brameld, *Japan*, p. 61.

73. Minami, *Konrei-shiki*, p. 16.

THE UNION: CEREMONIAL AND CELEBRATION

Once the matter of a match has been settled, a series of rites, exchanges and festivities follow in quite rapid succession to seal and announce the new status of the parties involved. The wedding is the climax, but there is usually a whole range of attendant ceremony and celebration, although registration of marriage is the only legal requirement (see p. 190). The whole process will form the subject-matter of this chapter. Customs vary quite considerably from one area to another and are constantly subject to the changing vagaries of fashion. Nowadays there is a good deal of Western influence, but many elements of today's more traditional celebrations have their origins in the Ise and Ogasawara schools of etiquette followed by the noble and warrior classes in pre-Meiji times.[1] The present practices often differ greatly from those on which they were modelled, however, some having quite changed their overt functions. In this chapter, the usual course of events from betrothal to co-residence will be described in chronological order, with practices as observed in the field in Kyūshū, but an effort will be made to indicate how representative or otherwise they are of national practices. Each element of the total process will also be considered to see how it has changed in recent years and how it varies from place to place, or even from household to household.[2] There is a wide range of choice about how a particular marriage ceremony will be celebrated, and the various options are presented in the section on 'Types of Wedding'. To avoid confusion, however, the chief elements common to all the different types are first considered, with some historical background, in the section on 'The Elements of the Marriage'. Finally, in the section on the cost and significance of weddings, a preliminary attempt is made to explain the enormous cost of wedding celebrations, already mentioned in the Introduction.

Betrothal

Kimeja *(Decide-Tea)* or Kugicha *(Nail-Tea)*

The first celebration associated with a marriage coincides with the announcement to relatives and neighbours of the engagement of the couple. Until this time, negotiations are carried out in the utmost secrecy, especially for the bride's family.[3] However, once a decision has been made and the proposal accepted, the boy's family immediately sends gifts to clinch the agreement, and the girl's family invites relatives to hear the news. In the Yame region these gifts consist of tea, known as *kimeja* (decide-tea) or *kugicha* (nail-tea), a bottle of *sake* and a large sea bream, which is shared with the visitors who come to celebrate. The significance of these gifts is to be found in their names: one bottle of *sake* is referred to as *isshō*, a homonym of an expression meaning 'one lifetime'; a sea bream is *tai*, referred to here as *ichidai* (one *tai*) which is a homonym of the expression for 'one generation'; thus the two become *isshō, ichidai*, to symbolise the shared lifetime to be initiated on this occasion. *Sake* and *tai* are used at most celebrations, the *tai* being particularly appropriate because it forms part of the word *omedetai* (congratulations). The words for the tea indicate that the decision has been made (*kimeja*) and that metaphorically a nail has been knocked in to secure it (*kugicha*) so that the agreement should not now be broken. The tea itself is usually purchased already packed by local professionals in a decorative box, adorned with representations of items used frequently to symbolise happiness and celebration, *shōchikubai* (pine, bamboo and plum),[4] a crane and a turtle. The crane is said, by informants, to live 1,000 years, and the turtle 10,000, so that together they symbolise longevity and long-lasting union.

The usual characters for writing *kugicha* may be replaced on the gift by characters which can have the same reading, but which have a meaning appropriate to the celebration, namely 'tea of long-lasting joy' (久 喜 茶). This practice of substituting loan characters (*ateji*) with the appropriate sound values, which can also be read semantically with a suitable meaning, is used frequently by the people who make decorations for the gifts given before a wedding. More examples will be given in the section below on 'The Trousseau', where the greater bulk of betrothal gifts are to be described.

In this region, these later gifts, which are taken only a few days before the wedding, are called *honja* (main-tea), and, together with the *kimeja*, form the betrothal gifts, also called *yuinō* (literally 'binding-settlement'[5]). Elsewhere all *yuinō* gifts are presented together at an earlier time to coincide with the public announcement following a favourable decision.[6] It seems that the practice of sending two sets of gifts, still found in Kyūshū, used to take place elsewhere under different names, but most areas now have only one engagement presentation.[7] The term *yuinō* is used widely in this context, but the terms for the first clinching gifts vary even within the central part of Kyūshū.[8]

The cost of the *kugicha* tea is not great, a mere fraction of the gifts which follow, but the sea bream may, according to fish merchants, cost over £40.

Decisions

The time between the *kugicha* and the wedding is not usually more than a few weeks, so the go-between may well try to settle dates for further celebrations on the occasion of the delivery of this first gift. Many people still like to choose a *dai'an*, the most auspicious of the days in the six-day cycle (see Appendix), for a wedding, although young people especially now scoff at this precaution. Some even choose the least auspicious day, when they will be certain to have no trouble with bookings at the hotels and halls where weddings are often held. More detailed calculations, based on Taoist ideology, are still sometimes made to determine an appropriate day, and, for this purpose, Kurotsuchi people may consult the same *ogamiyasan*, mentioned in Chapter 4, who advised about the compatibility of the couple. Wedding manuals recommend the consideration of more practical matters such as the avoidance of the days of the bride's menstruation period, and those of the summer, when the heat is too intense for dressing up.[9] When many of the guests are employed, Sunday is usually chosen, but in the country slack farming seasons are the best time for weddings. The autumn and spring are said everywhere to be the ideal seasons because the weather is then good. In Kurotsuchi these coincide with a period between the chrysanthemum and tea harvests, and a slack period after the chrysanthemum seedlings are planted. Most weddings did indeed take place at these times.

Further decisions must be made about the gifts to be exchanged, and about the type and venue of the wedding – the various options will be presented in the appropriate sections – and it is the business of the go-between to co-ordinate the ideas of the two families on all such matters. There is little contact between the two households until they are introduced at the wedding, except possibly for rather formal exchanges at the delivery of the betrothal gifts and the bride's trousseau. According to Norbeck, even people who previously knew each other would avoid contact at this time.[10] Nowadays the young couple may well continue to see each other, however, rather in the Western manner of dating and visiting each other's homes. Otherwise each house is plunged into the numerous preparations of various sorts: the bride's house with the trousseau, the groom's with the accommodation for the new couple, which not infrequently involves quite extensive house alterations.

Honja *(Main-Tea)*

The date of the wedding having been decided, another auspicious day can be chosen for the delivery to the bride's home of the main betrothal gifts from the groom's family. As the names suggest, these gifts are regarded as associated with the first clinching ones, but it is explained that discussion must precede a decision about the later gifts, since these are to help the bride with preparing her trousseau. Thus they may include kimonos and accessories, or there may be a large sum of money, although the bride's family is said invariably to spend a good deal more preparing their daughter than they receive in cash (see the section below on 'The Trousseau'). The sum given varies, of course, but a guide often mentioned for an employed groom is three months' salary.[11] The type of kimono given may well cost in the region of 500,000 *yen* (over £1,000 in 1979), and this is a figure mentioned frequently for the cash gift made by farming families. However, one presentation made by a Kurotsuchi family included no less than three kimonos with under-slips and jackets, and another family claimed to have received 1 million yen. There is also an impressive display of other gifts whose price may reach a similar sum again if an expensive engagement ring is included.

These gifts are delivered a few days before the wedding, when they are laid out on low wooden tables, which often spread around two sides of quite a large room. The arrangements and decorations are supplied by the same local manufacturers who make the *kugicha* tea, typically small family concerns which specialise in equipment for cere-monial, sometimes only for weddings. In this region, the first table is the place for the tea, green tea packed into brightly decorated cylin-drical boxes which are piled into two pyramids, a pink one and a red one, said to represent male and female respectively. This time many of the gifts are so divided, in contrast to the *kugicha*, where only one of each gift was made. Everyone points out that this tea is of poor quality because good tea can bear serving many times whereas poor tea will only give one good potful, which symbolises that the bride will only go once to be married, they explain. In Japanese the word *deru* (to go out/come out) is applied equally to tea being drawn from the leaves to emerge from a pot and to someone leaving home, so the metaphor is more appropriate than in English. One of the manufacturers further explained that tea is also a plant noted for its prolific qualities, four harvests being possible in a year, thus adding the symbolism of fertility to this gift. He added that tea plants in a row gradually grow into one long bush, which symbolises the unity of the members of the new family to be created as well as of the various 'bloods' being united in the match. He also said that, as the roots of the plant grow together under the ground,[12] the new couple should grow together in that part of their lives hidden from the world, as well as on the surface. After the wedding these cylindrical packets of tea are given to relatives and neighbours.

The next gift is purely decorative and symbolic. A little old man and woman stand in front of an arrangement of *shōchikubai* (pine, bamboo and plum, representing happiness, as found on the *kugicha*), again with models of a crane and turtle representing longevity. Informants referred to this old couple as Takasago, or *ojiisan* and *obāsan* (grandfather and grandmother), and explained that they symbolised long life since they had sworn to grow grey together until one was a hundred and the other 99.[13] Takasago is the name of a place in the old province of Harima, now Hyōgo prefecture, where, according to Redesdale, a legendary pine tree had two stems growing from a single set of roots, and the spirits of this 'pine of mutual old age' are represented by the old man and woman.[14] However, a decoration of this description was traditionally used at weddings with similar symbolism of longevity, happiness and conjugal fidelity.[15] Ema reports it to have represented an enchanted isle, named Hōrai, where a tree provided the fruit of eternal youth, and it is still known as the 'island-stand' (*shimadai*) but there is apparently also an alternative origin associated with specific sexual symbolism.[16] A local Shinto priest in Yame said that the ancient Shinto wedding was held before these models which represented Izanami and Izanagi, the mythical progenitors of the Japanese. The importance of this item in the betrothal gifts is suggested by the fact that one of the shops selling such gifts in Yame is named Takasago *ya* (Takasago shop).

Another table holds decorated dried cuttlefish (*surume*) and a large piece of a variety of seaweed called *konbu*.[17] This combination is used in Shinto ceremonies as part of a ritual feast, and, as is usual then, it is cut up and shared out, this time to relatives and other visitors after the wedding. These items have particularly appropriate loan characters to be written on the inventory which usually accompanies the gifts: those for *surume* (寿留女) mean 'long-life remain-female', and for *konbu* (子産婦) 'child-bearing-woman'.[18] Here too *tai* and *sake* accompany the gifts, but this time there are traditionally two of each. There must be a male and female fish, lying stomach to stomach to symbolise fertility. Again, this symbolism is used in other ceremonies. In particular, such fish should be offered to the deities at a Shinto ground purification ceremony before house-building to ensure the fertility of the household (see Chapter 6, p. 218). The Shinto symbolism is suggested specifically here because the *tai* are often decorated with a straw *shimenawa*, similar to that used to mark a shrine or other sacred object, which in season may include a sheaf of wheat or rice, again representing fertility. The *sake* may come in old-fashioned barrels, or in bottles, again usually some decoration distinguishing a male and female container.

Even if it is decided to make money rather than clothes the main part of the gift, an *obi* (the sash worn with kimono) is usually given. This symbolises the joining of the couple because it is used to *musubu* (tie up) something, in this case *en* (the fate of the two people), so that it is said to symbolise the *enmusubi*, the forging of a relationship between them. The *obi* is also very long, which again is said to symbol-ise a long-lasting marriage. Elsewhere, a sum of money 'for the *obi*' may be sent instead.[19]

On a separate table there are usually a few decorative paper packets, which may include the monetary part of the gift, appropriately wrapped. There will also be a *noshi*. This is properly a thin strip of dried abalone,[20] wrapped in a square of red and white paper folded into a long narrow hexagon, wider at the top than the bottom, and tied neatly round the middle. A representative of this is found on all envelopes and paper used exclusively for gifts for happy occasions, and informants explained that here it merely denotes the fact that this is a gift. Fish is prohibited to people in mourning, and scholars explain that this tiny fragment of fish is therefore indicative that on a happy occasion the sender is not contaminated by death or misfortune.[21] On this table there is often also a fan, or a pair of fans — a man's and a woman's — to symbolise that the marriage should open out and enlarge as the fan does when unfolded. In another packet a cord, again said to be symbolic of the joining of the couple, is included to represent white hair, written in the inventory *tomoshiraga*, literally 'companion-white-hair', but with the sense of 'growing old or grey together'. Here also will be found the list of contents, and even the heading *mokuroku* (inventory) may be written in loan characters: meaning 'luxuriant, long-lasting greenery' (茂 久 緑).

If a Western-style engagement ring is included, this is given a special table and background decoration as well as loan characters for *yubiwa* (finger-ring) which mean 'graceful, beautiful ring' (優 美 輪). The quality of the ring varies from an expensive diamond to a token birth-day stone of a much cheaper type.

The contents of *yuinō* gifts vary greatly from district to district, according to informants, and in no other recent ethnography is anything of the scale found here described. In the Tokugawa period, when *yuinō* gifts of this sort were established,[22] they were accompanied by presents for the future in-laws, all of which were limited according to the rank and means of the families concerned. They included various quantities of cloth of a particular quality, a fixed number of barrels of *sake* and another fixed number of condiments or fresh fish.[23] After Meiji, these gifts were simplified and money often sent for convenience.[24] In 1939, Embree reported of Suye Mura that only well-to-do families had *yuinō*, which seemed chiefly to be a garment to be worn by the bride at the wedding.[25] Since the war, a monetary gift for the purchase of clothes seems to have become common, sometimes supplemented by two further sums to replace the sake and fish, said by one writer to be for the bride's farewell feast.[26] Nowadays department stores sell abbreviated sets of the traditionally symbolic gifts such as *noshi*, *surume*, *konbu* and fans. These may be sent with an inventory in loan characters together with a sum of money.[27] Particularly unusual about the Yame district gifts seem to be the tea,[28] the Takasago *shimadai*, and the way huge pieces of *surume*, *konbu* and *tai* are each given their own display tables. These last have a function in this area, however, since they are afterwards shared with visitors who may thus take a small part in the festivities.

In cities, some people have dispensed with *yuinō* gifts and money altogether, perhaps holding a Western-style engagement party and exchanging rings. Young people sometimes claim to do this for ideological reasons, objecting to the possible interpretation of *yuinō* gifts as payment for the bride. This is an idea which was suggested by a Japanese scholar in the context of a rather speculative evolutionary theory,[29] but I follow Yanagida and Ariga in rejecting this interpretation.[30] Yanagida derives the word from *yuinomono*, a word for food and drink brought by the groom to share with his new in-laws in order to establish this bond, which is a plausible explanation of an earlier meaning of the gifts, to be discussed again in the section on 'The In-laws' Sharing of Cups'. The more commonly accepted etymology of *yuinō* is *ii-ire* (言 い 入 れ), which refers to an oral agreement, a proposal accepted.[31] Certainly the gifts have often been described as proof of the promise to marry,[32] and in many areas a return gift was traditionally made.[33] This is not the case in Yame, where the gifts are said to help the bride prepare her trousseau. However, nowhere in Japan do the gifts represent a bridewealth in the sense that the bride's brothers may take advantage of them to obtain their own brides, and in Yame, they fall rather into Goody's category of 'indirect dowry', since the bulk of them goes to the bride herself.[34]

The association of the *yuinō* gifts with the bride's trousseau was further emphasised in the past when both loads used to be packed up and suspended from long poles, carried by members of each family, who would sing appropriate songs as they went. Sometimes the two sets of bearers would arrange to meet at an inn or other fixed spot between the houses where they would exchange loads and perhaps enjoy a drink together.[35] Alternatively, the *yuinō* was taken to the bride's home on the morning of the wedding, where a reception (*mukoiri*) would be held to receive the groom into the family, after which the groom's party would return with the bride and her trousseau for the actual marriage at the groom's house that evening. Nowadays the goods are taken by cars and trucks. The *yuinō* is delivered a day or two before the trousseau is taken, which gives the bride's acquaintances a chance to see both at her home (see the section on 'The Farewell Party' below). According to the manuals, it seems to be standard procedure for these deliveries to be made by the go-between,[36] but in Kurotsuchi it is common for the parents and perhaps another senior male relative to make a formal visit to present the gifts and share a meal with the bride's family, who make a similar return visit with the trousseau. Such a visit will be described in 'The Trousseau'. In 1979, one family held an old-fashioned *mukoiri* for the groom and all his close relatives – parents, grandparents, siblings and *honke* uncle – on the occasion of the delivery of the *yuinō*. There was a measure of uncertainty about the procedure, but the bride served her husband-to-be with cold *sake* in the ceremonial red lacquer cups, then a similar cup was passed to each of the relatives and finally to the go-between. Some *utai* were sung, a feast was served and the guests took away gifts.

In the case of a family receiving a *yōshi* as husband for their daughter, the roles are reversed and *yuinō* gifts sent to the groom's house. There is apparently little difference in the items included, except that an expensive Western suit may be preferred to Japanese attire.

Separation

Hanamuke *(Parting Gifts)*

In the days before a marriage is to take place, a number of presents of money are received by the two families concerned. These are called *hanamuke* (parting gifts), although they are given to the families of boys who are receiving a bride as well as to those of the girls who are leaving home. They are given by relatives and neighbours, the amount increasing with closeness, and in Kurotsuchi, every household in the village makes a contribution at this time, as they do at house-building and when someone dies. This gift is distinct from that taken to the wedding by guests, again often money, but then called *oiwai* (happy occasion).[37] The bride's or groom's mother usually has a store of savoury snacks or some other small token gift to make in return when the *hanamuke* are brought. Many gifts to the household are placed in the *butsudan*, but it was interesting to note that in at least two households the *hanamuke* had been laid under the *kamidana*, as if this were more suitable for a celebration, although one family, when asked directly, denied they had thought of this.

Wakare *(Farewell Party)*

For a girl who will be leaving home, and indeed for a *yōshi*, a *wakare* or farewell party is usually held for age-mates, relatives and perhaps neighbours too. This is arranged where possible after the *yuinō* has been received and before the furniture and other effects are sent so that the guests may see the display. A meal may well be served and some *utai* (extracts from Nō plays) are usually sung at the beginning, after which guests relax and drink *sake*. One such occasion I witnessed in Kurotsuchi involved two separate parties on the same day, one at 2 p.m., and the other at 6 p.m. The earlier one was for women of the *tonari kinjo*, age- and workmates of the bride's mother, and female relatives; the second for male relatives and age-mates of both sexes of the bride.

The first guests gathered outside and came in together at 2 p.m., presenting first their gifts of money and then arranging themselves down from the top of the room in age order (see Plan 2). Helping in the kitchen were three sisters of the bride's father, her mother's elder brother's wife, the wife of the household's *bunke* in Kurotsuchi, and the bride's two sisters. These last brought tea to each guest, once they were seated, then the bride and her parents took their places at the bottom of the room for a formal greeting. This, which was made by the father, followed a fairly standard pattern of thanking the guests for giving up their busy time, apologising for there being nothing to offer, and asking them to take their time over what little entertainment there was.[38] A few low bows, by hosts and guests alike, completed the greeting and everyone was served with sake. Some confusion followed as guests vied modestly not to sing the *utai*, but eventually three were performed. These songs are extracts from Nō plays which

Plan 2: Seating at the Afternoon Session of a *Wakare* for a Bride

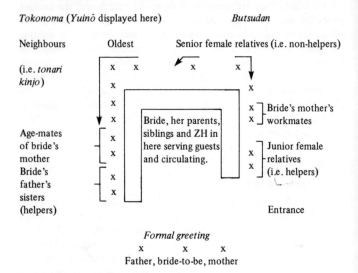

Tokonoma (Yuinō displayed here)   *Butsudan*

Neighbours   Oldest   Senior female relatives (i.e. non-helpers)

(i.e. *tonari
kinjo*)

Bride, her parents,
siblings and ZH in
here serving guests
and circulating.

Bride's mother's
workmates

Age-mates
of bride's
mother

Junior female
relatives
(i.e. helpers)

Bride's
father's
sisters
(helpers)

Entrance

Formal greeting
x   x   x
Father, bride-to-be, mother

Bride's furniture displayed here

are used for any appropriate occasion, although in this part of the country they are usually reserved for happy ones. Commonly three are sung, and the singer of each receives a ceremonial cup of *sake* from the nest of three lacquer ones before he starts and after he finishes, the same cup being taken to a different member of the celebrating family before the song, to be drunk after it. If various categories of guests are present, sometimes an effort is made for each to be represented with singers. On this occasion the *sake* was presented to the bride's father, the bride and her mother, in that order.

After this, everyone was entreated to relax their formal posture, and the feast already laid out on the tables was begun. The helpers came in, the closest relatives moving round inside the tables, serving *sake* and greeting personally each of the guests. Some less formal singing followed. At about 4 p.m. rice and soup was served, picnic boxes were distributed so that guests could pack up and take home their remaining food, and everyone left together. Each guest had also found gifts under the table. These often include fish paste or a few cakes of some sort, which may be shared out with the individual guest's household, and perhaps a more permanent souvenir of the occasion, such as plates or other household goods.

In the evening, most of the guests came much later than the time stated,[39] arriving in two groups. The first consisted of female age-mates of the bride, who greeted her formally, made a few polite inquiries into her new circumstances, and asked to see the *yuinō* and furniture. The former was soon shown, and though the bride was somewhat reluctant, the drawers and cupboards of the latter were all opened so that her friends could examine the clothes inside. The male guests arrived presently and took their seats, in age order round the top and *tokonoma* side of the table, the girls sitting opposite, again in age order. The same formal greeting and *utai* as before were performed. This time the drinking and feasting went on so much longer that the bride was asleep upstairs long before anyone else showed signs of leaving. Guests relaxed a good deal more than the women had in the afternoon, moving much more freely around the room, one or two even falling into a drunken sleep in odd corners.

Other families hold one party for all the guests at a *wakare*. One girl's family hired a room in a local restaurant to accommodate everyone better, although she took her guests home to see the *yuinō* and furniture before they went away. For this reason, the occasion is sometimes referred to as the *ochami* (tea-viewing), where tea is the *yuinō*, as already explained. A further *wakare* is usually held at the bride's home on the morning of the wedding for the final farewell to close relatives. Only a few of the bride's associates are invited to the wedding itself, but, by taking part in these farewell feasts, most are entertained at some time.

The Trousseau

The furniture and other items taken by a bride to her new home, referred to as *chōdohin* (utensils, furniture and household implements), may well cost several thousand pounds. As they are regarded as her part of the inheritance of the household, they may be compared to a dowry,[40] but they are here regarded as a trousseau because they are mostly for the personal use of the bride. The actual items taken will of course vary with economic circumstances, but the bride must take clothes, and she usually has chests and cupboards in which to store them. There is, apparently, always a dressing-table, with a long mirror, which arrives adorned with a red silk cover decorated with a peacock and pine motif and a crest of the Imperial paulownia tree, although I was unable to ascertain the significance of this. The mirror is said to be the woman's soul or spirit (*tamashii*), for this reason an essential part of the equipment.[41] Bedding is often also included, as is kitchen and electrical equipment, such as a washing-machine and a fridge, possibly even a new colour television. If the girl is to do farm work she may take along a bicycle to provide rapid access to the fields, and one *yōshi* took a new car with him, as well as a desk for paper-work. Sometimes *yōshi* are allotted one or two fields to retain when they marry, but this depends on the proximity or otherwise of the two villages.

The new couple are usually given a room of their own in the family house, a major alteration for this purpose being quite in order if necessary. Thus most of the new furniture can be accommodated there. It is delivered a day or two before the wedding if the couple will live with their family, but if they are setting up their own home they may wait until returning from their honeymoon so that they need not leave it unattended. Two descriptions of deliveries of this type follow, since one was more formal than the other, and these may be compared to the type of gathering which would take place in reverse on delivery of the *yuinō*.

The first example was the marriage described in the previous chapter as 'between *ren'ai* and *miai*'. Despite the previous acquaintance of the bride and groom, the two families met formally at a *miai* and held receptions for each other for the arrival of the *yuinō* gifts and the bride's furniture. The latter arrived in a fleet of four trucks 20 minutes before 10 a.m., the agreed time for the occasion, and a number of male relatives of both sides began the task of unloading. In a car which accompanied the convoy came the go-between's wife and the bride's mother, dressed in elegant kimono, who nevertheless huddled outside in the yard until they were formally invited to enter the house. They were then seated in a side room where, except for a brief exchange of bows, they were ignored until the time came for the formal greeting after the furniture had all been unpacked. Even the helpers who were not to stay were served tea before the procedure began. The main room had been thoroughly cleaned, and a special scroll for celebration hung in the *tokonoma*, where an arrangement of fresh flowers had been placed. In front of this were six cushions which were at last offered to the bride's father, in pride of place, his wife on his right, two male relatives on his left, and the go-between and his wife at either end (see Plan 3). The family then lined up at the entrance to the *zashiki*, where the father greeted the guests and welcomed them to his home. The

Plan 3: Formal Greeting on the Arrival of the Bride's Furniture

	Butsudan		*Tokonoma*

Bride's mother
x

Bride's father
x

Honke uncle
x

x
Go-between's
wife

Bride's mother's
x male relative

x Go-between

Zashiki
Gozen

x   Father

x   Groom

Groom's family

x   Mother

x   x   Sisters

A meal was served to the guests on trays.

Plan 4: Seating for the Meal at Another Such Occasion

> (Greetings had been made between house heads and go-between before these seats were taken.)

Butsudan   *Tokonoma*

Bride's father

Go-between's
husband

Table

Bride's brother

Groom's father
(house head)

Bride

go-between then presented the furniture with a formulaic expression of hope that they would keep it for a long time.[42] The father thanked them, then introduced his two daughters. Their husbands had helped to carry in the furniture, but their formal introduction was apparently to await the wedding itself. The guests introduced their two male relatives, the first the head of the household's *honke*, the second a male maternal relative. The bride herself was not present at all on this occasion and the groom came outside after the formal greeting and left his parents to entertain the guests. The two sisters brought tea and trays of food for each of the guests, but, before they began to eat, *sake* was served in the top cup of the ceremonial nest of three, and each member of the group took a drink to participate in the celebration.

The second example was also a farming family, but this time the bride came herself, dressed in nothing more formal than a pair of jeans. She had visited the house already on several occasions, as the groom had hers, but, for her father and brother, who accompanied her, it was a first visit. The go-between, in this case the groom's father's sister, and her husband had arrived a little earlier. The bride and her brother unloaded her belongings while their father was greeted formally by the groom's father, the go-between's husband and later by the groom's grandmother and mother. After this, the older women, including the go-between, remained in the kitchen while the bride and her brother took their places at the table with their father, the go-between's husband, who plays the formal role even if his wife has done the matchmaking, and the house head (see Plan 4). The groom had disappeared before the arrival of the guests and no one seemed to know where he was. The bride had been a little unsure about whether she should sit at the table, and she had gone into the kitchen to ask the go-between herself what she should do. The food for this occasion was delivered by a restaurant, but the group again shared a ceremonial cup of *sake* before the meal was begun.

It can be seen then that the arrangements for the delivery of furniture, as is the case for the *yuinō*, are fairly flexible, the details to be settled by the go-between in advance. The contents of the trousseau are not peculiar to this region. Many writers have described, regarding various classes and regions, how brides take clothes, bedding, furniture, kitchen and sewing equipment.[43] The quality and quantity of goods will depend on the household's financial status; most families make great efforts to see their daughters well equipped, saving for the occasion from the time they are small. According to Yanagida, marriages within villages did not involve so much, but, as they were made across larger distances, the trousseau became bigger and bigger.[44] The goods were on display as they were carried from one village to another, providing visible evidence of the status of the families, which across long distance could perhaps not be known by repute. Still today, the goods are displayed both at the bride's home before they are taken and often at the groom's home during the course of the wedding. Together with the *yuinō* they indicate to the world how well matched are the two households to be united. During the Tokugawa period the bride's trousseau was one of the things which was strictly limited by law,[45] and in recent times unnecessary expense has been discouraged on things the bride does not need.[46] Yet couples who are setting up home in the smallest apartments frequently find themselves compressed even further by the bride's expensive furniture, a luxury anyway in Japanese homes.[47] As Dore has commented, the bride's trousseau is a 'form of conspicuous consumption which has a very definite social significance'.[48]

Preparations

Early on the morning of the wedding, preparations will begin at the bride's home which are usually so complicated that a dresser is engaged for the day to help the bride with her various changes and hairstyles.[49] Some girls decide to do away with all tradition and choose to marry in a white Western wedding-dress, but the only such girl in Kurotsuchi in 1975 was to change into kimono during the course of the day. Many brides change several times, and, by 1979, most included a Western dress after the kimono. The stated aim of this is said to be to show themselves off in different lights. The custom is known as *ironaoshi* (colour-change), which, according to Japanese scholars, is an abbreviation of an older practice where the bride would wear white for the first and second day of her wedding and change into a coloured garment on the third.[50] At this time the bride used also to shave her eyebrows, blacken her teeth and change her hairstyle to indicate her new status,[51] although this teeth-blackening may also have been done at puberty or even earlier, at betrothal, or left until the first pregnancy.[52] Even now, a girl dresses differently to indicate her married status.

The main wedding garment is the *uchikake* (outer dress), a heavy gown with a stiff roll at the hem which must be carried when the bride moves. Under this the bride should wear a pure white kimono, the significance of which is now sometimes interpreted as representing purity, as does the Western wedding-dress. A more traditional interpretation refers to purity in a slightly different manner, likening the bride's white dress to the white in which babies and the dead are dressed, symbolic of a *tabula rasa* which starts a new period. Similarly pilgrims sometimes dress in white symbolically to wipe out past sins and to express an intention to lead a better life henceforth. The bride should forget entirely her past life and be prepared to colour herself in whatever way her husband desires.[53] This is consistent with the symbolism of a part of her head-dress which is called the *tsunokakushi*[54] (horn-hider) where horns refer to the bad traits of a woman's character which must be hidden to signify future obedience to her husband. Many people note that it is the bride who must change on marriage and not the husband, which is especially true when she moves into the man's family home, although, even where a new home is set up, it will usually be the bride who will, if necessary, change her religion and her ideas to match those of her husband.

One informant said that the bride wears white like a corpse and a baby because she is to die to her own *ie* and be born again to that of her new husband.[55] This is an interpretation which has been commonly reported, with the added implication that she will never return.[56] Other rites, also used for the departure of the dead, such as the breaking of the bride's tea-cup and the lighting of a bonfire to cut off her return path, support this idea.[57] Erskine also reported that brides fold their kimono right over left like a corpse to leave home, but change to left over right at the husband's house indicating that they are entering a new life.[58]

The outer wedding-gown and head-dress are usually hired for the occasion, and may be of various colours; shades of red and orange often predominate, since these are suited to a joyful occasion.[59] The head-dress may include tortoiseshell (usually mock or hired ones), said to symbolise a long marriage, and the bride usually carries a fan tucked into her kimono. The bridegroom sometimes wears a Western suit, but it seems to be quite fashionable for him also to dress in Japanese garments for the marriage and to change into a suit when the bride changes. The formal attire of the man, decided by government proclamation in 1877,[60] includes a black coat with house crests printed on it. Married women guests may also wear black with house crests.[61]

The Departure

Once the bride is dressed, she sits down for a farewell breakfast with her relatives, which may include an exchange of *sake* and the singing of *utai* again. Decorative drapes are often hung over the front door of the bride's home and visitors may call to wish her well. Some aunts will probably be there all day to take care of the empty house and receive well-wishers, for the uncles are more likely than they are to be invited to attend the marriage itself, even if a parent's sister must stay behind in deference to her husband (see p. 176). When it is time to leave, the bride kneels before the *butsudan* to say farewell and thank you to her ancestors for protection and blessings, for now she will worship those of her husband and only visit her own. Some of the neighbours may gather discreetly outside to see the bride in her finery as the go-between's wife leads her out to the car.[62]

The Wedding

There is a good deal of flexibility in the ways in which weddings can be performed, and these seem to follow certain fashions. In the past it was usual to hold the marriage and celebrations in the home, and, according to informants, many weddings continued for three days. Today, many people hold one grand reception in accommodation designed specially for weddings (*kekkon shikijō*), which also provide hire of clothing, photographic facilities, gifts for guests and several other services, as well as the rooms for the wedding and reception. These places have become thriving business concerns, although each individual one seems to have a limited period of success. A less plush atmosphere is available in some traditional Japanese restaurants (*ryōtei*) which have facilities for wedding receptions.

It has also become popular recently to hold a religious service for the actual marriage ceremony, followed by a reception, which probably represents an indirect result of Western influence, since this procedure coincides more closely with Western arrangements than that of more traditional weddings.[63] Most popular is the Shinto wedding (*shinzen* – 'before the *kami*'), which has flourished since the Meiji period,[64] and many Shinto shrines have invested in facilities for the reception so that they can provide the complete venue for a wedding. Members of some Buddhist sects prefer to marry in a Buddhist temple (*butsuzen* – 'before the Buddhist image'), and recently some Japanese have asked to be married in Christian churches, merely to make their weddings completely Western.[65] No doubt also in a Western vein, some modern couples in cities spurn the religious aspect altogether, perhaps referring to their weddings as *hitomae* – 'before people'. The manual by Fuji-saki suggests a procedure for a wedding based entirely on the new

Constitution, and also gives details of a 'tea party' wedding as well as of marriages held in the air, on top of a skyscraper, and in an Olympic stadium.[66] There are also still people who prefer to hold the whole procedure in as traditional a manner as possible, in the home. Examples of Shinto, Buddhist and home marriages, as well as their attendant receptions, will be given in the section on 'Types of Wedding', but for the sake of clarity certain common elements will be discussed first.

The Elements of the Marriage

The crux of the marriage is almost always a pledge through a sharing of cups between the bride and the groom. This rite is occasionally held in advance of other celebrations in a brief ceremony called a *karishūgen* (interim marriage ceremony). Since this isolates the essence of the nuptial rites, it will be described first. The next section will be concerned with another important part of any ceremony, the exchange of cups between the principals and their new in-laws, and it will be seen that this element has some interesting history attached to it. The marriage ceremony is followed by an announcement feast (*hirōen*), which will be considered on its own, although further celebrations are left to be discussed in the section on *Yorokobi*.

Karishūgen *(Interim Ceremony)*. A brief marriage ceremony may be held in advance of the main celebrations on the advice of a diviner, or perhaps because mourning restrictions necessitate the postponement of a happy occasion. One such marriage was arranged because the combination of the ages of the bride and groom were said to be incompatible with the date chosen for the main function. Another involved a bride who arrived from Shikoku to marry her cousin just as news came through that his brother had been killed. Also on the advice of a diviner, a *karishūgen* took place during my stay in Kurotsuchi on the same day that the *yuinō* was delivered. The groom and his parents went first to the bride's house, then returned for the ceremony to their own.

This ceremony was held before the *butsudan* to which the bride and her family paid their respects as soon as they entered the house. They were wearing kimonos, the older women's embroidered with the family crest, but the bride did not wear a bridal overgown, nor did she wear the wedding head-dress. She was accompanied by her mother, grandfather, elder brother and younger sister. The bride and groom sat in the centre,[67] with the go-between and his wife on either side, and their respective relatives seated as shown in Plan 5. The bride's sister,

Plan 5: Seating of Participants at a *Karishūgen*

Butsudan					*Tokonoma*
Go-between	x	Groom x	Bride x	x	Go-between's wife
Groom's father	x		sake served here	x	Bride's gF in place of her father
Groom's mother	x			x	Bride's mother
Groom's grandmother	x			x	Bride's elder brother

Role of
shikaisha

Role of *kageutai*
singer

another unmarried girl and a kindergarten pupil related to the groom
were all to help with the ceremony. Once everyone was seated, the two
families made a formal bow to each other, then the hosts thanked their
guests for the hospitality received earlier when they delivered the *yuinō*.
The go-between moved down below the groom's grandmother to play
the role of master of ceremonies (*shikaisha*), where he opened the proceedings by announcing the purpose of the gathering. The small girl
then carried in a little table on which a *noshi* was placed, laid this
before the couple and bowed. This is known as the *noshi no gi* (*noshi*
rite). After this, the two older girls carried in a nest of *sake* cups and
two ornate *sake* pourers. One girl presented the cups to the bride while
the other filled the top one with *sake*. At this point the bride's elder
brother moved out of the room behind the sliding door to sing a short
'hidden *utai*' (*kageutai*). When he had finished, the bride drank the
sake and the cups were moved to the bridegroom. Again *sake* was
served, and again it was drunk after another song was sung. Finally,
the cups were moved back to the bride, where the process was repeated once more. Before and after each song the girls and the bride
or groom bowed to each other. This completed the ceremony and

the go-between said a few words of thanks.

This rite is called the *san-san-ku-do* (literally, three-three-nine-times). It is performed in various ways, and there are a number of explanations of why it is so named. There are three cups in the nest, diminishing in size as they go up. Although in this case only the top one was used, many marriage rites make use of all three. Some informants explained that the *sake* was poured in three movements; sometimes the participants take three separate sips to finish the drink so that the combined sips of both partners total nine, three drinks of three sips each. However, several informants claimed that the number of sips has nothing to do with the 3-3-9 count, adding that the above version is an abbreviation of the correct process which should be as follows: the bride, then the groom, then the bride drink out of the first cup, the groom, then the bride, then the groom out of the second, and the bride, groom, bride out of the third (see Diagram 2). Thus, they have, together, drunk nine times.[68] The original rite of *san-san-ku-do*, also known by other names,[69] is said to have been developed by the Ogasawara school of etiquette for *samurai* weddings and only later introduced more widely.[70] The older form included the serving of soups and condiments between drinks from each cup, a sharing of the pouring by the bride and groom to symbolise the union being contracted, and the participation of a lady-in-waiting (*machijōrō*) so that three separate people drank from each cup.[71]

Diagram 2: Representation of a Complete *San-San-Ku-Do*

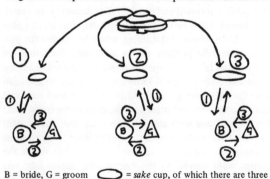

B = bride, G = groom   ⬭ = *sake* cup, of which there are three

However it is performed, the *san-san-ku-do* is the crux of the marriage rite, the one essential element.[72] The use of *sake* at marriage and other ceremonies is widespread and ancient.[73] The sharing of cups has been interpreted as the symbolic agreement of the bride and groom to share both joy and sorrow throughout life.[74] The reason why the number three is involved is more complex. Bownas suggests that the *san-san* may be used because it is homonymous with the words meaning 'birth after birth', thus acting as a fertility charm.[75] There were in the past three people taking part, but the groom was also to stay three nights during the Heian period,[76] a fire was sometimes kept burning for three days,[77] and three trays of food were served.[78] Ema suggests that three was symbolic of man, woman and child, or of heaven, earth and man,[79] and an informant likened it to the three Imperial Regalia of mirror, sword and jewel. Three is anyway an extremely auspicious number.

I was unable to obtain a satisfactory explanation of why a *noshi* was used in this context, although Embree regards it as representing the gift of the bride to the groom's father,[80] and Ema as representative of the older practice of serving fish at this time.[81] Here it was presented by a child, but this is not always the case, as will be seen. The *kageutai*, which may be sung by anyone with a reasonable voice, may also be omitted. The two persons who serve the *sake* are usually female, but in one Shinto and a Sōka Gakkai ceremony, a male priest performed the task. According to the literature, it seems to have been quite common for two children to do it, either a boy and a girl, or two girls.[82] The *sake* pourers are usually distinguished as male and female by having paper butterflies of each sex attached to them, and if the servers are a boy and a girl, each takes the server of their own sex, the *sake* is mixed, and then the boy serves the bride and the girl the groom.[83] The mixing of the *sake* has been reported as symbolising the mixing of blood,[84] but it has also been associated with more explicit sexual symbolism in that, while pouring, the butterflies were sometimes removed and placed male, face-down, on top of the female, face-up.[85] The use of butterflies is said to be because of the good conjugal relation and amatory constancy of this insect.[86]

It is appropriate to have isolated this section of the marriage ceremony, for in the past the sharing of cups used to be held in private or behind a screen, with only the go-betweens and serving-girls or children present.[87] Nowadays close relatives witness the rite. In Kurotsuchi these are called the *honkyaku* (main guests),[88] which include the parents and grandparents of the bride and groom, their siblings with their spouses, and siblings of the parents. They thus represent the present household and one generation of previous households of each of the bride and groom. However, the heads of the present households of the parents' siblings are usually invited, so that these may not be blood kin. As was seen in this example, the *karishūgen* involved only the members of the present households of the two participants.

In-laws' Sharing of Cups. Nowadays these *honkyaku* also partake in a ceremonial drinking of *sake* together soon after the *san-san-ku-do*. This may be done in various ways which will be described shortly as part of different types of wedding. It is usually followed by the formal introduction of each set of relatives by name and relationship to the bride and groom.

Before this, there is often also a rite during which the bride and groom each shares cups with their new parents-in-law. This is really a condensed version of the older sharing of cups which would take place previously at the *mukoiri* between the groom and his new in-laws, and at the *yomeiri* between the bride and hers.[89] Yanagida reports that only the bride used to share cups with her mother-in-law, if anyone, before the *san-san-ku-do* spread to rural areas.[90] The exchange of gifts, such as *yuinō*, and the sharing of food, drink and possibly fire seem to represent older ways of establishing marriage.[91] The custom of 'third-night-rice-cakes' (*mikka no mochi*) of the Heian period, when the bride's family would share *mochi* (rice-cakes) with the groom after he had stayed with his bride until the third night, is well documented.[92] It is said to have been a practice born among farmers in about the Nara period and adopted by the Heian nobility. Previously the groom would have visited his sweeatheart secretly so that the sharing of *mochi* is associated with a 'discovery' (*roken*) of this practice and a binding of the union by making the boy share food with and thus join the family.[93] In the Heian period, at least in the noble classes, the parents were apparently more instrumental in settling the union, arranging to receive the groom with a 'ceremony of the new pillow' (*niimakura no gishiki*), and removing his shoes so that he could not change his mind before the third-night sharing of food.[94]

This practice coincided with a period of uxorilocal residence in marriage, but with the rise of the *samurai* classes in the Kamakura and Muromachi periods, residence became virilocal and the more important ceremonies began to take place at the groom's home.[95] Nevertheless, a *mukoiri* frequently took place, sometimes before, sometimes after the *yomeiri*, although the significance of this practice varied regionally.[96] In some areas the *mukoiri* preceded a period of uxorilocal residence or work before the *yomeiri*, but in living memory in the Yame

region the two ceremonies usually took place on the same day. Typically the go-between would accompany the groom, his parents and
siblings to the bride's house on the morning of the wedding-day, when
other relatives and friends may also have carried the *yuinō* over. A
reception was then held at the bride's home to which her relatives and
probably some neighbours would be invited. This would be at about
noon. In the afternoon, the groom's family would return with the bride
and her parents and siblings, perhaps bringing the furniture, and the
marriage (*yomeiri*) would take place in the groom's home in the late
evening.

Since Meiji, the Western idea of marriage being the union of two
individuals, rather than the reception of each into the other's household, is said to have been symbolised in a new type of joint reception
called *deaishūgi* or *yoriaikon*.[97] This has only been practised in Kurotsuchi since the war, when celebrations were apparently much abbreviated, and never returned to what they were before. In 1975, the cost
of the reception was said sometimes to be divided between the two
families in a proportion agreed with the help of the go-between, but,
by 1979, the receiving family, or that of the husband where the couple
was to live alone, seemed to be taking total responsibility for this.

The Photograph. Nowadays a professional photographer is usually hired
to record the wedding in a large glossy hard-backed impression which
may be brought out over the years to come. In wedding halls there is
often a resident or contracted photographer who is kept busy all day
on auspicious dates. He will probably arrange the bride and groom in
a special studio, or, if the wedding is at home, he will take them in
front of the *tokonoma* and perhaps in the garden. There is frequently
also a group photograph with the front row as follows: (from left)
groom's mother, groom's father, go-between, groom, bride, go-between's
wife, bride's father, bride's mother. The remaining relatives arrange
themselves in rows behind, as far as possible on the side of their own
kin.

The Hirōen *(Announcement Feast).* Once the marriage ceremony has
taken place, a feast is usually served, which, according to its name, is
'to announce' the event.[98] If a Shinto or Buddhist ceremony has been
performed the participants move to a hall or restaurant where they may
be joined by other guests. For a home or restaurant wedding the marriage ceremony runs into the *hirōen*, although there is a distinction
made between the two with a transfer from cold to warm *sake* and

properly from earthenware to lacquer cups.[99] However, the order of proceedings at the feast varies according to the type of wedding, so this will be considered separately for each type. It was mentioned that some weddings take place in large halls which can accommodate all the guests to be entertained, but it is more usual in Kurotsuchi for several *yorokobi*[100] (celebrations) to be held in the groom's home after the ceremony and *hirōen* are over. These will be described separately under the heading 'Incorporation'.

Types of Wedding

Shinto (shinzen). Since the Shinto marriage seemed to be the most popular during field-work in Yame, this will be described first in detail. I witnessed five such ceremonies, four in three different marriage halls and one in a shrine, and each followed a fairly standard order, varying only in minor details.[101] The following is a synthesis.

The families of the bride and groom gather in separate rooms where they may be served a cup of tea while they are waiting. Some wedding halls have numerous marriages to accommodate on the same day and as one party leaves the Shinto altar room another is waiting outside to enter. When all is ready, the two families file in. At one end of the room is a Shinto altar where offerings are made of all that is necessary to sustain life: rice, water, salt, fruit, vegetables, *sake* and some *surume* and *konbu*. Two *tai* may also have been offered, belly to belly to symbolise fertility or the 'flourishing of descendants' (*shison han'i*).[102] Wedding-rings are also placed here, as are the nest of three *sake* cups and two pourers, distinguished by having one pointed tab for the male and two for the female, as well as by the colours red and pink, even if there are no paper butterflies attached.

To the right of the altar stands the Shinto priest (*kannushi*), and to the left the *miko*, who are maiden helpers dressed in red and white. Sometimes there is a tape-recording to provide background music at appropriate moments, but on one occasion there was a group of Shinto flute players seated behind the *miko* girls. The service may also include dancers.[103]

The bride and groom sit in the centre with the groom on the right of the bride, the go-between behind them, and the relatives of each in order of proximity and age down each side (see Plans 6 and 7). There is usually a table in front of each person with a *sake* cup and a small packet containing tiny pieces of *surume* and *konbu* which have first been offered to the deity. Thus all may participate in the ceremony. This is the case in other Shinto rites, a 'sacred, symbolic feast' being

Plan 6: Arrangements and Seating for a Shinto Wedding

Altar

(Musicians)	Offerings: rice, water, *sake*, salt, fruit, vegetables.		*Kannushi* (priest)
Miko girls (helpers)	*Surume* *Sake* cups, pourers, rings	*Konbu*	

Bride's relatives:			Groom's relatives:
Father	Bride	Groom	Father
Mother	Wife	Husband	Mother
	(Go-betweens)		
Siblings			Siblings
Aunts and uncles			Aunts and uncles

Plan 7: Alternative Arrangement of Principals (in Shrine)

Before Marriage		After Marriage	
Altar		Altar	
Bride	Groom		Groom
Wife	Husband		Bride
(Go-betweens)		Bride's	Groom's
Bride's	Groom's	father	father
father	father	and	and
and	and	mother	mother
mother	mother	Go-betweens	

During the course of the ceremony, the bride moves to the groom's family's side and the go-betweens move in between the two families. In the case of a *yōshi* marriage, the groom moves to the bride's side.

one of the four main parts of Shinto worship.[104] The other parts are the offerings, already described, purification (*harai*) and prayer (*norito*). The marriage ceremony shares these with all others.

The priests first greets the assembled company, offers his congratulations, then announces that the ceremony will begin. It starts with the purification rite. During this the priest chants then shakes his paper-decorated staff over the altar, the helpers, the bride and groom, and all present. This is followed by the *norito* prayer which is chanted from a scroll by the priest to summon the appropriate deities, in particular that of Izumo shrine, to pay attention to the couple named. The *san-san-ku-do* ceremony is then announced by the priest, as the *seiin no gi* (rite of the oath drink), for which the *sake* is brought by the *miko* girls to the bride and groom, the go-betweens sometimes moving to either side of the couple to help them if necessary. They made a point in the Shinto ceremonies of pouring the *sake* in three movements, the smallest cup filled with the male pourer, offered first to the groom, then to the bride; the second cup, filled with the female pourer would go in the reverse order; the third cup, a repeat of the first. This order was the same at all the ceremonies, although at one of them only a single pourer was used.[105] The couple then steps forward to the altar, where the groom reads from a scroll a pledge before the gods to the effect that they will spend married life in mutual harmony and respect, sharing pain, pleasure and peaceful living, measuring the way of prosperity for their descendants, unchanging until they die. The bride adds her name at the end. There may then be an exchange of wedding-rings, although this may take place later.

Once the bride and groom have been joined, the *sake* is brought out again to link the two families. First, the cups are taken to the bride-groom's father and, after he has drunk, to the bride, then the bride-groom's mother, and back to the bride. Then the bride's mother and father drink alternately with the groom. This is the *oyako-sakazuki* (parent-child cups). It is usually followed by the serving of each relative with a cup of *sake* which all drink together after standing up and chorusing *kampai* (cheers). This is the *shinseki-sakazuki* (relatives' cups). The *oyako-sakazuki* may be abbreviated to a general *kampai* as all drink together, it is said. The go-betweens seemed most often to drink with the relatives, but in one case they drank after the bride and groom and before the parents.

The final part of the ceremony, after some more chanting by the priest, involves the presentation of small paper-decorated *sakaki* branches (*tamagushi*) to the altar. This was explained by one priest as a thanksgiving to the deity. The branches are usually taken first by the bride and groom, then by the go-betweens, and finally by representatives of the two sets of relatives, usually the two fathers. The presentation of the branches is accompanied by two claps and two bows by each person, and as the fathers bow the other relatives join them. The exchange of rings took place at this point in some ceremonies, accompanied by clapping from the relatives. The introduction of relatives takes place either here, after the priest has left, or in a side room.

The *hiróen* is usually arranged by the catering department of the same hotel, marriage hall or shrine, and it follows on immediately the ceremony is completed. A feast is laid out, sometimes at Western-style tables, sometimes in Japanese style at individual trays or long low tables with cushions on the floor. Details in the procedure vary depending on the preferences of the clients and the institution concerned. Some receptions are quite Western, with a tiered wedding cake, one of which had no less than seven tiers. Typically, the guests are first seated, usually in places assigned to them, and the bride and groom then make an entrance with the go-betweens, often to the accompaniment of records such as Mendelssohn's or Wagner's Wedding March. On one occasion, curtains opened to reveal the couple on a stage from which they stepped down to walk to their places at the other end of the room. The bride sits on the groom's left with the go-betweens again on either side. There is usually a master of ceremonies who announces the events, and sometimes the proceedings start with a *noshi no gi*, as for the *karishúgen*. This would be done by a female employee of the wedding hall who walks slowly in, kneels down and places the table with the *noshi* on it on the floor, bows low to all the guests, picks up the table and walks slowly out again. It gives the occasion an air of solemnity, and the woman concerned on one occasion explained that the rite merely indicates that the *hiróen* has begun. Otherwise the first item is a speech by the go-between which includes a short life history of the bride and groom and expressions of hope that the union will be long-lasting. Short speeches are also made by the fathers of the two principals, and, where more guests have been included, there will be a speech by the chief guest of each of the bride and groom, usually a teacher or an employer, and perhaps one by a very old friend of each, although it is a relatively modern practice to invite friends of the bride to the wedding at all, it is said. *Utai* are usually sung by three of the guests, although no special dedications are necessarily made as they were at the *wakare*. These are followed by a general toast (*kampai*) to congratulate the bride and groom. The *sake* for this may be served cold, in red lacquer cups which are collected up afterwards, to distinguish the ceremonial drink from the warmed *sake* served through the rest of the celebration.

Guests are then asked to relax their formal upright posture and partake of the feast. Close relatives may move into the middle of the tables to make a round of greeting their new affines with an exchange of cups. For this, one person offers his own cup to another, filling it up for him, the recipient drinks the *sake*, returns the cup and fills it again. In this way inhibitions are soon discarded. If there is a microphone, or even if not, many guests will take to the floor for a song or a few words, and some may even dress up and do humorous dances. This kind of merrymaking follows the formal proceedings at any happy occasion.

During all this, the bride will leave the room at least once and return in a completely different outfit. If she can manage it she will enter quietly and return to her place almost unnoticed, but sometimes the master of ceremonies will catch her and insist that she walk down from the stage again. All the guests try to exchange cups once with the bride and groom, but the bride at least usually pours away the *sake* served before returning the cup. It would be much ruder to refuse to accept a cup offered in this way so that little fuss is made and the same practice is followed by anyone who feels they cannot take all the alcohol being offered. It means that a fair proportion of the *sake* purchased is not actually consumed, and most wedding halls take advantage of the custom by employing a number of women hostesses who join the festivities and work their way round the guests keeping all the *sake* cups filled. Sometimes these women are also professional entertainers who dance and sing on the stage during the celebration.

Several receptions may be held in such a hall in one day, so to bring the proceedings to a close, a new custom seems to have been adopted in some places – a presentation of bouquets by the bride and groom to the parents of the other. This was explained by one organiser as a kind of thank-you for having provided each other. It may be followed by a *banzai* (three cheers). Guests then pack up their remaining food in the boxes provided, tie these up with the gifts – often cakes to share at home and perhaps a household item such as a pretty plate or a tea-pot – and begin to move away.

Buddhist (butsuzen). Marriages in Buddhist temples are much less common, but one that I witnessed was for members of the Sōka Gakkai sect.[106] Otherwise informants expressed the opinion that temples were for funerals and memorial services, not for happy occasions such as weddings. The procedure was similar to other forms of marriage, except that the setting and altar ritual were Buddhist. The participants sat on cushions in much the same order as at the Shinto ceremony, facing the altar during the preliminaries and turning to face each other only for the *sake* rites. There were two priests officiating and the ceremony began as the younger banged a drum. The elder entered, sat down and began chanting sutras, accompanied by the occasional ringing of a bell.

After some time, a proclamation was read which announced the purpose of the occasion, and the relatives turned to face each other for the sharing of cups. The younger priest brought the cups and served the *sake*, and this time the complete process described on page 174 was performed. The cups were then taken to the bride's parents who each drank, then returned to the groom, who drank out of the same cup. This was repeated from the groom's parents to the bride. Similarly, they shared cups with each of their new relatives in twos, and finally the go-between and his wife drank together. There was then an exchange of rings and the elder priest read aloud a proclamation of the union which had been initiated and the promise which had been enacted by the couple to live in mutual love and respect, and to share sad and happy times together until they die. There was then further chanting[107] and the marriage was over. Guests were invited to attend a *hirōen* similar to that described at a conventional marriage hall, and a *yorokobi* was held later at the groom's house.

Home Marriage. It was rather paradoxical that two of the three home marriages which took place between 1975 and 1979 in Kurotsuchi involved people who were actually living away from home, in Kyōto and Osaka, both individuals who had returned to their own area to seek a spouse. It may be, however, that such couples had less need to indicate their independence and equality by holding the marriage ceremony on neutral ground. One such wedding, which will now be described, was that of the second son of the village head.

The marriage itself was held before the *tokonoma* in the *zashiki*, which opened out, by the removal of sliding doors, into the next two rooms to make one large, long room. It is sometimes said of home marriages that they are being held before the ancestors, but in this case the *butsudan* was in a separate room. Traditionally, however, the *tokonoma* had some religious significance (p. 82). The bride, groom and go-betweens sat at one end of the long room, as shown in Plan 8, and the relatives sat along each side of the length of the room. One of the groom's relatives had been designated master of ceremonies for the occasion and he sat at the bottom of the groom's side. Most of the formally seated relatives were men, except for parents, siblings and grandparents; the other women, the aunts, who were helping in the kitchen, occasionally offered advice on the proceedings from the open door. Three local girls, unmarried neighbours and relatives, were acting as *kyūjinin* (serving people), and these in particular were directed by the aunts from the kitchen. In front of each place, marked by a cushion,

Plan 8: Seating at a Home Marriage

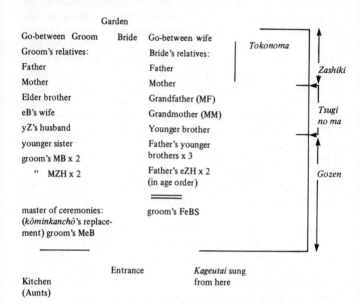

At the *yorokobi*, guests were seated in age order, and the family came down to the bottom of the room (by the entrance) for the formal greeting. Tables were set up in front of the guests, and family and intimate relatives stayed inside the tables to pour drinks and entertain the guests.

was a cup, two small cakes and a name card.

The proceedings began as usual with an introduction from the master of ceremonies, then the helpers came into the middle of the room to greet the guests. This was followed by the *noshi* presentation by one of the girls and then the cups and *sake* pourers were brought in. The *sakazuki* took place in the same abbreviated form as at the *kari-shūgen* and here too *kageutai* were sung from outside the door. A *sakazuki* for the relatives followed, using one cup down each side. After this, tea was brought in and served to each of the guests. The bride and groom stood up, and the groom read an oath to be bound in marriage to his wife, then gave her a wedding-ring. The master of ceremonies proclaimed the couple married, added a few words of congratulation, then asked the go-between to make his speech. This again included a brief biography of each partner and an expression of hope that the marriage would be long-lasting. Again the two fathers said a few words about the pleasure of the occasion. The next item was announced to be a greeting by the *kōminkanchō* (head of public meeting hall), apparently of the whole of Yame. He was not present, nor expected to be, according to informants, who explained that there would be too many weddings for him to attend them all. Instead, the master of ceremonies sang an *utai*, but the inclusion of this substitute for his greeting seems to serve the purpose of adding a public note to what would otherwise be a completely private ceremony between two families. After this, the two rows of relatives were introduced individually by the fathers of the bride and groom, and the ceremony, was complete. The guests then turned round to relax their legs while trays of food were brought in, and the feast with warmed *sake* followed. During this period there was much informal singing and dancing, and the bride changed her kimono. Photographs were taken of each outfit. After a suitable period, the guests were asked to rise and shout three cheers before the rice and soup were brought out to mark the end of the *hirōen*. Gifts were presented to each person as they left, and no sooner were they out of sight than the aunts moved in with the vacuum-cleaners to prepare the room for the first *yorokobi*.

Incorporation

Yorokobi *(Celebration)*

These *yorokobi*, of which there may be several, follow a fairly standard pattern whether they are held at home or in a public place. In Kurotsuchi, it seems to be common to invite neighbours in the afternoon, and age-mates of bridegroom and his father in the evening. The afternoon session was sometimes for women only, one member of each house in the *tonarigumi* being represented as well as age-mates of the groom's mother. Such guests would sit in age order, from the *tokonoma* down. Alternatively, the women of the *tonarigumi* and the men of the *tonari kinjo* may be entertained in the afternoon with the parents' age-mates, when all would sit in age order, men above women, while the evening session would be reserved for young people. Cousins and other relatives, who were not present at the marriage, are often entertained at an appropriate *yorokobi* too, so that the aunts in the kitchen may well sit down with the women of the neighbourhood. Yet another alternative is to hold one big reception, perhaps in a marriage hall, when all these categories may be accommodated at once. At one such occasion, a bus was provided to ferry the villagers to the marriage hall, and the different groups were seated in different parts of the room, men on one side, women on the other, and the groom's age-mates in pride of place at the top (see Plan 9). However, some women were to be seen sitting among the men, where an individual had been unable to attend and was represented by one of his family. Finally, there is sometimes also a *yorokobi* for a group of workmates, which may be held on the following day or even after the couple has returned from their honeymoon. A couple setting up a new home outside the village may well dispense with the *yorokobi* for villagers, for this is essentially to present the latter with their new member, and perhaps then the celebration for workmates will be more important. This was the case at a wedding I attended for a Town Hall employee who entertained all his colleagues on the evening of the marriage ceremony.

Plan 9: Seating of Guests at a *Yorokobi*

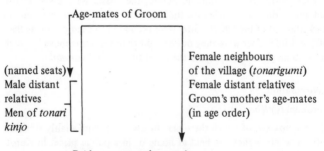

Age-mates of Groom

(named seats)
Male distant
relatives
Men of *tonari
kinjo*

Female neighbours
of the village (*tonarigumi*)
Female distant relatives
Groom's mother's age-mates
(in age order)

Bride, groom and groom's
parents greeted from here,
then circulated.

Within the village, the guests gather at a short distance from the house, waiting to be called in. This may take an hour or more, especially if there has been a *hirōen* elsewhere, for the bride must greet the ancestors as soon as she arrives, and it is more convenient if the guests do not move into their places until this task is fulfilled. While the guests are filing in, the bride may be taken by her mother-in-law to greet the *ujigami* at the village shrine, and at the home wedding this was done while the neighbouring women were being entertained. Women usually dress in kimono for such a *yorokobi*, although some may wear black Western clothes as a formal alternative, distinguished from mourning attire by white beads or a handkerchief at the neck. The female relatives, who wore black kimono with a coloured decoration at the wedding itself, usually changed into coloured kimono for the *yorokobi*, and this was the case also at the home marriage. The men usually wore Western-style suits.

Once the guests are seated, the bride makes a formal greeting by entering with the *noshi* and presenting it in the manner described on page 181). This time it initiates the *yorokobi* and the guests are able closely to scrutinise the bride. After this the groom and his parents will join the bride at the bottom of the room and the father will welcome the guests in the usual way: thanking them for giving up their time and apologising for the lack of entertainment. The *kyūjinin* may then be presented, and they will serve cold *sake* to everyone, sometimes in individual cups, sometimes in one cup passed down the line from guest to guest, so that all may take part in the celebration. Three *utai* are usually sung each time, sometimes presented to the bride, the groom and the groom's father, sometimes unspecified. Again, categories of guests may or may not be represented by each singer. An all-female occasion frequently involves a good deal of discussion before it is decided who will sing, and everyone joins in anyway.

The formal part of the proceedings over, feasting and drinking follow as at any other gathering, the all-female occasions being rather more subdued than those at which men are present. The former usually amuse themselves by singing together, while the latter tend to jump up and sing solos or make speeches. The party for the groom's age-mates usually includes one or two of his seniors, perhaps a teacher from the agricultural college, and such a person would be asked to make a formal speech. The Town Hall party for workmates also included several speeches, but in the village things were generally less formal, although the bride may well change once or twice.

The purpose of these *yorokobi* is said to be to introduce the bride to her new community,[108] and Yanagida goes further, saying that the approval of the community used to be required for the bride's acceptance and for a successful marriage.[109] Certainly the categories of groups in the village are redefined at every wedding in this way, as is the order of age priority re-emphasised in the seating arrangements. The degree of closeness of each household in the village is also illustrated by the amount of money given in gifts at such a time, and by who receives what gifts in return.

Honeymoon

At the end of the feast, the go-between used traditionally to see the couple to their bridal chamber, where they would supervise a further sharing of cups before leaving them alone.[110] The room was laid out ready for the two, who were advised to lie facing particular directions according to the rules of geomancy.[111] Recently, however, the practice of going away on a honeymoon has become popular, and in Kurotsuchi this has been going on since about 1960, it is said. It usually involves a few days or a week in some pleasant part of the country, or even abroad if funds permit. This is probably the only time for many years that the couple will be alone for an extended period if they are to live in the family home, for many people in Kurotsuchi commented that, until they retire, they never go away as a couple after the honeymoon is over. The break is also seen by older people in Kurotsuchi as a chance for the bride to recover from the ordeal of the marriage celebrations, for several commented that it is now unnecessary for them to spread the festivities over three days, because the couple can get away on holiday afterwards. One woman said that previously girls were allowed to do a 'sitting-down task', like sewing, for a few days after the marriage until they recovered.

There is a certain amount of pride expressed, particularly by a husband and his father, when a baby appears to have been conceived during the honeymoon. Thus, if the final *yorokobi* before the couple's departure is witnessed by age-mates, it provides an opportunity for a good deal of horseplay as these find some novel way to indicate to the couple what is expected of them during their trip.[112] On one occasion, a line of boys brandished bottles and carrots, while another line waited with sheets of paper, and, after some chanting and cavorting, the first line charged forward to pierce the pieces of paper held by the second line. On another occasion, several boys covered themselves in blankets and made noises and movement to indicate that they represented two horses, which then proceeded to simulate copulation wildly for some minutes. This all took place while the bride and groom, changed into ordinary clothes, were made to sit formally and watch the show. Finally, the whole group made an archway through which the couple was jostled, the groom being thrown up and down at the end, before they were finally allowed to board the taxi waiting outside.

Satogaeri *(Home Visits)* and Kinjo-Mawari *(Neighbourhood Round)*

Traditionally on the third day after the wedding, but now as soon as possible after the honeymoon, the bride pays a formal visit to her parents. She may well dress in kimono for this occasion, perhaps one she received in her betrothal gifts. Her parents may also send back rice-cakes *(mochi)* which are then delivered by her to her new neighbours in the *tonari kinjo* and to close relatives of her husband's family. In this area, this visit home is called the *mitsumearuki* (the third-day 'walk'), and it is the first of a series of visits home by the bride (or *yōshi*), generally referred to as *satoaruki* (home-walks), which is a dialect variation of the more widely used term *satogaeri* (home-return).[113] Traditionally these visits were made at fixed times, usually during slack periods in the agricultural cycle such as after rice-planting and after rice and chrysanthemum harvest, as well as at the annual holidays of Bon, New Year and Sekku (see Chapter 6). Nowadays there is more flexibility, but the visit soon after the wedding seems to be a part of the proceedings everywhere.[114] In some areas this occasion coincides with the *mukoiri* (reception of the groom) and his parents and other relatives may accompany the bride.[115]

The bride's delivery of *mochi* is one form of the *kinjo mawari* (neighbourhood round), which usually involves the bride's being introduced by her mother-in-law to each of their near neighbours.[116] Even in their own home, a newly married couple would be expected to pay a courtesy visit and present a small gift to each of their near neighbours, a practice which is general when people move into a new neighbourhood. The introduction of *mochi* makes this practice the first of a series of links between the neighbourhoods of the two households joined by marriage. More of these will be described in the next chapter, particularly in the section on birth.

Meanwhile, on the first New Year's Eve after the marriage the bride and groom again visit the bride's parents with a large fish called a *buri* (yellowtail), which can be cut up and offered later by the bride's family to their New Year visitors. Again this visit is an occasion for dressing up. The gift is said to signify the gratitude of the couple for the part played by the bride's family in bringing about the union. A further visit is made once New Year has begun, and another gift may be taken, probably together with a large rice-cake for the ancestors. The young couple usually also visit their go-between at this time, and perhaps again at Bon.

Civil Registration

Before a marriage is recognised in the eyes of the law, it must be reported at the local registry office, where a new family sheet is started. The bride and groom must both be present, bringing with them their personal seals (*inkan*), and the registration must be witnessed by a third party. This is all that is required by law, as it is in the case of divorce by mutual consent, and couples wishing to avoid all tradition and ceremony may merely register their marriages in such a way. As has already been discussed, the registration is usually completed within a few weeks of the ceremony nowadays, although previously it often used to be left until a child was expected.

The Cost and Significance of Wedding Celebrations

The total cost of a marriage depends, of course, on the type of wedding and celebrations provided, but figures quoted to cover the whole affair ranged from 500,000 to 3 million *yen*, which is between one and seven thousand pounds approximately. The groom's family must provide the *yuinō* gifts and now usually all the expenses of the marriage, reception and *yorokobi*, although the guests bring monetary contributions as an aid to this outlay. The greatest expense for the bride's family is the purchase of furniture and other equipment, although the position is of course reversed in the case of a family receiving a *yōshi* husband for their daughter. Since many families also choose to rebuild or alter their homes before receiving a *yome* or *yōshi*, this adds even further to the expenses associated with the marriage.

   In some cases, a young man who has savings may contribute to his own marriage expenses and even to those of his brothers or sisters if his parents have difficulty in meeting the cost. The weddings which involve children leaving home, or those who have left home, can be less expensive, especially if they are held in the place of adoption rather than the home village, when only workmates and close relatives would be invited. For a son inheriting the farm, the whole range of associates must be entertained, and a prosperous family may wish to do this even for sons who have left home. This was the case for the wedding of the second son of the village head, although his mother did comment that the marriage of the elder inheriting son had occasioned an even more splendid affair. Another family in the village had held the wedding of their eldest, inheriting son in the house, and those of his younger brothers in *ryōtei*. However, some families claimed that all their sons had been or would be treated alike, whether they were to inherit or not. This and the choice of location and type of marriage vary from household to household. The impressions of neighbours and associates are likely to be formed by evidence of expenditure at a wedding, whatever the details of the event.

This is an occasion when the household is making adjustments, accepting or losing a member, creating a new alliance, and the wedding feast, trousseau and gifts provide evidence that it can or cannot maintain or improve its standing in the community.[117] On the one side, guests at the wedding feast are witness to the provisions made, on the other, the bride's furniture and betrothal gifts have been displayed, and small helpings of *surume*, *konbu*, tea and *tai* shared out within the community. All these things are also evidence to each of the families involved that the other measures up to expectations. As Fujisaki warns, there is no point in prejudicing future married life and affinal relations by making an issue of the expenditure at the time when these decisions are made.[118] Furthermore, evidence that the match has been an appropriate one maintains the status of the two households concerned.[119] The marriage of a child is worthy of the use of lifetime savings, or even the incurring of debt, for the public display called for is one of the biggest chances to establish or confirm the status of the households concerned within the lifetimes of the members of each.

Notes

1. Rules of etiquette have been consciously drawn up and taught in Japan since the Heian period (Bun Nakajima, *Japanese Etiquette* (Japan Travel Bureau, Tokyo, 1955), p. 1), or earlier (J.M. Dixon, 'Japanese Etiquette', *Transactions of the Asiatic Society of Japan*, vol. 13 (1885), p. 1). From about the fourteenth century until the end of Meiji a family by the name of Ogasawara was associated with the most popular school (Dixon, 'Japanese Etiquette', pp. 1-2), followed at first by the warrior classes, but afterwards by many people of all classes, especially in the Kantō district, but with branches in Kyūshū (Tsutomu Ema, *Kekkon no Rekishi* (*History of Marriage*) (Yūzan-kaku, Tokyo, 1971), p. 122). The Ise school was associated rather with the Court and with Kyōtō (Nakajima, *Japanese Etiquette*, pp. 1-2; Ema, *Kekkon no Rekishi*, pp. 74, 121-2; Tarō Nakayama, *Nihon Kon'in Shi* (*A History of Marriage in Japan*) (Shunyō-dō, Tokyo, 1928), p. 818). Since Meiji there has been a great deal of Western influence, but some of the old rules are still remembered.

2. In different regions some of these elements have traditionally appeared in a different order, or perhaps with a much greater time between betrothal and permanent co-residence. Some of these variations are summarised in Tokuzō Omachi, 'Kon'in' ('Marriage') and 'Konrei' ('Marriage Ceremony') in T. Omachi

et al. (eds.), *Nihon Minzokugaku Taikei (An Outline of Japanese Folklore)* (Heibonsha, Tokyo, 1962), Vol. 3, pp. 175-202, and Vol. 4, pp. 247-74.

3. One family in Kurotsuchi had a daughter who fell in love during a stay in Osaka, and rumours about her engagement reached me before the official announcement, but despite several leading questions, they maintained their silence, the daughter even stating with a poker face that she thought she would like to marry in a couple of years' time. The daughter of another family, owners of a shop I used frequently, even asked me to keep an eye open for a suitable husband for her only a month before she was married!

4. Although informants merely explained that *shōchikubai* was used for happy occasions, various documentary sources attribute specific symbolism to the components: pine, as an evergreen, is symbolic of an unchanging virtuous heart and of longevity; bamboo of an upright and straight mind and, because of its pliancy, of gentleness; and the plum (*ume*), which flowers in the snowy season, thus symbolises fidelity in adversity (Lord Redesdale, *Tales of Old Japan* (including a translation of *Shorei Hikki*, a 'Record of Ceremonies', published in 1706 by Hayashi Rissai) (Macmillan, London, 1908), p. 378; Nakajima, *Japanese Etiquette* p. 159; Jukichi Inouye, *Home Life in Tokyo* (Tokyo, 1910), p. 183.) Ema reports that together they represent the symbolism of three periods, pine, the Heian, bamboo, the Kamakura and plum, the Momoyama period (Ema, *Kekkon no Rekishi*, p. 110).

5. The etymology of this word will be discussed shortly.

6. Robert J. Smith, 'Kurusu', in J.B. Cornell and R.J. Smith, *Two Japanese Villages* (Greenwood Press, New York, 1969), p. 78; Edward Norbeck, *Takashima* (University of Utah Press, Salt Lake City, 1954), pp. 177-8; B.H. Chamberlain, *Things Japanese* (John Murray, London, 1902), p. 309; Hiroshi Fujisaki, *Kankonsōsai Jiten (Dictionary of Ceremonial)* (Tsuru Shobo, Tokyo, 1957), pp. 44, 47; Ryōhei Minami, *Konrei-shiki to Kekkon no Kokoroe (On Marriage and the Marriage Ceremony)* (Taibunkan, Tokyo, 1953), p. 36.

7. Omachi, 'Konrei', p. 253; Kunio Yanagida, *Japanese Manners and Customs in the Meiji Era* (trans. and adapted by Charles S. Terry, Obunsha, Tokyo, 1957), pp. 174-5.

8. Yutaka Chikushi, *Nihon no Minzoku (Folklore of Japan)*, no. 40 (Fukuoka), Tokyo, 1974, pp. 200-3; Kunio Yanagida and T. Omachi, *Kon'in Shuzoku Goi (Popular Terms Associated with Marriage)* (Minkan Denshō no Kai, Tokyo, 1937), pp. 99, 101, 109.

9. Fujisaki, *Kankonsōsai Jiten*, pp. 66-7; Yaeko Shiotsuki, *Kankonsōsai Nyūmon (An Introduction to Ceremonial)* (Kōbunsha, Tokyo, 1970), pp. 32-3; cf. Norbeck, *Takashima*, p. 178.

10. Norbeck, *Takashima*, p. 177.

11. Cf. Shiotsuki, *Kankonsōsai Nyūmon*, p. 25.

12. I do not know whether this is true or not, but the individual bushes certainly grow into one continuous bush above the ground.

13. *Anata ga hyaku made, washa kyūjūkyū made, tomo ni shiraga no haeru made . . .*

14. Redesdale, *Old Japan*, p. 368fn. Takasago is also the name of an *utai* (extract from a *Nō* play) sung usually at weddings, and, according to the introduction by Shimazaki to the Nō play of the same name, a legendary pine growing there became famous because of a reference to it in the Preface to the *Kokinshū* (a tenth-century anthology of Japanese poetry, compiled by imperial command). This explains that two pines, at Takasago and Suminoe, now Sumiyoshi of Osaka, were looked upon as *ai-oi*, which, in the context, is interpreted as meaning 'to grow old together' (Chifumi Shimazaki, *The Noh*, Vol. 1, *God Noh* (Hinoki Shoten, Tokyo, 1972), p. 105).

15. Fujisaki, *Kankonsōsai Jiten*, pp. 103-4; Minami, *Konrei-shiki*, p. 56; Inouye, *Home Life in Tokyo*, p. 183; Ema, *Kekkon no Rekishi*, pp. 105-6; Naomi Tamura, *The Japanese Bride* (Harper and Bros., New York and London, 1904), p. 48.

16. Ema, *Kekkon no Rekishi*, p. 109; Nakayama, *Nihon Kon'in Shi*, pp. 339-41.

17. *Konbu* is said widely to be used because it is part of an adaptation of the word 'to celebrate' or 'to be joyful', *yorokonbu* (cf. Ema, *Kekkon no Rekishi*, p. 111). Ema reports that *surume* was chosen by the warrior classes because of its 10 legs, and possibly because it emits ink to hide from, and therefore to protect itself in the face of the enemy (ibid.).

18. Cf. Fujisaki, *Kankonsōsai Jiten*, p. 55; Shiotsuki, *Kankonsōsai Nyūmon*, p. 23; Ema, *Kekkon no Rekishi*, p. 191.

19. Fujisaki, *Kankonsōsai Jiten*, pp. 51-2.

20. The abalone is stretched through a process of steaming and beating, hence *noshi*, from *nosu* (to stretch), according to Ema, who reports that because the word for 'to beat' (*utsu*) is homonymous with the word for 'to defeat', the *samurai* chose this as symbolic of defeat of the enemy and therefore of celebration (pp. 111, 224). However, the use of *noshi* would seem to pre-date the *samurai* period, since it is reported mentioned in the *Ise Monogatari* (*The Tale of Ise*) of the ninth century (Mock Jōya, *Japanese Customs and Manners* (The Sakurai Shoten, Tokyo, 1955), p. 72).

21. Harumi Befu, 'Gift-giving in a Modernising Japan', *Monumenta Nipponica*, vol. 23 (1968), pp. 445-6; Yanagida, *Manners and Customs*, p. 186; cf. Yaeko Shiotsuki, *Zukai Kankonsōsai* (*Illustrated Ceremonial*) (Kōbunsha, Tokyo, 1971), p. 26.

22. Itsue Takamure, *Nihon Kon'in Shi* (*A History of Marriage in Japan*) (Nihon Rekishi Shinsho, Tokyo, 1963), p. 227.

23. Dixon, 'Japanese Etiquette', p. 16; L.W. Küchler, 'Marriage in Japan', *Transactions of the Asiatic Society of Japan*, vol. 13 (1885), p. 120; Redesdale, *Old Japan*, pp. 364-5; Ema, *Kekkon no Rekishi*, pp. 138-9.

24. Ema, *Kekkon no Rekishi*, p. 190.

25. John F. Embree, *Suye Mura* (University of Chicago Press, Chicago, 1939), pp. 204-5.

26. Norbeck, *Takashima*, p. 177; Smith, 'Kurusu', p. 78.

27. Fujisaki, *Kankonsōsai Jiten*, pp. 53-5; Shiotsuki, *Kankonsōsai Nyūmon*, pp. 23-5.

28. Elsewhere it is regarded as unlucky, at least if served (Fujisaki, *Kankonsōsai Jiten*, p. 48; Shiotsuki, *Kankonsōsai Nyūmon*, p. 28), although tea has been used at such a time as far away as Tōhoku (Takamure, *Nihon Kon'in Shi*, p. 227).

29. Nakayama, *Nihon Kon'in Shi*, p. 217.

30. Kunio Yanagida, *Minzokugaku Jiten* (*Dictionary of Folklore*) (Minzokugaku Kenkyūjo, Tokyo, 1953), p. 648; Kizaemon Ariga, *Nihon Kon'in Shiron* (*A Study of the History of Marriage in Japan*) (Nikko Shoin, Tokyo, 1948), pp. 203-6.

31. *Nihon Kokugo Daijiten* (*Large Dictionary of the National Language of Japan*) (Nihon Daijiten Kankōkai, Shōgakukan, Tokyo, 1976); Nakayama, *Nihon Kon'in Shi*, p. 822; Ema, *Kekkon no Rekishi*, p. 136.

32. Küchler, 'Marriage in Japan', p. 120; Chamberlain, *Things Japanese*, p. 309; Ema, *Kekkon no Rekishi*, p. 136; Tamura, *The Japanese Bride*, p. 32; Redesdale, *Old Japan*, p. 364; Ichiro Kurata, 'Rural Marriage Customs in Japan', *Contemporary Japan*, vol. 10 (1941), p. 373.

33. Kurata, 'Rural Marriage Customs', p. 373; Minami, *Konrei-shiki*, p. 38; Shiotsuki, *Kankonsōsai Nyūmon*, p. 26.

34. Jack Goody and S.J. Tambiah, *Bridewealth and Dowry* (Cambridge University Press, Cambridge, 1973), pp. 2, 5, 61.

35. Cf. Chikushi, *Nihon no Minzoku*, p. 198; Omachi, *'Konrei'*, pp. 256-7.

36. Shiotsuki, *Zukai*, p. 14; Fujisaki, *Kankonsōsai Jiten*, pp. 48-9; Minami, *Konrei-shiki*, p. 51.

37. The name of the gift is usually written on the *noshi* envelopes in which money is placed, although there are sometimes discrepancies in what is written on different gifts received at one occasion. The name of the giver, or the head of the household concerned, is written beneath the type of gift, which makes it easy for the recipients to keep a record of their benefactors.

38. *O-isogashii toki dōmo arigatō gozaimasu, nanimo gozaimasen ga dōzo go-yukkuri . . . (agatte kudasai)*

39. Cf. David W. Plath, *The After Hours* (University of California Press, Berkeley, Los Angeles and London, 1964), p. 105.

40. Cf. Goody and Tambiah, *Bridewealth and Dowry*, pp. 17, 62.

41. Cf. Gail Bernstein, 'Women in Rural Japan' in Joyce Lebra *et al.* (eds.), *Women in Changing Japan* (Westview Press, Boulder, Colorado, 1976), p. 28. Mirrors feature in Shinto ritual and symbolism, a mirror being one of the three items of Imperial regalia symbolising authority which were given to the son of the Sun Goddess when he was sent to rule the nation and found the Imperial Dynasty (Sokyo Ono, *Shinto: the Kami Way* (Tuttle, Rutland, Vermont and Tokyo, 1969), pp. 5, 13). They also feature in shrines where they are said to symbolise the stainless state of the *kami* (ibid., p. 23). Mirrors are also said to be symbolic representation of the presence of the *kami* (Kenji Ueda, *'Shinto'* in Hori *et al.*, *Japanese Religion*, trans. Yoshiya Abe and David Reid (Kodansha International, Tokyo and Palo Alto, 1972), p. 37).

42. *Hanayome-san no chōdohin de gozaimasu. Sue nagaku osame kudasaimase.*

43. I.L. Bishop, *Unbeaten Tracks in Japan* (John Murray, London, 1900), p. 214; Tamura, *The Japanese Bride*, p. 33; William Erskine, *Japanese Festivals and Calendar Lore* (Kyo Bun Kwan, Tokyo, 1933), p. 153; Embree, *Suye Mura*, p. 211; Norbeck, *Takashima*, p. 178; Fujisaki, *Kankonsōsai Jiten*, pp. 80-1; Minami, *Konrei-shiki*, pp. 49-50; Inouye, *Home Life in Tokyo*, p. 181. Pfoundes reported that two poisonous beetles were included in the noble bride's trousseau for the wife to swallow should she need to save her honour or expiate her unfaithfulness (C. Pfoundes, 'On Some Rites and Customs of Old Japan', *Journal of the Anthropological Institute*, vol. 12 (1882), p. 226). Ema, *Kekkon no Rekishi*, pp. 75-6, 98-9, describes how brides used to take 360 clam shells, one for each day of the year, to symbolise the harmonious union of the couple, since although all the shells were divided into left and right ones, they still fitted into each other.

44. Yanagida, *Manners and Customs*, p. 178.

45. J. Carey Hall, 'Japanese Feudal Law', *Transactions of the Asiatic Society of Japan*, vol. 38 (1911), p. 316.

46. E.g. Fujisaki, *Kankonsōsai Jiten*, pp. 80-1.

47. Cf. Robert J. Smith, *Kurusu* (Dawson, Folkestone, 1978), pp. 137-8.

48. R.P. Dore, 'Japanese Rural Fertility', *Population Studies*, vol. 7 (1953), p. 68.

49. Cf. Norbeck, *Takashima*, p. 179. A description of a Meiji bride having her hair done up for her wedding is to be found in Bishop, *Unbeaten Tracks*, p. 248.

50. Nakayama, *Nihon Kon'in Shi*, p. 828; Ema, *Kekkon no Rekishi*, pp. 90-1. One writer reports that the bride changes into a ceremonial garment to show her willingness to serve the ancestral gods of her new home, and then into a more home-like garment to show her acceptance of house tasks and her willingness to

work for the future of her new house (Erskine, *Japanese Festivals*, p. 155; *Japanese Customs* (Kyo Bun Kwan, Tokyo, 1925), p. 9). Others merely refer to the fact that she changes into a garment received from the bridegroom (Redesdale, *Old Japan*, p. 370; Ema, *Kekkon no Rekishi*, p. 154). For details of such garments, see Ema, *Kekkon no Rekishi*, pp. 196-203. Shiotsuki, *Kankonsōsai Nyūmon*, p. 79, sees the main advantage of this practice as an opportunity for the bride to have a rest.

51. Ema, *Kekkon no Rekishi*, pp. 90-1; Nakajima, *Japanese Etiquette*, pp. 108-11; Tamura, *The Japanese Bride*, pp. 34, 37-8; Chamberlain, *Things Japanese*, p. 62.

52. Ema, *Kekkon no Rekishi*, pp. 79, 192; Bishop, *Unbeaten Tracks*, p. 97; Redesdale, *Old Japan*, p. 373.

53. Cf. Kawashima, *Kekkon*, p. 98.

54. This is a recent simplified version of the *watabōshi* (silk-floss veil), which used to be worn by noblewomen to go out, by women of the Ikko Buddhist sect to visit the temple, and later came to be used for ceremonial occasions, finally limited to the bride at her wedding (Chikushi, *Nihon no Minzoku*, p. 200; Jōya, *Japanese Customs and Manners*, pp. 30-2; Fujisaki, *Kankonsōsai Jiten*, pp. 97-9; Nakayama, *Nihon Kon'in Shi*, pp. 320-3). The original function is interpreted variously as to hide the face and avoid the evil eye (*jashi*) (Nakayama, p. 321), as a head covering, and to stop the horns of jealousy (Joya, p. 31). These 'horns of jealousy' are sometimes represented by holding two fingers up to the forehead (cf. Helmut Morsbach, 'Aspects of Non-verbal Communication in Japan', *Journal of Nervous and Mental Diseases*, vol. 157 (1973), p. 268).

55. Blacker reports use of this symbolism by pilgrims, and for the initiation of a spirit medium who 'marries' the deity who takes possession of her (Carmen Blacker, *The Catalpa Bow* (Allen and Unwin, London, 1975), Chapter 11 and p. 147).

56. Cf. Dixon, 'Japanese Etiquette', p. 17. However, Ema, *Kekkon no Rekishi*, p. 104, says that the notion of white as a symbol of death so that the bride will not return is mistaken, and the marriage ceremony is the foundation or source of human relations, so white is worn because it is the foundation of the five colours.

57. Chamberlain, *Things Japanese*, p. 309; Norbeck, *Takashima*, pp. 181, 190; Douglas Sladen and Norma Lorimer, *More Queer Things about Japan* (Anthony Treherne, London, 1904), p. 24; Tamura, *The Japanese Bride*, pp. 49-50; Lafcadio Hearn, *Japan: an Attempt at Interpretation* (Macmillan, New York, 1924), pp. 77; Yanagida, *Manners and Customs*, p. 177; Chikushi, *Nihon no Minzoku*, p. 202.

58. Erskine, *Japanese Festivals*, pp. 154-5; *Japanese Customs*, pp. 39-40.

59. Purple and violet are said to be avoided by bride and groom since they fade soonest and divorce may result (Bishop, *Unbeaten Tracks*, p. 254).

60. Yanagida, *Manners and Customs*, p. 12.

61. More details of ceremonial dress and how it should be worn are given in Nakajima, *Japanese Etiquette*, pp. 94-101, and Shiotsuki, *Zukai*, pp. 34-43.

62. In the past there would have been a palanquin for the bride of rich families, and the bridal procession provided a colourful display for onlookers (e.g. Redesdale, *Old Japan*, pp. 365-6; Nakayama, *Nihon Kon'in Shi*, p. 827; Ema, *Kekkon no Rekishi*, pp. 97, 124, 139-40).

63. Cf. Inouye, *Home Life in Tokyo*, pp. 185-7; Takamure, *Nihon Kon'in Shi*, p. 260.

64. The first Shinto wedding was held in Hibiya shrine in 1898 (Ema, *Kekkon no Rekishi*, p. 169), and reported from Izumo shrine in 1915 (Erskine, *Japanese Customs*, p. 8), but the rise in popularity of shrine weddings seems to

be a largely post-war phenomenon (Keiichi Yanagawa, 'The Family, the Town and Festivals', *East Asian Cultural Studies*, vol. 11 (1972), p. 126.)

65. Descriptions of Japanese Christian weddings are to be found in Minami, *Konrei-shiki*, pp. 79-82; Shiotsuki, *Kankonsōsai Nyūmon*, pp. 58-62; Ema, *Kekkon no Reshiki*, pp. 186-8; Fujisaki, *Kankonsōsai Jiten*, pp. 154-70. The current interest in Western, and particularly British, weddings as illustrated in England when a party of twenty-odd Japanese wedding organisers was in the news after visiting a society wedding in Henley-on-Thames to learn about British practices (*Henley Standard*, 30 June 1978; *Henley Times*, 30 June 1978).

66. Fujisaki, *Kankonsōsai Jiten*, p. 170.

67. Whether the bride sits on the left or the right of the groom has varied in the past, although at all the occasions I witnessed the bride sat on the groom's left. In the past, the position of the *tokonoma* would determine the top seat (that nearest the middle of the room, or the *tokobashira*), and the groom would sit there, but later the bride was given this seat as, until they were married, she was the guest of the house (Ema, *Kekkon no Rekishi*, p. 83). This may have varied regionally, however (Fujisaki, *Kankonsōsai Jiten*, pp. 105-6).

68. Other descriptions of the rite are to be found in several works including Dixon, 'Japanese Etiquette', pp. 16-17; Küchler, 'Marriage in Japan', p. 124, Sladen and Lorimer, *More Queer Things about Japan*, p. 23, Tamura, *The Japanese Bride*, pp. 51-2, Nakajima, *Japanese Etiquette*, p. 134, Fujisaki, *Kankonsōsai Jiten*, pp. 106-9, Ema, *Kekkon no Rekishi*, p. 205, and, of the Imperial wedding of the Emperor Taishō, in Erskine, *Japanese Customs*, pp. 41-2.

69. Fujisaki, *Kankonsōsai Jiten*, p. 106.

70. Yanagida, *Manners and Customs*, p. 179.

71. Ema, *Kekkon no Rekishi*, pp. 87-8, 114-15, 153; Redesdale, *Old Japan*, p. 367. Norbeck, *Takashima*, p. 183, reported that the go-between's wife played this part in Takashima.

72. Cf. Inouye, *Home Life in Tokyo*, p. 183; Embree, *Suye Mura*, pp. 101-2; H. Byron Earhart, *Religion in the Japanese Experience* (Dickenson, Belmont, California, 1974), p. 189.

73. Ema, *Kekkon no Rekishi*, p. 16; Nakayama, *Nihon Kon'in Shi*, p. 327; U.A. Casal, 'Some Notes on the Sakazuki and on the Role of Sake Drinking in Japan', *Transactions of the Asiatic Society of Japan*, vol. 19 (1940), pp. 1-186.

74. Tamura, *The Japanese Bride*, p. 52; Sladen and Lorimer, *More Queer Things about Japan*, p. 23; Bishop, *Unbeaten Tracks*, pp. 215-16.

75. Geoffrey Bownas, *Japanese Rainmaking and Other Folk Practices* (Allen and Unwin, London, 1963), p. 70.

76. Ivan Morris, 'Marriage in the World of Genji', *Asia*, vol. 11 (1968), p. 66; Omachi, 'Konrei', p. 263; Takamure, *Nihon Kon'in Shi*, pp. 76-7; Ema, *Kekkon no Rekishi*, p. 60.

77. Takamure, *Nihon Kon'in Shi*, p. 115.

78. Ema, *Kekkon no Rekishi*, pp. 53-4.

79. Ibid., p. 52.

80. Embree, *Suye Mura*, p. 208.

81. Ema, *Kekkon no Rekishi*, pp. 204-5.

82. Dixon, 'Japanese Etiquette', p. 16; Küchler, 'Marriage in Japan', p. 123; Embree, *Suye Mura*, p. 207; Fujisaki, *Kankonsōsai Jiten*, p. 102.

83. Fujisaki, *Kankonsōsai Jiten*, pp. 101, 103, 106-7; cf. Shiotsuki, *Kankonsōsai Nyūmon*, p. 56; Küchler, 'Marriage in Japan', pp. 123-4; Casal, 'Sakazuki and Sake Drinking', p. 39.

84. Norbeck, *Takashima*, p. 182. The drinking of water mixed from that of the bride's and groom's houses has also been reported as part of an ancient ceremony (Nakayama, *Nihon Kon'in Shi*, p. 327), as has the mixing of fire from

the two houses (Takamure, *Nihon Kon'in Shi*, p. 115).

85. Redesdale, *Old Japan*, p. 367; Ema, *Kekkon no Rekishi*, pp. 151, 159.

86. Ema, *Kekkon no Rekishi*, pp. 85, 112; Casal, 'Sakazuki and Sake Drinking', p. 39.

87. Dixon, 'Japanese Etiquette', p. 16; Inouye, *Home Life in Tokyo*, p. 183; Küchler, 'Marriage in Japan', p. 123; Embree, *Suye Mura*, p. 207.

88. This word seems to be peculiar to Kyūshū (Yanagida and Omachi, *Kon'in Shūzoku Goi*, p. 145).

89. E.g. Ema, *Kekkon no Rekishi*, pp. 207, 160, 116, 61; Redesdale, *Old Japan*, pp. 370-2; Yanagida, *Manners and Customs*, pp. 175, 180.

90. Yanagida, *Manners and Customs*, p. 180; cf. Omachi, 'Konrei', p. 262.

91. Yanagida, *Manners and Customs*, p. 174; Takamure, *Nihon Kon'in Shi*, p. 115.

92. Morris, 'Marriage in the World of Genji', p. 66; Ema, *Kekkon no Rekishi*, p. 50; Omachi, 'Konrei', p. 263.

93. Takamure, *Nihon Kon'in Shi*, pp. 76-7.

94. Ibid., pp. 111-12; Morris, 'Marriage in the World of Genji', p. 66; Ema, *Kekkon no Rekishi*, p. 48.

95. Ema, *Kekkon no Rekishi*, p. 66; Morris, 'Marriage in the World of Genji', p. 66; Nakayama, *Nihon Kon'in Shi*, p. 741.

96. Embree, *Suye Mura*, pp. 206-7; Norbeck, *Takashima*, p. 181; Smith, 'Kurusu', p. 81; Takamure, *Nihon Kon'in Shi*, p. 223; Bernstein, 'Women in Rural Japan', p. 28; Küchler, 'Marriage in Japan', pp. 121-2; Omachi, 'Konrei', pp. 263-8, 247-8; 'Kon'in', pp. 178-89.

97. Yanagida and Omachi, *Kon'in Shūzoku Goi*, pp. 1-2; Takamure, *Nihon Kon'in Shi*, p. 243.

98. In some parts of the country this has traditionally taken place as much as a year or two after the actual marriage ceremony, perhaps in the fifth or sixth month of pregnancy (Omachi, 'Konrei', pp. 261-2).

99. Casal, 'Sakazuki and Sake Drinking', p. 60, fn 115.

100. This appears to be another local word (Yanagida and Omachi, *Kon'in Shūzuko Goi*, p. 159.)

101. Further general descriptions of Shinto weddings are to be found in Fujisaki, *Kankonsōsai Jiten*, pp. 136-46; Minami, *Konrei-shiki*, pp. 75-7; Shiotsuki, *Kankonsōsai Nyūmon*, pp. 54-8; *Zukai*, pp. 44-53; Ema, *Kekkon no Rekishi*, pp. 179-81; Nakajima, *Japanese Etiquette*, pp. 129-35.

102. In the past, similar offerings were placed on the raised dais of the *tokonoma*, typically including fish such as carp and *tai* and fowl such as pheasant, together with the *shimadai*, now used in the *yuinō* gifts in Yame, and the *sake* pots and pourers (Inouye, *Home Life in Tokyo*, pp. 181-3; Redesdale, *Old Japan*, pp. 366-7; Minami, *Konrei-shiki*, pp. 56-62; Fujisaki, *Kankonsōsai Jiten*, pp. 101-4, 114-15; Ema, *Kekkon no Rekishi*, pp. 81-7, 150). The carp is said to be the most courageous fish since it can swim against the current, and the pheasant is the legendary messenger of the gods (Ema, *Kekkon no Rekishi*, pp. 87, 112).

103. Yoneo Okada and Sadatoshi Ujitoko, *Shinto Shrines and Festivals* (Jinja Honchō, Kokugakuin University, Tokyo, 1958), p. 19.

104. Ono, *Shinto*, pp. 51, 57.

105. This was the reverse of the order at the *karishūgen*, when the bride drank first, which was also that practised at home and *ryōtei* marriages, said to be because the bride is a guest until the couple is actually married. In Fujisaki's description of the rite performed by children (pp. 221-2), the male and female pourers were served to groom and bride respectively, the opposite of here.

106. More general descriptions of Buddhist weddings are to be found in Fujisaki, *Kankonsōsai Jiten*, pp. 147-53; Minami, *Konrei-shiki*, pp. 78-9; Shiotsuki,

Zukai, pp. 62-9; Nakajima, *Japanese Etiquette*, pp. 136-7; Ema, *Kekkon no Rekishi*, pp. 181-6.

107. I was unable to understand the language used at either this or the Shinto wedding during the periods of chanting, but in this I was apparently not different from any lay participant. Requests for explanation produced general answers such as 'this is calling up/thanking the *kami* or Buddha'. With the possible exception of the Sōka Gakkai and other new-religion adherents, participants pay very little attention to any ideology the religion may possess with regard to marriage. Thus they can without qualms seek a Christian union as easily as marry in their own home where there is no direction further than that provided by older people.

108. Cf. Embree, *Suye Mura*, p. 210.

109. Yanagida, *Manners and Customs*, p. 180.

110. Inouye, *Home Life in Tokyo*, p. 185, Chamberlain, *Things Japanese*, p. 310; Tamura, *The Japanese Bride*, p. 54.

111. Ema, *Kekkon no Rekishi*, pp. 90, 161-3; Minami, *Konrei-shiki*, pp. 70-1. According to Minami, for example, the pillow should face east, then the man lies on the south side of the woman (p. 71).

112. Traditionally this may have been part of the sex education of the young people of the village (cf. Kamishima, *Nihonjin no Kekkonkan*, pp. 184-92). More explicit sexual symbolism was also said to have been found in the decorations in the past (Nakayama, *Nihon Kon'in Shi*, pp. 339-42).

113. Cf. Toshimi Takeuchi, 'Satogaeri' in *Nihon Shakai Minzoku Jiten* (1954), p. 502; Yanagida and Omachi, *Kon'in Shūzoku Goi*, pp. 209, 205; Chikushi, *Nihon no Minzoku*, p. 200.

114. *Konrei-shiki*, p. 88; Fujisaki, *Kankonsōsai Jiten*, pp. 127-8; Shiotsuki, *Kankonsōsai Nyūmon*, p. 96; Takamure, *Nihon Kon'in Shi*, pp. 228-9; Küchler, 'Marriage in Japan', p. 125. There also seems to have been a practice for the bride to be visited by her mother in her new home before she returned to visit her old one. This was called the *heyamimai* (room-visit). It is reported by Smith, 'Kurusu', p. 81, and Ema, *Kekkon no Rekishi*, pp. 164, 209.

115. Tamura, *The Japanese Bride*, p. 63; Norbeck, *Takashima*, p. 183; Omachi, 'Konrei', p. 265; Ema, *Kekkon no Rekishi*, pp. 164-5.

116. Cf. Minami, 'Women in Rural Japan', p. 28; Minami, *Konrei-shiki*, p. 89; Fujisaki, *Kankonsōsai Jiten*, pp. 126-7; Yanagida and Omachi, *Kon'in Shūzoku Goi*, pp. 153ff.; Takamure, *Nihon Kon'in Shi*, p. 229; Tamura, *The Japanese Bride*, pp. 63-4.

117. Cf. Yanagida, *Manners and Customs*, pp. 122-3; Dore, 'Rural Fertility', p. 67; Ronald Dore, *Shinohata* (Allen Lane, London, 1978), p. 205.

118. Fujisaki, *Kankonsōsai Jiten*, pp. 79-80.

119. Cf. Chie Nakane, *Kinship and Economic Organization in Rural Japan* (University of London, The Athlone Press, London, 1967), p. 158.

6 FURTHER CEREMONIAL: SOME OF THE WIDER IMPLICATIONS OF MARRIAGE

In this chapter, a number of other ceremonies and life crises will be considered. One of the purposes of this is for comparison so that the rites associated with marriage may be assessed in a wider context of ceremonial and celebration. Many of these events also provide excellent illustration of some of the broader implications of marriage, and the relations and obligations established at this time.

The first section will treat other important events in the life cycle of the individual, but it will be seen that these are frequently associated with membership of a household or community, and with the consequences for those groups of the development of the individual. Marriage involves the change of status of individuals, but the relations established are also very much between households and communities, as will be illustrated. It was mentioned at the end of Chapter 3 that most relations between households are initiated by marriage, either because this creates direct affinal links, or because it gives the individuals setting up their own households the status of adults and householders. In the developmental cycle of the household, marriages provide the important definitions required for each new generation. A group of siblings includes only one permanent member of the household; all the others must move out. As these siblings marry, one of them will receive a spouse into the natal household, others will move into or set up other households, and thus a new set of related households will be formed. During the course of this chapter, some of the implications of these relationships and the obligations involved will be illustrated in descriptions of the ceremonial occasions at which they are expressed. As was also noted at the end of Chapter 3, relations with the neighbouring households of the *tonari kinjo* are often as frequent as those with relatives, particularly at life crises, and the ceremonies of marriage included appropriate attention to these groups. What follows will indicate the extent to which these different kinds of relationships between households are similar, and to what extent they are distinguished.

The second part of the chapter is concerned with some important annual events which provide regular occasions for interaction between households linked through mutual descendants and ascendants. Finally, the third part is concerned with house-building, the physical redefinition of the *ie*, which, like the redefinition of its living members at marriage, involves considerable ceremony and participation of related households.

The Life Cycle

Pregnancy, Childbirth and Subsequent Rejoicing

News of a pregnancy may well leak out before the fifth month, especially through the proud husband or his father, but during this month a public announcement is made. This is referred to as the *obi-iwai*, the celebration of the *obi*, which is a long piece of corseting in which the mother-to-be wraps herself from that time until after the baby is born.[1] It is said that the date chosen for this *iwai* is a dog day of the Chinese calendar, because the dog has an easy delivery as a rule,[2] and this is like a request to higher powers that this birth will be likewise. The doctor's advice is sought about how the corseting should be worn, and sometimes he signs the garment with a character of congratulation (*kotobuki*). The garment itself is often a gift from the wife's family, which comes accompanied by a trayful of rice-cakes, to be distributed to households of the *tonari kinjo* and relatives of the family. The wife's parents may be invited to a celebration at their daughter's new home, where the two families will probably share a meal including *tai* (bream) to denote the occasion for congratulation (*omedetai*).

About two or three weeks before the birth, at least for a first baby, the mother-to-be returns to her own parents' home where she remains until a month or more after the delivery.[3] Until the late sixties, informants said, most babies were delivered at home with the help of a midwife who lived locally. Now most are delivered in hospital, and the change-over has been so complete that the previously much-respected midwives have had to find themselves work in hospitals if they are to continue their jobs. These hospitals are private in the Yame area, typically with one obstetrician who lives on the premises. The facilities often include such luxuries as free photographs of the new baby, but a relative or friend of the patient must be present 24 hours a day to see to more mundane needs. This relative is usually the new mother's mother or sister.

When the mother-to-be goes home before the birth, she usually takes some cakes again, this time for her own parents' neighbours and relatives, sent by her new household. After the birth, the recipients of these and the cakes sent at the time of the pregnancy announcement make gifts to the baby, and some may arrange a visit to the hospital.

These include neighbours and relatives of both sets of grandparents, all of whom will receive more cakes when the baby arrives back – from hospital for the mother's side, and from the mother's home for the father's side. It can be seen then that this life crisis involves the whole network of close households in an exchange of gifts to mark the occasion.

The two sets of grandparents usually meet again at the mother's home after she and the baby return from hospital to celebrate the naming (*nazuke*) of the child. Traditionally this took place on the seventh night after the birth and was often called *shichiya* (seventh night).[4] The return from hospital is usually about a week after delivery, and the birth must be registered within two weeks, so the old practice need not be greatly modified. Apparently this is just a quiet celebration between the two families, the first of a series to mark the growth and development of their new link through the child. For a second or subsequent baby, some mothers remain in their husband's home, when their own parents would come there for the *shichiya* celebration. This may even be dispensed with after the first one or two babies.[5]

It is usual for a mother to rest for a month after childbirth, and many girls who remain in their husband's home right up to the time they go into hospital will go to their own parents for the month afterwards. This is a clearly defined pollution period which ends 30 days after the birth of a boy and 33 days after that of a girl with a *hibare* or *hi no hare* (literally, clearing up).[6] During this time, the mother and baby remain mostly indoors;[7] the mother does not go to the communal bath, nor does she do any work or even watch television, which is said to be possibly harmful to the eyes at this time. No one could explain the difference in the period of pollution for a girl and boy baby, except to indicate that it was evidence of the usual superiority of the male sex. Women are traditionally more polluted than men with regard to the shrine because of their association with menstruation and childbirth.[8] Appropriately, then, it is at the shrine that the end of this period of pollution is celebrated with the *miyamairi*,[9] when the baby is presented for the first time to the local deity. In case the mother does not feel well enough to return to her husband's house on this occasion, she may take her baby with her own mother to her local shrine, and visit the one at her husband's village when she does return. Otherwise the visit to the shrine coincides with her return to her husband's home. For this visit, the baby is dressed first in white robes, as it was at birth (and will be at death and marriage, if a girl), to symbolise its purity and unmarked state. A boy baby is then further wrapped in a black kimono with blue or green decoration and marked with the house crest, a girl in an uncrested one of red and orange colours. These garments, which are expensive, are usually big enough to be worn for later celebrations. They are given by the mother's family, or, in the case of a *yōshi*, by his family.[10]

Villagers may gather at the shrine to join the celebration, young children and toddlers especially being encouraged to come and see their new playmate. The baby arrives with its mother and two grandmothers, who lay the baby down and kneel before the shrine, where they light a candle and greet the deity with bows and claps in the usual way. They then play with the baby for a while, trying to encourage it to cry or make some sound, so that the *ujigami* will be aware of its new parishioner, for it is said that this visit is for the purpose of registering the new member of the village with the protective deity.[11] Once the rite is completed, the women give *sake* and rice with beans (*sekihan*, for celebration), which have been offered to the deity, to the waiting villagers. In this way, all partake in the happy occasion. It is said locally to be a good idea to visit briefly one or two relatives before returning, but, once back in what will be the baby's home, the two families take their places round the table, with the baby at the head. Cold *sake* is then shared out of the celebratory red cups, a *sake*-wetted finger being touched three times to the baby's lips for good fortune in life. The child's name may be hung up over the *butsudan*, which is usually open so that the ancestors too may welcome the new addition to the family. Before eating, the father's family will formally thank the mother's for taking care of the baby until now, and the latter will thank the former for lending it to them. A murmur of similar thanks was to be heard at the shrine from the villagers when the mother's mother arrived with the baby, which informants explained was thanks from the village on behalf of one of their members, albeit new, for hospitality received. Only the two families share the meal, which includes *tai* and other food eaten on joyful occasions, but later, cakes are taken to the households of relatives and neighbours as a gift from the baby. One informant likened this practice to the visits made by people when they move into a new neighbourhood. Relations are established and everyone is made aware of the new situation.

There are variations in the celebrations if, for example, the mother returns directly from the hospital to her husband's home, or if she has received a *yōshi* and is therefore with her parents there anyway. Then the *miyamairi* celebration may be held at the grandparents' home not yet visited by the baby, and the grandmother who has least seen it will probably carry it to the shrine. The money spent and the extent of the celebration usually diminishes with each subsequent child, it is said, which is true of many of the celebrations for children.[12]

Another small celebration for the baby takes place 100-110 days[13] after the birth. This is called *momoka* (written 100 days) or *kiuzome* (first eating), when the baby is given a little rice for the first time and probably receives a bowl and a tiny pair of chopsticks from his mother's family. Again the two sets of grandparents may meet to celebrate this occasion.

The most important celebration held during the first year of a baby's life falls on one of the traditional national holidays of *osekku*. For a girl, this was the third day of the third lunar month, for a boy, the fifth of the fifth month, now celebrated on 3 March, which is known as the Doll's Festival, and 5 May, which is officially Children's Day, respectively.[14] When a girl baby has been born, the mother or *yōshi*'s parents are expected to buy a set of dolls dressed in the traditional costumes of the ancient Japanese court, which are set out on tiers with various pieces of furniture, utensils, lanterns and trees, to be displayed in the *tokonoma* that day.[15] For a boy baby, warrior dolls and large cloth carp, both credited with qualities of courage and energy, are given, the latter to be hung like flags over the house for some time before the day itself. In either case, the baby is dressed in its *miyamairi* kimono, and a gathering of the same relatives who attended the marriage ceremony (*honkyaku*) is held, to which, at least for a first child, the go-between is also invited as a special guest. This celebration in particular is greater for the first child, which suggests that it is as much a celebration of the cementing of the marriage as that of honouring the new member, who nevertheless symbolises the new strength of the union. A feast is served, with the usual food for happy occasions as well as special items for *osekku*, which symbolise the fortune and health of the child as it grows. *Utai* are usually sung, and this celebration resembles others already described, providing a good opportunity for the two families linked by the marriage to know each other better and relax in each other's company.

At the baby's first New Year, the mother or *yōshi*'s parents are again expected to provide gifts in this area, this time a bow and arrow for a boy – not a toy, but an ornament enclosed in a glass case – and a *hagoita* (badminton racquet) displaying an exquisitely dressed doll, made of padded pieces of material attached to the wooden background, again in a glass case, for a girl. These gifts, which are kept in the *tokonoma* afterwards, are more or less ornate depending on the economic circumstances of the family concerned. Since they are on display to all visitors to the house, they provide a tangible representation of the appropriateness of the match made when the bride or *yōshi* was chosen. One such item given by a wealthy Kurotsuchi family included not only the expected *hagoita*, but a set of flashing lights and a musical box to play a tune as one admired the gift. The cost may well be in excess of £100, but such expensive gifts are usually only given for a first baby of each sex.

The next celebration for a baby is held on its first birthday. In the past, in Japan, ages were reckoned to start with one at birth, increasing every New Year, so that a child born on New Year's Eve would be two the following day.[16] Thus generally the birthday had no special significance, and the baby's first birthday, which was celebrated, was often referred to simply as 'the birthday' (*tanjōbi*). Although young people now often follow the Western custom of sending each other cards and gifts, the baby's first birthday is still often referred to in this way. On this occasion, in Kyūshū, the mother's parents provide a large, flat rice-cake on which the child is made ritually to take its first steps.[17] Some people say that as the step is taken the phrase associated with Takasago (Ch. 5, n13) should be said so that the baby will live for a long time. Others add that the baby should wear a handkerchief filled with money on its back to make sure it will always have enough. At the other side of the cake are placed several items to attract the attention of the child, and the first one it selects is supposed to indicate its inclinations for the future. For example, a pair of scissors chosen might suggest that the child will become a seamstress or a tailor, an abacus might indicate a mathematical bent, a ruler perhaps a carpenter and a writing brush a clerk or secretary. The rice-cake is then cut up into pieces, which are later distributed to relatives and neighbours, five pieces to the former and three to the latter, one family explained. A celebration is usually held in the house for at least the two grandmothers and perhaps more of the close family for a first child.

Several traditional rites to celebrate the first time a child was allowed to wear grown-up clothes[18] have recently been amalgamated into a single day of celebration known as 7-5-3 (*shichi-go-san*) on 15 November. On this day, children of three, five and seven throughout the land are dressed in fine new clothes and taken to visit shrines. The Shinto priest conducts a purification rite involving the usual elements of worship and the mention of the name of each child whose parents have paid the appropriate fee. Afterwards each child receives a bag containing sweets and one or two toys as well as a small piece of dried cuttlefish (*surume*) and seaweed (*konbu*), which represent the sharing of a ritual feast. The rite is said to be for protection against misfortune, a prayer for health, wealth and long life, and the prayer should be repeated by mothers at the local village shrine if the visit was made to a larger one with a resident priest.

This occasion was treated rather casually in Kurotsuchi, as it falls at a busy period, and for convenience children's ages may be calculated according to either the new Western or the old indigenous system. One mother took her son and daughter to the shrine together when the daughter was three by Western reckoning and her son five by Japanese reckoning. In the evening a special meal for the children was arranged, to which one or two relatives and neighbours were invited, but this did not seem to represent an important gathering. Another mother, whose child was of an age to go, claimed to be too busy and remarked that the child would be all right because he was always playing in the shrine compound anyway.[19] Nor did it seem to matter in Kurotsuchi to which shrine children were taken, though most apparently go to Fukushima. Several families reported having taken their children at three for girls and five for boys, but I found no one who bothered going again at seven. Perhaps this is anyway irrelevant now. There used to be an important rite at that age in this area involving the presentation of a white loincloth for a boy and a red petticoat for a girl,[20] garments elsewhere presented at or around puberty.[21] Seven was an important age[22] at which children were said to gain entry into the community and *kodomogumi* and come under the constant protection of the local deity.[23] Nowadays entry into the community at this time would seem to be adequately marked as entry into primary school, which also involves a celebration when the maternal family may send pencils and other equipment. Mothers may also start regular meetings for age-mates at this time. Interestingly, the first-year pupils in their seventh year of life are involved especially on the festival of Tanabata, which takes place on the seventh of the seventh month,[24] when they are expected to practise the Chinese characters they have been learning at school. This seems now to have little connection with the legend that two crossed lovers who were turned into stars may meet on that one day of the year after being separated for the rest of time by the Milky Way.[25] Instead, the first-year pupils and their older siblings write out wishes on coloured pieces of paper which they hang on a bamboo branch to be displayed in the *tokonoma*. Water-melon is usually served and the children are given fireworks by their maternal relatives, though in one case in Kurotsuchi a paternal aunt made such gifts to her nephew, and in another a little girl received a blouse from her paternal great-aunt, so this is in no way limited.

By now, the child's life crises have taken on more of a concern for his or her individual progress than a representation of the strengthening of family ties. As the child becomes a full member of the community by attending school, the mother is drawn into the activities of the parent-teachers' group, which also gives her a community place in her own right. Gradually, then, the mother and her children become fully incorporated into village activities, and the mother's family, through celebrations connected with the children, are known and accepted as relatives of the household. While marriage redefines the household concerned and its relations with other households, birth and subsequent celebrations serve in part to emphasise and strengthen this redefinition, and in part to bring the new individuals involved into full membership of the community.

The Attainment of Adulthood

Since the war, a formal civic celebration takes place in every town and city of Japan on 15 January to welcome into adulthood all young people who have gained the age of twenty and thus the right to vote, smoke, drink, and bear responsibility for their own actions. Various civic dignitaries make speeches about the rights and duties of adulthood and the qualities of a good and upright adult citizen to an assembly of these young people, whose representatives reply and read poems and essays on the topic of becoming an adult. For many people questioned, the most striking feature of this occasion was concerned with dress, for attendance at the ceremony is made in the most formal attire. Girls wear a kimono which might cost in the region of several hundred thousand yen (several hundred pounds),[26] beside which the cost of a boy's new Western suit pales into insignificance. Photographs are taken of the young adults after the ceremony, in groups which graduated from the same middle school, and most of their families will purchase an expensive, hard-backed copy of this to keep with those of other important occasions. The Youth Group presents a small gift to each new adult to commemorate the occasion.

There would seem, however, to be a good deal more to becoming an adult than attendance at this civic ceremony. Indeed, one member of the village, a girl of the appropriate age of twenty, had married a few months earlier, and this change of status was legally sufficient (Article 753) to override the necessity of attending the ceremony at all. It would seem, in fact, to be marriage itself, rather than any national celebration, which brings community recognition of adulthood. Two cases in Kurotsuchi illustrate this. The house which was not recognised in 1975 as a household by the village was owned by a 27-year-old employed man, who was single, and, according to the village head, as soon as he married, his house would be included in village affairs. Another household, whose oldest male member was 28, was registered in the name of his mother 'until he marries'. This association of marriage with the attainment of adulthood has been noted by several writers.[27] In fact, marriage represents the completion of a transition period which begins as children leave school to take up training or employment.

In the past, this period was often spent in the *wakamonogumi*, which took an active part in arranging the marriages of its members (p. 23), as well as providing a good deal of community activity and training in the lore and skills required of villagers.[28] Entry into the group was often subject to the successful completion of initiation ordeals which typically involved physical tests, possibly a pilgrimage, and usually the sponsorship of a foster parent.[29] These were part of the ceremonies of adult initiation which usually took place at puberty or a fixed age such as thirteen or fifteen.[30] They marked the beginning of the transition to adulthood. After Meiji, celebrations associated with conscription into the military services became the mark of entry into adulthood, and these are reported by villagers to have been the predecessors of the present celebrations of 15 January.

It seems nowadays that young people enter the period of transition with graduation from school. At this time they begin specific training for their life ahead, they may now enter the Youth Group and, as members of such, they often take an active part in community affairs. Some boys, particularly first sons, are undecided for some time about their future. They may even spend a period living away from home. Other sons, who eventually expect to leave, often work for this period from their family home. Girls usually remain at home, even if they are working, but they are frequently thinking and planning ahead for the time when they will become housewives. As each young person marries, his or her future is decided. A boy will either agree to stay in the house, with a view to inheritance, or he will leave, either as a *yōshi*, or to set up his own home. A girl will marry out as a *yome* to another household, usually in another village, or she will agree to receive a *yōshi* and remain. At marriage, the future household and community is settled, and the individual achieves recognition as an adult permanent member of that household and community.

Yakudoshi *(Unlucky Years)*

No special ceremonies are held for the individual during the middle years of adult life, but there are certain ages which are regarded as especially vulnerable and inauspicious, during which care should be taken to avoid accidents and other misfortune. These are called *yakudoshi* (bad or unlucky years), and especially mentioned in Kurotsuchi are the 33rd year for a woman and the 41st for a man.[31] More generally these are said to be 33rd and 42nd, sometimes supplemented by 19th and 37th for women and 25th and 60th for men.[32] Villagers reported that sometimes people make a trip to a shrine in Kurume, perhaps as an age-mate group, preferably at the start of the year, in order to seek protection through the usual purification ceremony. It is possible that the origin of the shrine visit at 7-5-3 may have been of this type, since Wakamori suggests that seven was thought to be the first 'critical and climactic age'.[33] There does not seem to be a great deal of importance attached to these rites either, and one man in Inobu related how he and his age-mates had arrived in Kurume only to decide the fee charged by the shrine was too expensive, so they went to the horse races instead. It was commented, however, after the death of the 37-year-old farmer that his wife, who was 33 that year, had not been for a purification rite.

Kanreki *(Return of the Calendar) and Old Age*

The next celebration of a particular age in the life cycle is at 61. This is called *kanreki*, which means 'return of the calendar' since, according to the Chinese cycles of the zodiac (see Appendix), this is the first return of the same year in which a person was born. This was the year in which traditionally the head of the household and his wife passed on their duties to the younger generation,[34] thus returning to being dependants, this time on the younger rather than on the older generation. The occasion is referred to as a return to childhood, symbolised by the presentation to the person concerned of red garments of underwear, since red is a colour worn by children. These are usually given by the offspring, who are by now married and settled in their adult roles, settled in a network of links and relationships among themselves. A party may also be held in celebration. In Kurotsuchi, women are given a petticoat called a *koshimaki*, the same garment which was given to a girl of this area at seven and elsewhere at puberty, so there is a clear parallel, which was mentioned by informants. Another local parallel with the 7-5-3 ceremony, which is not mentioned by other writers, is that both may involve a visit to the shrine for the purificatory rite. These two occasions, linked in the minds of informants, could be interpreted as part of the marking of entry into and exit from full participation in community life. I accompanied one Kurotsuchi woman to a shrine in Kurume in her 61st year and the rite closely resembled that for children. She paid the fee, for which the priest made supplications to the deity, which included mention of her name and place of origin. She was then offered the ceremonial *sake*, which is the ritual feast, and also given an amulet, some cakes and a pair of chopsticks. There was a notice in the shrine which indicated the ages at which individuals are especially in need of such rites, particularly the *yakudoshi*, and interestingly enough 61 was not among them for women, only for men. However, the priest did not complain, neither did he object to the informant's insistence on the inclusion of the author, though my age was not one indicated for either sex. This woman had received the money for her trip to Kurume from a young relative who lived away in Nagoya. Another family held a formal celebration in their home on the first day of the year in which the two grandparents would become 61. This was organised by the three children, two of whom returned from some distance for the occasion. A feast was served, ceremonial *sake* drunk, and *utai* were sung. Sometimes red and white rice-cakes are distributed among members of the *tonari kinjo* after such a family celebration.

Just as age celebrations are frequent at the beginning of life, so it seems are they at the end. After 61, there may be further similar gatherings at 77 and 88 in Kurotsuchi, and as well as these, at 79, 80, 90 and 100 elsewhere.[35] The one at 88 seems to be the most important. It is known as the 'rice celebration' since the character for 'rice' (米) may be regarded as an inverted 8 (八) over 10 (十) over another 8. I witnessed none, but typically these occasions are said to involve invitations to relatives and neighbours and the distribution of red and white rice-cakes.

Death and Ancestor Memorials

When a person dies, neighbours and relatives gather to make preparations for the funeral. Equipment is borrowed from the temple and an altar is set up at one end of the main room of the house. This is brightly lit with lanterns sent by relatives of the dead, and often adorned with flowers, especially in the chrysanthemum season. The body is washed with alcohol by the spouse, parents, siblings and children, in order to purify the corpse, which is then dressed in a white kimono fastened the opposite way to usual, and laid out facing north, a direction usually avoided.[36] A printed version of the fee, said to be required to cross the river dividing this world from the next, is tied in a bag around the neck, together with a bowl of rice for the journey. The coffin is laid in front of the altar, and in the evening, representatives of every house in the village come round to express their condolences to the family, who receive the visitors and explain the circumstances of death. A sum of money is presented in a black-banded envelope, and, when a few days have passed, the household sends round return gifts worth about one third of that received, or alternatively, sends an equivalent sum to the city welfare fund. The first night, the bereaved usually sit up with the corpse, a practice called *otsuya*, which resembles the wake practised in some Roman Catholic countries.

The following day the body is cremated, by law more than 24 hours after death,[37] and the family returns with a box of ashes which is placed on the altar for the funeral. This is usually held the day after death, but there is one day in the six-day cycle of the old Chinese calendar (*tomobiki*) which is held to be inauspicious for funerals since the dead may drag another with it on that day, so it is avoided. A Buddhist priest is called to officiate, and the gathering of relatives, workmates, neighbours and other associates often spills out of the house so that the priest's voice is relayed to them by loudspeaker. A container holding burning incense is passed round, first to relatives in order of proximity and age,[38] then gradually to everyone present, each of whom adds a pinch more to the fire, thus making a symbolic farewell or separation (*wakare*) with the deceased.

As Embree has pointed out, neighbours and relatives are distinguished at funerals since the former take over the practical details and the latter assemble to mourn and participate in the rituals.[39] Members of the *tonari kinjo* group serve tea and snacks before the ceremony starts. They also keep a record of everyone who attends, handing out a handkerchief and a printed acknowledgement from official mourners to each person as they arrive. Chief mourners of the same household are mentioned by name, but even close family who have left are represented on this card by the name of the head of their new household. Thus, at the funeral of an old lady, her daughter's name was not mentioned, rather that of her father-in-law. A list of representatives of relatives (*shinzoku daihyo*) indicates clearly the households which are in a first-order relationship with that of the deceased, whether affinal or consanguineal. Thus the names shown are those of the heads of the households of, for example, the mother, sisters, daughters, son's wife and wife (or *yōshi*) of the deceased, even if the spouse is already mentioned by name as chief mourner. The list of attendance is kept by the family and referred to in future so that reciprocal attentions can be paid to the families represented. Within the village, it is only to the wake that every house sends someone. Attendance at the funeral is more variable. If a woman dies, all the village women whose households share the same temple attend the funeral as members of the temple women's group, and, for both sexes, there will be someone there from at least every house in the *tonarigumi*. When the parent of schoolchildren died, a group of the children's classmates was taken to the funeral by a teacher. Age-mates of the deceased are certainly present, where possible, and these may take an active part in helping the afflicted family. Much seemed to depend on the case, and on the affiliations which the deceased had in life, so it was difficult for people to lay down general rules.

After the funeral, visitors may well throw salt[40] on their clothes 'to prevent the soul from sticking to them', and members of the deceased's household are regarded as particularly polluted and therefore subject to various prohibitions. Sometimes the soul is said at this stage to be reluctant to leave on its journey to the Buddhist paradise of *Gokuraku* and to be staying close to the roof of the house.[41] Further rites should therefore be held every seven days for seven weeks, until *hibare* or *hi no hare*,[42] the name given to the 49th day after death, when the pollution period ends and the soul is said to be safely converted into a *hotokesama*. During this time, a notice is pinned up on door of the house which indicates that the occupants are in mourning or, literally, under pollution taboos (*kichū*). A piece of plain white paper is pinned up over the *kamidana*, and members of the family should not visit the shrine compound.[43] Dietary restrictions are usually observed for a few days, in particular a ban on meat and fish, but few people continue for the whole 49 days. The seven-day rites are usually limited now to the first, when a posthumous name is given, the fourth called *hatsumeinichi* (first death-day) celebrated on the same date of the following month as death occurred, and the seventh. On each of these occasions the priest is called to perform a *kuyō* (memorial service) in front of the *butsudan*. On at least one of these occasions, a feast is held to repay the relatives, who brought gifts, and neighbours, who helped at the funeral. A specific example will illustrate the way such obligations are discharged, and also again how they are obligations to households rather than to individuals.

Special attentions are also made to the memory of the deceased on the first celebration of the Bon festival (see pp. 215-16) in the year after death, and this was so close to the *hatsumeinichi*, one month after the death of a certain old lady, that her household combined the two dates in one gathering. After the priest had finished his prayers, tables were laid up for a feast and gifts were arranged at each place under the table. The chief guests were as follows: the head of the family into which the deceased's daughter had married, in fact her husband's father; the head of the household's *honke*, who had downed tools immediately on learning of the death and spent the rest of the day making preparations for the funeral; the head of another *bunke* of the same *honke*, both descendants of the brothers of the deceased's father; the head of the household from which the deceased's mother had married into the present household (the deceased had no brothers and she received a *yōshi*); and members of the households of the *yōshi* husband of the deceased, and of that from which her son's wife had come. The actual relationship between the deceased and even the four topmost guests was quite distant: DHF, FBSS, FBSDH, and MZSS, but these represented quite clearly households which had a first-order relationship with the household of the deceased. Later in the afternoon, members of the *tonari kinjo* households, who also helped on the day of the funeral, were invited to take part and receive some kind of return for their efforts. In the kitchen helping during the day were the wives of the same *honke* and *bunke* guests at the table, the daughter of the deceased, and other female relatives including the son's wife's sisters, all of whom ate a very inferior meal in a side room after the chief guests had been served. Later, however, at the celebration 100 days after death, these helpers too were served by the family in return, and the obligations incurred at the funeral were properly discharged.

The celebration 100 days after death is the first of a further series of rites, again for the benefit of the soul, to which a priest is also called to perform a *kuyō*. These continue on the anniversary of death after one, three, seven, 13, 25, 33 and 50 years.[44] The descendants of the individual should gather on these occasions, share a vegetarian meal, and perhaps visit together the *nōkotsudō* where the remains are kept. Members of the *tonari kinjo* may also be invited to drink tea, or be sent cakes, on these occasions. Such rites may cease when no one remembers the individual concerned, or if a subsequent death day is designated for the memory of more than one individual, although diligent families will remember their dead on every *meinichi*, perhaps making special offerings to the *butsudan*, if not actually calling a priest. If the rites are faithfully observed until the 50th anniversary, this becomes a happy occasion (*iwai*),[45] signified by the consumption of meat or fish. The departed spirit is then allowed to merge with the other ancestors, remembered as the general category of *senzo*, and the related households created during his generation of marriages have usually moved into the category of *mukashi no shinseki* (distant relatives). In practice, of course, some relatives will stop attending memorials long before the 50th anniversary of the death of their linking ancestral relative, particularly if they have moved away, and other households will maintain close relations and mutual aid even after such time. In general, however, this is the last formal occasion that households linked since that time would meet as such a group, although a general *senzo matsuri* may be held annually among a wider group of more distantly related families in the same village.

Annual Festivals

Regular occasions for members of related households to visit each other are provided annually during the celebration of festivals. A certain amount of visiting takes place during village shrine festivals, described in Chapter 2, but by far the most important times for this activity are the national holiday celebrations at New Year in the winter, and Bon in the summer. On both these occasions previous members of a household return if possible to pay respects to their own ancestors. *Bunke* members pay formal visits to their *honke*, wives and *yōshi* take a few hours or even a couple of days to visit the household of their birth, and long-distance trains are jammed with holiday-makers which include among their numbers many urban migrants and their families returning to visit their villages of origin. A day or two on each of these occasions usually finds households temporarily transported back to a previous generation of occupants, now usually scattered in their new circumstances, but joined once again briefly as they were during childhood.

Although these two festivals are said by some scholars originally to have been identical occasions for remembering the ancestors, which divided the year exactly into two,[46] there are now a number of clear differences. They will thus be considered separately.

Shōgatsu *(New Year)*

This is without doubt the most celebrated time of the Japanese year. During the last weeks of the old year, all debts are paid, unfinished business transacted and other affairs brought into order. Properties are thoroughly cleaned out, and food is prepared for the visits of the first few days, when women should do no housework. Special rice-cakes are made in vast quantities, some of which are decorated and offered to the *kamidana* and various other deities around the household, typically Kōjin, a kitchen god, and Suijin, who protects the water. Less specifically, offerings are placed in all the motor vehicles for safety, on children's desks for luck and aid with their studies, and in places which may be dangerous, such as the shed where gas cylinders are kept in the shopkeeper's household. Much symbolism is associated with these New Year offerings, which are concerned with the year ahead: for example, a fern is placed under the rice-cakes to symbolise prosperity for the *ie*, a vine leaf is added for health, and on top, a *daidai* variety of orange is placed because *dai* also means 'generation', and this therefore symbolises the continuity of generations in the future.[47]

Little attention seems to be paid to celebrating the actual change of year at midnight. New Year's Eve, now celebrated according to Western dates, on 31 December, is spent watching a special three-hour television variety show in many homes in Kurotsuchi, although newly-weds take a present to their in-laws. Buddhist temples play their only part at this time of mostly Shinto and folk activity by tolling out the old year with 108 booms of the large temple bell, which are said to represent the 108 worldly passions (*bonnō*) one must try anew to control in the New Year. Some young people climb one of the nearby peaks to see the first sunrise, but for most people celebrations begin at breakfast when the family joins in a toast of spiced sake (*tososhū*), said to protect from illness, and each makes a formal congratulatory greeting to the others. This greeting, which is repeated as each acquaintance is met for the first time in the New Year, includes the phrase 'kotoshi mo onegai shimasu' ('this year, too, please'), which seems to represent a formal renewal of the relationship.

Men are supposed to rise first, light the fire under the rice, and present the rice-cake offering to the *kamidana*, informants explained, though many added that this was only the theory, and the first riser, was, as usual, the daughter-in-law. In one household, the latter woke her father-in-law, who then proceeded to do his duty. The first day of the year is a quiet one, often spent at home with the family, perhaps including sons and daughters returned from far-off homes for the occasion, and no work is supposed to be done. Shops are closed, some for their only holiday of the year, but everyone goes out to make their first prayer at the village shrines, and possibly at the *nōkotsudō* too.

Others climb a nearby hill to pray at a shrine or image at the top, but it is said in Kurotsuchi that women should not really go out on the first day, for this sets a precedent for the whole year.[48] New Year cards sent between dates in December advertised by the Post Office are delivered on the first, but these are not sent and few are received by families who have been bereaved during the year. This is a happy occasion, an occasion for congratulation, and, as such, must not be confused with death and mourning. In one household which had lost a member during the year, the grandfather explained that he had sprinkled salt around the house first thing to purify the place and remove the pollution of death.

During the first few days, women often dress in kimono. A traditional activity observed is to visit three Shinto shrines in the area,[49] appropriate ones sometimes chosen in accordance with directions determined auspicious for that year by the calendar. Talismans are purchased and brought home to the *kamidana*, and in this way good fortune, health and luck for important ventures expected during the year, is said to be accrued. Throughout the first half of January, rites of the New Year continue, even after everyone has gone back to work. On the seventh, a special soup is made with seven herbs, on the 11th, the age-mate groups hold their first meeting of the year and check their books, on the 15th there is the civic ceremony for the new adults of the community, and only on the 17th[50] are all the decorations burned and the festivities officially brought to a close. After this a new *yome* or *yōshi* may be allowed to visit home for a few nights.

Bon[51]

Bon is a three-day period in midsummer when the souls of departed ancestors are said to return. Extra offerings are made to the *butsudan*, perhaps of things that the dead liked,[52] although packets of noodles, sugar, fruit or powdered-rice-cakes are typical gifts taken by visitors to the ancestors. This is also a time when gifts may be made to people to whom one feels an obligation of some sort. In Kurotsuchi, every household in the village sends a small gift, usually money wrapped in an appropriate black-banded envelope,[53] to families which have been bereaved during the previous year. These are celebrating *hatsubon*, the first Bon after a death, when before the *butsudan* are set up the lanterns which were received for the funeral. Many visitors usually call at this time and a large pile of presents and offerings collect in front of it. A big family gathering is likely to be held in such houses, which may also choose, if convenient, to discharge some of the obligations they incurred at the funeral at this time.

These three days are taken as holiday by most people, but in Kurotsuchi in 1975 they coincided with three days of warm dry weather after a period of rain which had impeded the planting of chrysanthemum seedlings for the New Year crop, so that many farmers were out in their fields, except for the actual hours when visitors had to be entertained. They were a little sheepish about working on these days,[54] providing excuses at the first opportunity, but determined too to set their fields in order for the biggest crop of the year.

Informants explained that on the third day of Bon a candle-lit procession used to accompany the souls back the the graveyard, when these were still used, but now visits are made to the temple and the *nōkotsudō*. In many parts of the country special Bon dances are held on the evening of this last day, and in Yame, where lanterns are manufactured, a big dance is held in front of the ruins of the old castle, the shape of which is reconstructed out of hundreds of lanterns. Similar smaller dancing sessions are held in front of the *nōkotsudō* in several other parts of the city.

House-building

Just as marriage provides a redefinition of the internal composition of the household, house-building is concerned with the redefinition (or definition in the case of a new family) of its accommodation, its external composition. Again, just as for a wedding, everyone in the village sends a gift, and many are more directly involved. In Chapter 3 the type of construction was described, and it was noted that these houses need replacing about once in the lifetime of a single inhabitant, although recent affluence has encouraged more reconstruction than there might otherwise have been. There were thus several families in the village who were involved during the study in some stage of this redefinition, for although the actual building takes only a few months, the complete process, from planning to final celebration, may take a couple of years.

The first stage is to make plans with a carpenter. This is a matter of some complexity, since various rules of geomancy must be taken into consideration to avoid future misfortune in the house, and an *ogami-yasan* may also be consulted at this time. These ideas are based on originally Chinese theories of yin and yang and the five elements, as well as the 12 zodiacal periods (see Appendix) and the location of a certain deity named Konjin.[55] Carpenters are able to allow for these factors to some extent by consulting a guide, and a Kurotsuchi master of the trade showed me a flat perspex piece of equipment, resembling a protractor, which, if placed correctly on a house plan, would indicate the lucky and unlucky places for various parts of the house. The centre of the building is the principal post (*daikokubashira*), and from here, the north-east corner is the most inauspicious place, known as 'demons' gate corner' (*kimonzumi*), unlucky for the kitchen or lavatory, but a good place for the protective *butsudan* or *kamidana*. The opposite south-west corner is called the demons' back gate (*urakimon*), and it is said to be associated with women, who would fall sick if the lavatory were placed here. According to Norbeck, these are directions associated with Konjin, who would be offended and cause harm if 'unclean' places were located there,[56] and other writers note that the north-east is an unlucky direction for doors, gates or windows too.[57] Certain temples in Kyoto and Tokyo are said to be in the north-east to protect the cities, and Jōya's explanation is that the north-east was in China said to divide the opposing elements of yin and yang, such as day and night, positive and negative.[58]

Another common idea is that the front of the house should not face north, and this is illustrated clearly in Kurotsuchi, where the east-west road has a pleasant row of house fronts to the north, but just a series of backs to the south. The usual explanation is that north is avoided because the dead are laid out with their heads to the north, but this does not explain why that should be so.[59] With such considerations in mind, then, the householders and the carpenter plan the new construction. The following description provides an example of the procedure which follows.[60] As is often the case, it involved a family with children in the transition period between school-leaving and marriage, so that the new house is ready for the redefinition of its internal composition.

An auspicious day for demolition was fixed, which was then made known by the house head to all his relatives, neighbours and acquaintances. At 8 a.m. on the appointed day helpers began to arrive, proceeding straight to work by climbing up on to the roof to dismantle the tiles. In the work-shed of a neighbouring relative's house, women were beginning to sort out provisions for the day's meals. The wife of the household concerned had been adopted as a child by the now deceased barren couple from whom she and her husband had inherited, her husband being received as a *yōshi* from the next village of Tachiyama. The women in the 'kitchen' were mainly close family of the two, including the wife's mother, her sister, her brother's wife and her husband's brothers' wives. These worked together with apparent harmony, nobody giving orders or allocating tasks, but everybody managing to find something to keep them occupied most of the day. They set up tables, prepared and laid out two main meals and two snacks for the work-force of about thirty men, served them, and ate their own meals amongst the debris left after the house-demolishers had finished. Over at the house, work also proceeded without much evidence of direction, the house-owner himself wandering rather forlornly from place to place as the building was gradually dismantled. The helpers included relatives from the actual families of the husband and wife, as well as from households related to their household through the barren grandparents, one member per household of the *tonari kinjo*, and the age-mates of the husband. There were also a few other people, who explained that the house-owner had helped at their house-building so they were providing reciprocal aid, which is an example of how a man can save up a certain amount of aid by investing in the works of others.

The work of demolition was completed by lunch-time on the following day, and the ground was cleared. New foundations were then to be laid by professionals, and it was not until three weeks later that a similar gathering was held for the official first day of building. Meanwhile, a Shinto priest was called to perform a purification ceremony. He first constructed an altar in the middle of the site, putting a big *sakaki* branch in the middle with four bamboo branches at the corners of the square surrounding it. A thin straw rope was hung all round this to mark off the sacred area, and a table was set before it for offerings. These included rice, salt, water, dried fish and vegetables, as usual items thought necessary to sustain human life, *sake*, and a special fresh fish. The priest complained that there should, by rights, be two fish since they are supposed to represent the husband and wife of the household, and placed stomach to stomach, they symbolise the continuation of the household through descendants. The priest then prepared his *gohei*, a staff decorated with streamers of paper used in all Shinto ceremony, which he later left to be hung in the entrance porch of the new house. Meanwhile the carpenters had marked off the space which would eventually be the area covered by the house, laid a post across the *kimonzumi*, and arranged a pile of earth and their instruments by the table. Only the carpenters, the head and his wife took part in this ceremony, although the Shinto priest noted that ideally the plasterers should be there too.[61] He explained that the main purpose of the rite is to inform the deities of the earth, of carpentry, of water, the sun and protection, that this person intends to build a house on that site, to apologise for disturbing the earth, and to ask them to bring no harm upon the workers involved or the members of the household concerned.

When he was ready to begin, the priest called the participants to the east of his table, which faced north, and first chanted to summon the deities concerned. He then purified the altar, the earth and instruments, and the assembled people, by shaking his staff over them. This was followed by a longer chant at the altar, some of which was read from a scroll, which stated what was occurring at that site and requested benevolence and protection. The priest then took his staff again and shook it in each corner of the territory, starting with the *kimonzumi*, and proceeding to the well. After this the household and the carpenters performed symbolic tasks with the tools, and then the priest and each of the participants took a little *sakaki* branch and presented it to the altar, completing their worship with a bow and a clap in the usual way. The priest then tied up his long sleeves and distributed the offerings, shaking a little rice, water and *sake* over the pile of earth, the altar itself, the four corners and the well, finishing by drinking some *sake* as an *omiki*[62] and handing a cupful to each of the participants. Later, some other relatives and the children of the household came to the altar, bowed, clapped, and partook of the offerings.

This ceremony contains the usual Shinto elements occurring also at purification of the shrine at festivals, at the marriage ceremony, and at 7-5-3, varying only in the detail concerned with the particular event. The ceremony before house-building may also be a Buddhist affair, however, a procedure followed by the Sōka Gakkai households and also apparently by a household of the Nichiren sect in the village. In Suye Mura the rite was performed by a *kitōshi* (praying priest),[63] the specialist known in this area as an *ogamiyasan*, who is sometimes consulted about geomancy, sickness and marriage prospects. Such a specialist also performed rites for one house which was extensively modernised in 1979 in Kurotsuchi.

A similar person was consulted in this case about an auspicious day for the building to commence, but the best day clashed with the summer festival in Tachiyama, so it was changed. To be on the safe side, however, the family decided with the carpenters to erect one post of the building on the most auspicious day, that chosen being the corner post in the *kimonzumi*. Another illustration of the concern with possible upset to the deities during house-building was provided when the housewife involved here found that her ankles were swollen shortly after the house had been knocked down. She thought that this might be retribution from some deity for their having demolished the old house, and went to consult the *ogamiyasan* about it. However, she was reassured that it was no such thing, and her ankles apparently returned to normal of their own accord.

Early on the day finally fixed for building, people began to gather at the house site. The posts for the framework of the house had been fashioned at the carpenters' workshop and were piled up waiting to be assembled. As people arrived, the housewife gave them each a towel died red at one end (*hachimaki*), to symbolise the *iwai* or ceremonial happiness associated with their labour on this occasion. They were also given a cup of *sake*, the *omiki* from the purification rite, and a pinch of salt, rice and the fishes which had been offered to the deities, to protect them from injury during the day. Work could then commence, and as most people tied their towels around their straw hats, there was a gay atmosphere to suit the occasion. There were more people helping than at demolition, and apparently anyone in the village with the time and inclination goes along, confident that the more times they help, the more aid they will receive when it is their turn to rebuild. Three women joined the men for building this time. They were representing their households in the *tonarigumi*, and although they started off helping with the catering, they must have decided they were superfluous there and moved to other tasks.

Other people arrived throughout the day with bottles of *sake*, boxes of beer, or money in the red-banded envelopes used for *iwai*. Every household in the village takes a gift of some sort, and as these were received, the housewife sent back little parcels of bean-cakes as a return gesture. A similar parcel was given to each helper as they left. This is a practice found at most gatherings, which ensures that people do not leave empty-handed and provides them with something to share out from the occasion when they return home.

The framework took about a day to assemble and the shape of the roof was discernible by evening, leaving the tiling to be completed the following day.[64] The main ridge roof-beam (*mune*) was inscribed with the date of construction and the names of the owner and carpenter. As the roofing was nearing completion on the second day, children and passers-by began to gather in front of the house. Over in the cooking area, pink and white rice-cakes were being prepared by the dozen, some rolled with a small coin inside, the total amount being 333 *yen* (some 50p) it was said. The head carpenter explained that this was for the completion of the purification rite which had been carried out by the Shinto priest at ground level. Now that the roof was in place, he and the house head would climb to the top, erect three branches of bamboo, and offer 12 specially prepared rice-cakes to the deities, one for each month of the year. They then sprinkled rice, salt and small fish over the house, as the priest had done below, offered one wrapped rice-cake to the house head, and finally hurled into the air the dozens of other cakes, including the ones containing coins, for the waiting people to scramble for below. The head carpenter explained that this was to protect the occupants of the house from sickness and misfortune; one of the participants added that it was to give the house a birthday, and an apparent but unmentioned effect was to allow anyone in the village to participate on this happy occasion, collecting rice-cakes to enjoy later at home.

The rest of the construction is carried out by professionals, who complete their work in about two or three months. Many people buy a good deal of new equipment to match the new wood, so that a complete return to order may take longer than the construction itself. Once finished, however, the final celebration may be held. This is the *shinchiku iwai* (new-building celebration), at which the carpenters and plasterers have seats of honour and are given gifts, money, or both, if the members of the household are pleased with their new home. Relatives too are invited, a feast is served, and *utai* are sung. On one occasion, the head carpenter sang first, his cup being presented to the head and only man of the house; a male relative sang second, and his cup was taken to the older woman; and a female relative sang the final *utai*, after which her cup was taken to the younger woman of the house. All this followed a formal statement of thanks for the work of the previous year from the head of the house, and was followed by feasting, drinking and less formal community-type singing. The guests leave with gifts, perhaps plates or a tea-pot, and a parcel of cakes to share out when they get home.

It can be seen, then, that this is an event which involves no mean amount of ceremony. The redefinition of the house, just like the redefinition of its occupants, is fraught with possible dangers and adverse consequences. Propitiation of supernatural powers is required, as is the involvement of all the relatives and neighbours. As an occasion which prompts a gift from every household in the village, it is to be ranked only with marriage and death. Members of neighbourhood and age-mate groups offer their aid with only a long-term return in view. Relatives are entertained in the final finished product, together with the workmen responsible for it, who are feasted and gifted in a manner much greater than that required of a merely economic contract. The house is the external manifestation of the *ie*, the most important and basic unit of society, and as such, its reconstruction is an event of considerable moment.

Notes

1. This practice dates back at least to the Edo period since it was included in the *Sho-rei Hikki* (*Record of Ceremonies*) (published 1706 by Hayashi Rissai, translated in Lord Redesdale, *Tales of Old Japan* (Macmillan, London, 1908), p. 357); cf. C. Pfoundes, 'On Some Rites and Customs of Old Japan', *Journal of the Anthropological Institute*, vol. 12 (1882), p. 223. It appears since to have been widespread. See, for example, Robert J. Smith, 'Kurusu' in J.B. Cornell and R.J. Smith, *Two Japanese Villages* (Greenwood Press, New York, 1969), p. 70; Edward Norbeck, *Takashima* (University of Utah Press, Salt Lake City, 1954), p. 164; William Erskine, *Japanese Customs* (Kyo Bun Kwan, Tokyo, 1925), pp. 1-2; *Japanese Festivals and Calendar Lore* (Kyo Bun Kwan, Tokyo, 1933), p. 151; Yutaka Chikushi, *Nihon no Minzoku* (*Folklore of Japan*) no. 40, (Fukuoka, Tokyo, 1974), p. 189; Jukichi Inouye, *Home Life in Tokyo* (Tokyo, 1910), pp. 220-1.

2. Mock Jōya, *Japanese Customs and Manners* (The Sakurai Shoten, Tokyo, 1955), pp. 20-1, reports that in the eighth century the Empress Kōmyō made the Hoke [*sic*] temple in Nara give clay dogs to pregnant women for a smooth delivery; and sometimes a pair of dog-shaped powder boxes called *inu-bako* (dog-box) were taken as part of the bridal trousseau. Papier-maché dogs are also given to newborn babies to symbolise healthy growth.

3. This custom seems to be quite widespread (Tokuzō Omachi, 'Kon'in' ('Marriage') in T. Omachi *et al.* (eds.), *Nihon Minzokugaku Taikei* (Heibonsha, Tokyo, 1962), p. 193; Takao Sofue, 'Childhood Ceremonies in Japan', *Ethnology*, vol. 4 (1965), pp. 149-50). Ichiro Kurata, 'Rural Marriage Customs in Japan', *Contemporary Japan*, vol. 10 (1941), p. 375, saw it as possibly related to an older practice where the bride stayed at home until she became the housewife when her husband inherited. Takeyoshi Kawashima, *Kekkon* (*Marriage*) (Iwanami Shoten, Tokyo, 1954), pp. 80-1, suggests that the way the wife's family provides her with things needed at the time of childbirth, as well as having her home for the birth itself, indicates that the bride is like a servant in her husband's home in the early part of her marriage.

4. This custom has also been very widely reported, for example, Geoffrey Bownas, *Japanese Rainmaking and Other Folk Practices* (Allen and Unwin, London, 1963), p. 68; Hiroshi Fujisaki, *Kankonsōsai Jiten* (*Dictionary of Ceremonial*) (Tsuru Shobo, Tokyo, 1957), p. 226; Inouye, *Home Life in Tokyo*, p. 223; Norbeck, *Takashima*, p. 167; Smith, 'Kurusu', p. 70; Alice M. Bacon, *Japanese Girls and Women* (Gay and Bird, London, 1891), p. 3; Erskine, *Japanese Festivals*, p. 151, although naming is occasionally said to take place on the third day (Shōji Inoguchi, 'Tanjō to Ikuji' ('Childbirth and Infant Care') in Omachi *et al.* (eds.), *Nihon Minzokugaku Taikei*, p. 208; John F. Embree, *Suye Mura* (University of Chicago Press, 1939), p. 180; Sofue, 'Childhood Ceremonies', p. 150. Redesdale (*Old Japan*, p. 380) adds, of the Edo period, that the name was changed again on the attainment of adulthood with the cutting of the forelock. The baby's head used to be shaved on the seventh day (B.H. Chamberlain, *Things Japanese* (John Murray, London, 1902), p. 92; Naomi Tamura, *The Japanese Bride* (Harper and Bros., New York and London, 1904), p. 82.)

5. Cf. Norbeck, *Takashima*, p. 167.

6. This is a local word to mark the end of the pollution period (cf. Chikushi, *Nihon no Minzoku*, p. 192), elsewhere known as *hiaki* (Sofue, 'Childhood Ceremonies', p. 152; Morimitsu Ushijima, *Nihon no Minzoku*, no. 43 (Kumamoto), p. 219; Edward Norbeck, 'Pollution and Taboo in Contemporary Japan', *Southwestern Journal of Anthropology*, vol. 8 (1952), p. 281; Embree, *Suye Mura*, p. 183) and *kiake* (Bun Nakajima, *Japanese Etiquette* (Japan Travel Bureau,

Tokyo, 1955), p. 157). The number of days varies too (Sofue, 'Childhood Ceremonies', pp. 152-3; Inoguchi, 'Tanjō to Ikuji', p. 209; Fujisaki, *Kankonsōsai Jiten*, p. 227; Chikushi, *Nihon no Minzoku*, p. 192), and, according to a local Shinto priest, it should be 31 days for a girl, not 33 as said in Kurotsuchi.

7. It is reported that in the past there used to be separate parturition and menstruation huts in parts of Japan, to which the mother was confined during the pollution period (Kunio Yanagida, *Japanese Manners and Customs in the Meiji Era*, trans. and adapted by Charles S. Terry (Obunsha, Tokyo, 1957), p. 201; Kizaemon Ariga, *Nihon Kon'in Shiron* (*A Study of the History of Marriage in Japan*) (Nikko Shoin, Tokyo, 1948), pp. 65-9; Donald Philippi, *Kojiki* (trans.) (University of Tokyo Press, Tokyo, 1969), p. 66; G.B. Sansom, *Japan: a Short Cultural History* (The Cresset Press, London, 1952), p. 51; Inoguchi, 'Tanjō to Ikuji', p. 203).

8. Cf. Norbeck, 'Pollution and Taboo', pp. 271-3, 276-7; *Takashima*, pp. 140-1; Inoguchi, 'Tanjō to Ikuji', pp. 202-6; Carmen Blacker, *The Catalpa Bow* (Allen and Unwin, London, 1975), p. 42; Toshiaki Harada, 'Nyonin Kinsei' ('Prohibitions on Women'), *Shakai to Denshō*, vol. 2, no. 4 (1958), pp. 162-71; Kiyoko Segawa, 'Menstrual Taboos imposed upon Women' in Richard M. Dorson, *Studies in Japanese Folklore* (Kennikat Press, Port Washington, New York, London, 1973), pp. 239-50. This seems to be a common explanation (Bownas, *Japanese Rainmaking*, p. 69; Sofue, 'Childhood Ceremonies', p. 153), but in some areas the periods of pollution are identical, and, in a few, the period for a boy baby even longer than for a girl (Sofue, 'Childhood Ceremonies', p. 153).

9. *Miya* is shrine, *mairi* is visit for the purpose of worship or prayer. This custom has also been widely reported (Tamura, *The Japanese Bride*, pp. 83-4; Yanagida, *Manners and Customs*, p. 203; Erskine, *Japanese Customs*, p. 3; *Japanese Festivals*, p. 152; Bacon, *Japanese Girls and Women*, p. 4).

10. Further necessities, such as a baby's mattress, a chest of drawers for its clothes, napkins, etc. are often also provided by the parents of the mother or *yōshi* (cf. Kawashima's comments in footnote 3 of this chapter).

11. Cf. Yanagida, *Manners and Customs*, p. 203; Inoguchi, 'Tanjō to Ikuji', p. 209; Sofue, 'Childhood Ceremonies', p. 152.

12. Cf. Norbeck, *Takashima*, p. 157; Sofue, 'Childhood Ceremonies', p. 158; Chikushi, *Nihon no Minzoku*, p. 196.

13. The number of days varies between 100 and 120 (Sofue, 'Childhood Ceremonies', p. 153; Inoguchi, 'Tanjō to Ikuji', p. 210; Fujisaki, *Kankonsōsai Jiten*, p. 227; Chikushi, *Nihon no Minzoku*, p. 193; Inouye, *Home Life in Tokyo*, p. 225; Redesdale, *Old Japan*, p. 376).

14. These are two of the five traditional festivals, held also on the first or seventh of the first month (New Year), the seventh of the seventh month (Tanabata), and the ninth of the ninth month (Chrysanthemum Festival). Much historical detail of an anecdotal nature is given in U.A. Casal, *The Five Sacred Festivals of Ancient Japan* (Tuttle and Sophia University, Tokyo, 1967). See also Ernest Clement, 'Calendar (Japanese)' in James Hastings (ed.), *Encyclopaedia of Religion and Ethics* (Edinburgh, 1910), Vol. 3, p. 116, and Erskine, *Japanese Customs*, p. 4. These festivals were cancelled in 1873 (Yanagida, *Manners and Customs*, p. 260), but the third of March is still celebrated as the dolls' festival and the fifth of May as Children's Day.

15. More details of these dolls, the warrior dolls given to boys, and the associated celebrations, are to be found in, for example, Casal, *Five Sacred Festivals*, pp. 36-78; Fujisaki, *Kankonsōsai Jiten*, pp. 190-3, 197-201; Norbeck, *Takashima*, pp. 148-51; Inouye, *Home Life in Tokyo*, pp. 292-3, 297-8.

16. Some old people still reckon their ages in this way, especially if they wish to emphasise their age rather than their youth.

17. This seems to be a local custom, and elsewhere a baby is made to walk with rice-cakes on its back (Sofue, 'Childhood Ceremonies', pp. 154-6; Ushijima, *Nihon no Minzoku*, p. 220), or with enough rice on its back to make it fall if it can walk alone, since it is said to be inauspicious to walk so early (Inouye, *Home Life in Tokyo*, p. 225).

18. These include previous rites for the termination of a child's head-shaving, for the boy's first *hakama* (garment like a divided skirt worn as part of men's indigenous dress), and for a girl's first *obi* (kimono sash). See, for example, Redesdale, *Old Japan*, pp. 377-8; Chamberlain, *Things Japanese*, p. 161; Fujisaki, *Kankonsōsai Jiten* p. 217; Erskine, *Japanese Customs*, p. 3; Jōya, *Japanese Customs*, p. 179.

19. The casual attitude to these rites supports Sofue's findings that ceremonies involving social interaction with neighbours and relatives are more often held than those concerned with mere 'supernatural effect' (p. 159).

20. Cf. Chikushi, *Nihon no Minzoku*, p. 196; Tarō Wakamori, 'Initiation Rites and Young Men's Organizations' in Dorson (ed.), *Studies in Japanese Folklore*, p. 295.

21. Wakamori, 'Initiation Rites', pp. 292-3; Ariga, *Nihon Kon'in Shiron*, p. 52; Omachi, 'Seinenshiki' ('Coming of Age') in Omachi *et al.* (eds.), *Nihon Minzokugaku Taikei*, p. 240; Sofue, 'Childhood Ceremonies', pp. 156-7; Hitoshi Miyake, 'Folk Religion' in I. Hori *et al.* (eds.), *Japanese Religion*, trans. Yoshiya Abe and David Reid (Kodansha International, Tokyo and Palo Alto, 1972), p. 133.

22. Wakamori, 'Initiation Rites', p. 295; Edward Norbeck, 'Age-Grading in Japan', *American Anthropologist*, vol. 55 (1953), p. 374. Court nobles in the Heian period celebrated an adult initiation rite as early as this (Wakamori, p. 295), as did Tokugawa *shōgun* families (Omachi, 'Seinenshiki', p. 230).

23. Sofue, 'Childhood Ceremonies', p. 156.

24. This connection of sevens was pointed out by a schoolgirl informant as a possible explanation of why first-year pupils were particularly involved at this time.

25. More details of this festival are to be found in Fujisaki, *Kankonsōsai Jiten*, pp. 206-7; Casal, *Five Sacred Festivals*, pp. 79-94; Jōya, *Japanese Customs*, pp. 90-2; Bownas, *Japanese Rainmaking*, pp. 95-7; Embree, *Suye Mura*, pp. 283-4; Norbeck, *Takashima*, p. 151; Erskine, *Japanese Festivals*, pp. 88-91; I.L. Bishop, *Unbeaten Tracks in Japan* (John Murray, London, 1900), pp. 247-8.

26. This is probably an overt expression of recent prosperity in Japan. Some families with more than one daughter may well insist that the same kimono be passed down, which is quite reasonable since the garment is of a style which will not anyway be worn after marriage, and only on very formal occasions before.

27. E.g. Embree, *Suye Mura*, p. 213; Ariga, *Nihon Kon'in Shiron*, pp. 104, 108-9; Richard K. Beardsley *et al.*, *Village Japan*, Phoenix edn (University of Chicago Press, Chicago, 1969), p. 289; Fujisaki, *Kankonsōsai Jiten*, p. 18; Jirō Kamishima, *Nihonjin no Kekkonkan (The Japanese View of Marriage)* (Chikuma Sōsho, Tokyo, 1969), p. 151.

28. Kamishima, *Nihonjin no Kekkonkan*, p. 144.

29. Ichiro Hori, *Folk Religion of Japan* (University of Chicago Press, Chicago, 1974), p. 28; Kamishima, *Nihonjin no Kekkonkan*, pp. 151-2; Norbeck, 'Age-Grading', pp. 377-8; Omachi, 'Seinenshiki', pp. 234-6; Wakamori, 'Initiation Rites', pp. 293-4; Yanagida, *Manners and Customs*, pp. 223-5.

30. Details of such ceremonies varied from district to district, and among classes, elements of the upper-class rites gradually spreading to lower ones during the Meiji period. Descriptions of such details, and their association with the youth group, may be found in several sources, among them Wakamori, 'Initiation Rites'; Omachi, *'Seinenshiki'*; Fujisaki, *Kankonsōsai Jiten*, pp. 16-7; Hori, *Folk Religion*,

pp. 26-8; and Ariga, *Kon'in Shiron*, pp. 48-75.

31. Cf. Chikushi, *Nihon no Minzoku*, p. 203.

32. Erskine, *Japanese Festivals*, p. 41; Fujisaki, *Kankonsōsai Jiten*, p. 40; Jōya, *Japanese Customs*, p. 74; Edward Norbeck, '*Yakudoshi*, a Japanese Complex of Supernaturalistic Beliefs', *Southwestern Journal of Anthropology*, vol. 11 (1955), p. 107. These are also the ages advertised as inauspicious in Shinto shrines. Explanations include references to inauspicious alternative meanings of the pronunciation of some of these ages, such as *shini* (towards death) for 42, *sanzan* (trouble-trouble) for 33, and *jūku* (heavy suffering) for 19 (Fujisaki, *Kankonsōsai Jiten*, p. 40; Norbeck, '*Yakudoshi*', p. 118; Erskine, *Japanese Festivals*, p. 41); and the idea that they originated as being critical times in life when people undergo mental and physical changes, viz. at 25 men reach manhood, at 42 the height of their development, and at 60 the beginning of their decline; women attain womanhood at 19 and are in full bloom at 33 (Jōya, *Japanese Customs*, p. 75).

33. Wakamori, 'Initiation Rites', p. 295.

34. Yanagida, *Manners and Customs*, p. 118. This life crisis is still recognised widely and an academic may have a *festschrift* published by his students or colleagues to celebrate his 61st year.

35. Erskine, *Japanese Festivals*, pp. 156-7; Inouye, *Home Life in Tokyo*, pp. 236-7; Chikushi, *Nihon no Minzoku*, p. 204; Sofue, 'Childhood Ceremonies', p. 157.

36. Other things, such as screens and hanging scrolls, may also be reversed at this time (cf. Bownas, *Japanese Rainmaking*, p. 73; Embree, *Suye Mura*, p. 218; Robert J. Smith, *Ancestor Worship in Contemporary Japan* (Stanford University Press, Stanford, 1974), p. 94). For other descriptions of funerals, see Yanagida, *Manners and Customs*, pp. 183-98; Embree, *Suye Mura*, pp. 215-8; Beardsley *et al.*, *Village Japan*, pp. 338-43; Inoguchi, 'Sōshiki' ('Funerals') in Omachi *et al.* (eds.), *Nihon Minzokugaku*, pp. 291-329; Norbeck, *Takashima*, pp. 188-94; Erskine, *Japanese Customs*, pp. 92-105.

37. Cremation is the usual practice nowadays, although burials were common in the past (e.g. Embree, *Suye Mura*, p. 215). According to Chamberlain, p. 107, cremation was prohibited in 1873 as it was said to be un-European and barbarous, but when it was discovered to be a goal of European reformers, the law was rescinded in 1875.

38. Cf. U.A. Casal, 'Incense', *Transactions of the Asiatic Society of Japan*, Third Series, vol. 3 (1954), p. 53.

39. John F. Embree, 'Some Social Functions of Religion in Rural Japan', *American Journal of Sociology*, vol. 47 (1941), p. 188.

40. Salt is commonly used for the purpose of purification, cf. Norbeck, 'Pollution and Taboo', pp. 271, 275; *Takashima*, p. 142; Harumi Befu, *Japan: an Anthropological Introduction* (Chandler, San Francisco, 1971), p. 107; Jōya, *Japanese Customs*, pp. 122-3; Erskine, *Japanese Customs*, p. 98; Yanagida, *Manners and Customs*, p. 191; Smith, *Ancestor Worship*, pp. 93-4.

41. Cf. Narimitsu Matsudaira, 'The Concept of *Tamashii* in Japan' in Dorson (ed.), *Studies in Japanese Folklore*, p. 188; Smith, *Ancestor Worship*, p. 94.

42. Cf. the end of the pollution period following birth. Smith (*Ancestor Worship*, pp. 51, 95), refers to this as *imi-ake* (cf. Norbeck, 'Pollution and Taboo', p. 281).

43. Death is regarded as extremely polluting in the Shinto order of things (Kunio Yanagida, *About Our Ancestors: the Japanese Family System* (trans. Fanny Mayer and Yasuyo Ishiwara, Japanese National Commission for UNESCO, Tokyo, 1970), pp. 85-6; *Manners and Customs*, pp. 183-7), and although there are Shinto funeral rites practised by the families of Shinto priests and a few

others, priests usually try to avoid contamination, and before the end of the nineteenth century, even they were sometimes buried according to Buddhist rites (R.P. Dore, *City Life in Japan*, Phoenix edn (University of California Press, Berkeley, Los Angeles and London, 1971), pp. 457-8; Erskine, *Japanese Customs*, pp. 106-12; Smith, *Ancestor Worship*, pp. 73-4; Nakajima, *Japanese Etiquette*, pp. 150-1, 155).

44. The years when these are celebrated vary with Buddhist sect and area, sometimes being completed after 33 years (Smith, *Ancestor Worship*, p. 95; Hiroji Naoe, 'A Study of *Yashikigami*' in Dorson (ed.), *Studies in Japanese Folklore*, p. 207; Matsudaira, 'Concept of *Tamashii*', p. 190), or continuing up to 61 (R.J. Smith, *Kurusu* (Dawson, Folkestone, 1978), p. 156).

45. This custom apparently has no Buddhist support. Several writers report that the spirit loses its individuality, and some that it becomes a *kami* at this time (Yanagida, *About Our Ancestors*, pp. 118-19; Miyake, 'Folk Religion', pp. 123, 134; Naoe, 'A Study of Yashikigami', pp. 207-8; Smith, *Ancestor Worship*, p. 96).

46. Bownas, *Japanese Rainmaking*, p. 39; Smith, *Ancestor Worship*, pp. 17-18; Yanagida, *About Our Ancestors*, pp. 55-60.

47. These explanations are found all over Japan, it seems. For more details of New Year decorations and their history and symbolism, see Casal, *Five Sacred Festivals*, pp. 1-35; Jōya, *Japanese Customs*, pp. 1-14; Fujisaki, *Kankonsōsai Jiten*, pp. 179-87; Bownas, *Japanese Rainmaking*, Chapter 2.

48. Japanese people usually refer to New Year as Shōgatsu, literally 'standard month', also used for the whole of January, which should set a standard for the rest of the year (Jōya, *Japanese Customs*, p. 3; Casal, *Five Sacred Festivals*, p. 1).

49. The popular Meiji shrine in Tokyo is said to have four million visitors in the first three days of New Year (Yoneo Okada and Sadatoshi Ujitoko, *Shinto Shrines and Festivals* (Jinja Honchō, Kokugakuin University, Tokyo, 1958), p. 18).

50. This date seemed to vary even from village to village in the area.

51. This midsummer festival is now very much a Buddhist affair, and its name is usually said to be an abbreviation of the Sanskrit *Ullambana* where *bana* and *bon* are also words for a 'tray' on which food can be offered on behalf of the dead. Further details of Ullambana may be found in Jōya, *Japanese Customs*, pp. 99-100; Bownas, *Japanese Rainmaking*, pp. 94-5; Erskine, *Japanese Festivals*, pp. 101-2; cf. Miyake, 'Folk Religion', p. 130.

52. Smith, *Ancestor Worship*, p. 133; David W. Plath, 'Where the Family of God is the Family', *American Anthropologist*, vol. 66 (1964), p. 308.

53. Envelopes for gifts of money may be purchased, with a red band for happy occasions and a black one for affairs of mourning.

54. A proverb advises that it is lazy people who need to work on a holiday (Chamberlain, *Things Japanese*, p. 396), and a story quoted by Yanagida, *About Our Ancestors*, pp. 140-1, warns of the possibility of adverse supernatural consequences.

55. Tokutarō Sakurai, 'The Major Features and Characteristics of Japanese Folk Beliefs' in K. Morioka and W.H. Newell (eds.), *The Sociology of Japanese Religion* (Brill, Leiden, 1968), p. 16; Norbeck, *Takashima*, p. 64, 137.

56. Norbeck, *Takashima*, pp. 124-5; cf. Smith, 'Kurusu', p. 105.

57. Miyake, 'Folk Religion', p. 125; Jōya, *Japanese Customs*, p. 145.

58. Jōya, pp. 145-6; cf. Smith, *Ancestor Worship*, p. 60.

59. One Sōka Gakkai house faced directly north, but when untimely death and sickness occurred in the family, they refused to blame this and complained to the village assembly that their bad luck was due to the fact that public paths ran all round their house; this was presumed to be on the advice of a Sōka Gakkai specialist.

60. Though several houses were in the process of being built while I was in Kurotsuchi, there was only one which completed the process during my stay, and this will be described in detail, comments being added where others appeared to differ in some way. This case was that of the family who ran the rice-polishing shop. Their previous kitchen was situated behind the shop, so the parents stayed here throughout the proceedings, sending the children out to stay with relatives or schoolfriends. They stored their furniture in a neighbour's barn. Rice-polishing continued throughout the time. Other families with more land available sometimes knock down a barn or an outhouse and build their new house on that site before demolishing their old one, or they may leave a part of the old house to stay in during building. Since the whole process only lasts a few months, hardship is not too prolonged.

61. The carpenters hold a simplified version of the ceremony themselves if the house-owners neglect to do so, it was said, because one of its purposes is to protect them from harm during building.

62. *Omiki* is the name given to *sake* when it is drunk for ceremonial purposes, usually after people have taken part in a religious ceremony.

63. Embree, *Suye Mura*, pp. 125, 251-2.

64. It is interesting that the first object when building a Japanese house is to get the roof completed. The walls are left as a basic framework until the tiling is done, after which attention is given to filling in the side spaces. Edward Morse, in his detailed discussion of Japanese homes notes that the word for 'roof' is *yane*, literally 'house root', and he refers to a Korean acquaintance who suggested that as a tree without root dies, so a house without a roof decays (*Japanese Homes and their Surroundings* (Boston, 1886), p. 107).

7 CONCLUSION: THE PIVOTAL ROLE OF MARRIAGE

It should by now be clear that marriage in a village like Kurotsuchi involves much more than a contract between individuals. Even for a couple living alone, like those where the wife's family provided a plot of land, or a newly formed branch house, marriage immediately establishes the house head as a member of the village assembly, and various obligations follow for the household. These were described in detail in Chapter 2. Membership in a *tonarigumi* involves tasks such as the collection of taxes, and every year one house must discharge the duties of head, which include the entertainment of all the other members. As member of a *zagumi*, a turn must be taken in care of the shrines, and as member of a *tonari kinjo*, aid must be given when someone dies, marries or rebuilds their house. Once a year, there are the village roads to mend, and someone must be sent to join celebrations for the river festival. . .

For individuals who establish themselves on marriage as permanent members of an extended household, these obligations are shared among more people, but such an established household usually has more obligations with other such units than a new one would have. Regular visits are required or received at New Year and Bon, ancestor memorials must be remembered, and due attention must be paid to all life crises within the network of related households.

However, in both village and household, various concessions have been made to the post-war demands for individual dignity, which were discussed in Chapter 1. In Chapter 2, a whole section ('Age Groups') treated of groups which are now joined on an individual basis, whereas previously these, like other village groups, were joined as a matter of course when individuals reached an appropriate age. Now they are only joined by those who wish to join, in practice still a majority. Within the household, several changes, described in detail in Chapter 3, may be detected. First, in the very construction of the house, adaptations have made it possible for children to have their own rooms, and for a young married couple to have a place apart from the rest of the family. Second, individual members of the household are now frequently employed in separate capacities, rather than in one household endeavour, although many households maintain a communal purse.

Others, however, report that each member is responsible for his or her own money. Hope is expressed by elders that the eldest, or another, son will remain in the household and take care of his parents when they retire, but it is recognised that the individual concerned must make his own choice about this. Similarly, in the case of a girl with no brothers, she must decide whether she wants to remain in the family home and receive a *yōshi*, if one can be found. When it comes to marriage, a new *yome* or *yōshi* is said to be treated much better than hitherto, and registration of the union takes place promptly. Individual choice is also taken into consideration with regard to the selection of marital partners, and if all other factors are satisfactory, an individual may even make his or her own selection.

Nevertheless, *ren'ai* marriages are still in a minority, and courtship among young people is not widely practised. The aid of the go-between is still sought in a majority of cases, and family opinion is usually of concern to young people. In Kurotsuchi, as many cases came to light of marriages which were not made due to parents' objections as those made against parental wishes. The celebration of a marriage is still an event of considerable importance and a good deal of money is spent on seeing that it is performed properly. At the end of Chapter 5, it was suggested that the expenditure was due to the importance of marriage as a time for a household to confirm or increase its status, indeed, as the only time when a family which has risen socially may have its new status recognised. It has also been pointed out that marriage redefines a household with a new generation of permanent members, and establishes individuals as adults and sometimes as householders in their own right. Marriages transform a group of siblings into a group of related households. Each marriage represents the definition of a household, created legally as a new entry in the registry, and redefines the relationships between households in a particular generation. I hope to show, in this final chapter, that marriage also plays a structural role in this society which I shall, for want of a better word, call pivotal. To do this, I start by considering marriage in relation to other life crises, discussed in detail in the previous chapter, and move on to suggest some of the possible implications of this relationship in the wider social organisation.

In Japan celebrations of life crises, and of rites of passage in general, involve some or all of the following activities: gatherings of relatives and neighbours, the consumption of *sake* and food, the wearing of certain garments, and the exchange of gifts. These gifts are often made to the household concerned in the form of money, and are received by relatives and neighbours in the form of cakes. Depending on the nature of the occasion, the gifts are presented in one of two outward forms. If it is a happy affair, the money or gift will be wrapped in an envelope or paper decorated with a representation of a *noshi*, and tied round with three or five strands of string called *mizuhiki*, usually red and white, although it may also be gold and silver, or red and gold. Paper for gifts comes printed with *noshi* and *mizuhiki* of an appropriate hue. For an occasion of mourning, however, the gift is wrapped in paper or an envelope with a black and white, blue and white, or yellow and white *mizuhiki* and an appropriate motif such as a lotus flower. Even if the gift comes in a plain wrapping, the way the paper is folded may differ in each case.[1] Cakes may be individually wrapped in pink or red paper for a celebration and in green or blue for mourning, or the colouring may even be incorporated into the ground rice from which they are made. They will often be delivered for distribution in a box, which when opened will reveal a sprig of leaves on top of them, right side up for a celebration, facing downwards for condolence.

Thus are distinguished two types of event, classified in Japanese as *keiji* or *iwai*, and *chōji*, occasions of joyful celebration and occasions of mourning, and all features of such gatherings can be divided clearly in the same way. The food served provides another illustration. At *chōji*, meat and fish are avoided and special vegetarian dishes are served. Joyful occasions are marked by the use of sea bream, because its name *tai* is part of *omedetai* (congratulations), spring lobster, *sekihan* (rice with beans) and the ritual consumption of *sake*, using a special nest of three red lacquer cups. Formal dress is also different. Black may be worn for both types of gathering, but there will be a white or coloured relief for *keiji*, when kimono or hair decorations may be red or other bright colours. The division of colours in this way is illustrated well in *hanawa*, large wreaths used particularly for the opening of business ventures, and when someone dies. The former involve bright colours such as red, orange and pink, the latter use blues, greens and yellows. Both serve the purpose of announcement, one makes public the happy news of new premises to attract business, the other the unhappy news of a death in the district. The first celebration is not strictly a life crisis, and the distinctions being drawn here can indeed be applied more widely. *Noshi* appear on envelopes containing money for many purposes. They indicate merely that the enclosed is a gift, and originally that the giver was not contaminated with restrictions associated with mourning. Rather, these distinctions are made between affairs connected with the living and those connected with the dead. In fact, the presentation of a mourning gift (*kōden*) may be made at a memorial so many years after the death of a person that the occasion is not an especially sad one; for example, the rites held 33 years after someone's death are bound to involve people who hardly, if at all, knew him. Nevertheless, a *kōden* gift is always associated with the dead. Again, the so-called 'happy' occasions may be tinged with sadness, as we shall see shortly, but they are classified quite clearly as *keiji* (or *iwai*) when they are concerned with the living, and these are opposed, again quite clearly, to *chōji*, affairs of the dead.

Where an occasion is marked by some form of religious activity, and here I include various practices which informants sometimes describe as superstition (*meishin*) (see p. 63), there seems to be a definite tendency to turn to Shinto for happy occasions of the living, and to Buddhism for those of mourning. A new baby is taken to the Shinto shrine for the *miyamairi*, and a manual about ceremonies associates other rites held in the home for babies with the *kamidana* rather than the *butsudan*.[2] For the 7-5-3 celebration for children of 7, 5 and 3, a visit to a Shinto shrine is again in order, and it is usually a Shinto priest who is called to conduct the purification ceremony which precedes the building of a house. On the other hand, funeral rites and memorial services are almost always conducted by a Buddhist priest, and the dead are remembered at the *butsudan* and the temple. As Morioka has put it: 'The former (Shinto) is for this-worldly prosperity; the latter (Buddhism) is of other-worldly concern'.[3] There are exceptions to this rule. Shinto priests and their families conduct their own Shinto funeral and memorial services, although even these are apparently mostly recent adaptations of Buddhist rites. Some Buddhist sects, such as Sōka Gakkai, permit no attendance at Shinto rites, providing their own versions of the *miyamairi* and house-building purification. However, the vast majority of informants readily accept this opposition of Shinto and Buddhist worship as associated with *keiji* and *chōji* respectively. People also sometimes express it indirectly by their reactions to, for example, my attendance at the wedding of a Sōka Gakkai adherent which was held in a Buddhist temple. It seemed to be a contradiction in terms, like the idea of Shinto funeral rites, as reported by Smith.[4] This whole division of Shinto and Buddhist spheres was first suggested to me explicitly by an informant as an explanation of why a sheet of paper is hung up over the *kamidana* during mourning, and the shrine compound should not be visited at this time for fear of pollution. Thus, so far, we have a series of oppositions, as follows:

Living	Dead
Keiji	*Chōji*
Shinto	Buddhism
Kamidana	*Butsudan*
Shrine	Temple

There is also a rather hazy middle area of shamanistic and divinatory activity to which recourse is had in times of sickness, when life may be threatened by death. Such activity is practised by faith healers who are associated specifically with neither Shinto nor Buddhism by their lay clients, although individual practitioners may claim allegience to either one, or even both.[5]

More generally, the opposition between Shinto and Buddhism can be shown to be associated with other distinctions in the ordering of the wider society. The association of Shinto with the community as a whole and Buddhism with the household is well documented.[6] The village shrine includes as parishioners all the members of the community, who take it in turns to attend to its upkeep. The disapproval and ill-feeling expressed when the Sōka Gakkai households tried to withdraw from these duties illustrates the extent to which it is regarded as a community obligation. Affiliations with a Buddhist temple, on the other hand, are not uniform throughout the village, and the household is regarded as the fundamental unit of the parish, since it is with memories of household ancestors that Buddhist worship is concerned. The *butsudan*, within the household, devoted to the memory of dead members, is perhaps regarded with more respect than the *kamidana*; and within the village, which is the chief community of its residents, there are two Shinto shrines but no Buddhist temple. Even the *nōkotsudō*, where the physical remains of the dead are stored, are all outside the village boundaries. Funerals and memorial services are usually held within the household, where the priest comes to perform the rites; but celebrations for children, the attainments of certain ages, marriages and other affairs of the living frequently involve trips to shrines within the wider community, if not within the village. The two big festivals of the year, New Year and *Bon*, now also polarise into illustrating Shinto and Buddhist practices respectively, although they may both have originally been identical indigenous soul festivals. Nowadays the former involves attentions to Shinto deities such as Suijin and Kōjin, trips to shrines to seek good fortune throughout the year, and the renewal of relations within the community through the New Year greetings. The latter, Bon, involves attentions to the *butsudan*, visits to the Buddhist temple and graveyard or *nōkotsudō*, and the renewal of relations with departed ancestral spirits, who are said to return at this time. At New Year, gifts are made to households in which new babies have been born, whereas at Bon they are sent to the households which have been bereaved that year.

Embree pointed out that ancestor worship serves to unite kin groups, based on connections of blood, while other aspects of village religion unify the local group whose relations are based on territory. He showed how this distinction is manifested at a funeral when the neighbourhood group comes to the aid of the stricken family while the extended kin group assembles to mourn and participate in the rituals. This 'horizontal, spatial' kin-group he also contrasts to the 'perpendicular, temporal family', whose continuity through generations is revivified at Bon.[7] Befu, too, has discussed this opposition between the spatial, immediate existence of bilateral kindred related by blood, marriage and adoption, and the temporal continuity of the group which operates chiefly on the principle of patrilineal descent.[8] The spatial/temporal opposition can in more general terms be applied here to the community/household, Shinto/Buddhist ones already discussed. The Shinto rites are concerned with the living, synchronic community at any one time; the Buddhist with the diachronic aspect of the household and its continuity through time.

The opposition pair Buddhist/Shinto: :*Chōji/Keiji* is in some senses complementary, but in others not. Shinto observances are prohibited during the period of pollution immediately following death, whereas the family *butsudan* is frequently open during an *iwai* in the house. However, a comparison of rites following birth and death brings out an interesting series of parallels. There is, for example, after each a period of pollution which terminates with what is locally called *hibare*, elsewhere *hiaki* and *kiake*. These periods are different, 49 days being that set by Buddhist rules for the period following death, and 30 and 33, with local variations, for the periods following the birth of a boy and girl baby respectively. However, the restrictions are similar. Certain foods must be avoided, and neither the family of the dead, nor the mother who gave birth, may visit the Shinto shrine during this period. Again, salt is used for purification: in the one case it is said to be to prevent the soul of the dead sticking to people who attended the funeral; in the other to appease the deity of the river when the rags of childbirth have been washed there. The concern during the two periods of pollution is apparently with the attachment and detachment of the soul from the body. The baby's soul could, if care were not taken, escape from its body at any time before the end of this period, or indeed, some say it does not arrive until then.[9] Likewise, the soul of the recently dead person may stay around for some time after death, so that various rites must be performed to see it on its journey, a process held certainly to have been achieved by the end of the 49 days.

After birth, there is a naming rite (*shichiya*) on the seventh day, the *miyamairi* after approximately one month, and the *momoka* or *kuizome* after 100-110 days. After death, the rites most often observed are after the first seven days (*hatsunanoka*), after one month (*hatsumeinichi*), and further rites after 100 days. There is another celebration one year after each of birth and death – the *tanjōbi*, and the *isshūki*, the first annual *meinichi*. Then the Shinto observances which happen on 15 November are 7-5-3, which number of years include two of those when Buddhist memorials for the dead are especially observed (three and seven). Miyake has commented, 'From this symmetry it may be inferred that in the thinking of many Japanese people, the souls of the living and the souls of the dead go through much the same process of development.'[10] Later memorial celebrations are also after numbers of years which represent important times in life: 13 being the change from primary to middle school, and 25 and 33 *yakudoshi* for men and women. There are even places where ancestral rites continue until the 61st anniversary of death,[11] which has a clear parallel with the *kanreki* celebration of 'return to childhood' for the living. This whole phenomenon is regarded as characteristic of the syncretic nature of religious observances at folk level, wholly to be explained by neither the Shinto nor the Buddhist specialist, whose doctrines do not always coincide with the collective ideas of them expressed when lay people request clerical services. Among ordinary people religious activities are remembered and passed down in a form which is consistent with other categories of social organisation. I hope I have shown that the total picture includes a set of oppositions into which Shinto and Buddhism are incorporated as associated with *keiji* and *chōji*, with life and especially birth and with death, with the community and the household, the synchronic and diachronic elements of organisation of society, and with New Year and Bon.

If we now consider marriage in this context, we are without doubt concerned with an occasion of celebration, for the gifts are made in red-banded envelopes, the food and clothes are those for a celebration, and the whole event may be referred to simply as the *iwai*. However, there are aspects of marriage which are not entirely happy. The bride must leave her home and take up residence in a strange household, often share her bed with a man she hardly knows, and her parents and family must lose her company and aid in the home. The husband's family, too, must make adjustments, and although in principle they may be happy to receive a wife for the heir, it will be some time before the former intimacy can be re-established, if it ever is. The arrival of a baby does much, according to young wives, to make them feel at home, and a birth plays a great part in the consolidation of the union between the two households as well as the couple. As long as the mother and child are healthy, birth and the subsequent celebrations are unqualified in being joyful.

Nor is marriage exclusively associated either with Shinto or Buddhism. It is my contention, in fact, that marriage plays a part in bringing together various institutions such as Shinto and Buddhism, birth and death, even village and household which are more usually opposed. In recent years, the Shinto wedding has become popular, but this is a relatively new phenomenon, and the marriage ceremony is equally valid whether held in a Buddhist temple, a secular restaurant, a marriage hall, or in the home. In the last case, it may be described as being held before the ancestors in the *butsudan*, or it may be held in front of the *tokonoma*, which has had associations with Shinto worship. The bride, on arrival at her new home, must remember to greet her new ancestors in the *butsudan*, and thus join the household; and she is taken to greet the *ujigami* at the village shrine, thus joining her new community.

Where the importance of the *ie* is emphasised, one of the most usual reasons given for marriage is to ensure its continuity, and even where it is not, the creation of descendants (*shison*) is frequently expressed as the purpose of the institution. When members of a household are asked about their concern for the continuation of the unit, the occupational need is not mentioned first, rather it is the question of care in old age and the need to be remembered after death which predominate. Thus marriage is the vital link in the sequence, at once associated with the birth of the next generation and the death of the previous one. Both birth and death are brought to mind at the wedding ceremony, when the bride dresses in white to express her symbolic death in her own house and her rebirth in that of her husband. She must erase her past life, hide her 'horns', the bad traits of her character, in her headdress, and start afresh with a clean slate. In white, she is dressed like a corpse, and like a baby. According to Blacker, this symbolism of the wedding ceremony is used as a model for the initiation of a blind spirit medium who 'marries' the deity who takes possession of her, when 'dying to her old self, she is reborn in the dazzling garb of the bride of the deity implanted in her at the moment of death'.[12] Thus, while the rites of birth and death are themselves opposed, if parallel, the marriage rite, which falls between them in the life cycle of an individual, also incorporates elements of the other two.

That marriage joins households has been well illustrated, and this is symbolised at the ceremony in the exchange of cups between the two sets of relatives as well as between the bride and groom. Speeches made during the receptions also frequently refer to the union of households (*ke*) which has been set up, and for a marriage held in a wedding hall, a board outside usually announces the event as the celebration of X *ke* and Y *ke* where X and Y refer to surnames. In practice, a series of exchanges and visits is set up, strengthened greatly with the arrival of mutual descendants, and the two families may call on each other for aid. In the future such affinally linked households may well provide the connections necessary for further marriages. In the past, these were often simple reinforcements of an existing affinal link through a cousin marriage. Nowadays, they are more likely to be unions created by introductions through related families to their neighbours or relatives by a different connection. In this way, marriages between specific villages persist, so that inter-community affinal links are also created.

Thus marriage is at once concerned with the diachronic aspect of the continuity of the family through time, and the synchronic one of forging links between households and communities existing at any one time. It is marriage which defines the members of Embree's 'horizontal, spatial family', as well as playing a role in the continuity of the 'perpendicular, temporal family'. All these categories are remembered and reinforced during the course of the wedding celebrations. The bride's farewell to her own *butsudan* and the greeting at that of her husband's home, before any living members are acknowledged, indicates her awareness of the ancestral line she is joining. Even at the marriages of sons who will not inherit an established household, reference is made during the introduction of relatives to the household from which he is to branch off, and sometimes the antecedent of that household is referred to by the naming of an uncle as 'of the main house' (*honke*).

The guests who attend the marriage ceremony itself, the *honkyaku*, are the closest members of Embree's horizontal kin-group of Befu's bilateral kindred: parents, grandparents, siblings of the bride and groom, their aunts and uncles – in other words, present and previous members of the households from which they come and with which they enjoy first order consanguineous and affinal links. Further guests, who in the Yame area are often invited to separate home celebrations called *yorokobi*, emphasise the categories of territorial relations, those based on membership in the community: the women of the *tonarigumi*, the men of the *tonari kinjo*, the female age-mates of the mother of the groom and the male age-mates of the groom and his father. During these *yorokobi*, female relatives, perhaps wives of the male *honkyaku* who attended the actual ceremony, are often called in to help in the kitchen, but these and more distant relatives usually have a chance to be entertained at one of the *yorokobi*. At the wedding I attended where all the guests had been invited to one large reception in a wedding hall, the above categories were so well preserved that an old grandmother, who was there to represent an absent son, found herself among the men of the *tonari kinjo*, and another woman, whose son was also unable to attend, was seated with the groom's age-mates. The *honkyaku* relatives, who had attended the actual Shinto ceremony, had had a separate feast earlier, but some of them came to the second gathering and moved round inside the tables, greeting the guests and exchanging cups with them. Thus the wedding rites serve to redefine all these categories, and bring them together on the one occasion.

It could be argued that funerals are affairs which serve a similar purpose, though partly in reverse, since this time it is the neighbours who come in to help entertain the relatives, who take part in the rites, and these same neighbours are entertained later at one of the memorials. Also, the birth of a child is followed by gatherings which involve both neighbours and relatives, particularly at the first *osekku*. The difference is in the way the marriage rites incorporate aspects of both of these. At a funeral or memorial service, the participants are descendants of the deceased, a group of kindred peculiar to that individual; at celebrations for the birth of a child, the participants are ascendants of that individual, again a group of personal kindred. At a marriage, the ascendants of both partners are present, each with a concern in the mutual descendants they hope will result from the union. Marriage is thus a pivot on which these groups of kindred are balanced, from which groups of kindred are created.

Marriage is also associated with both of the now otherwise opposed festivals of Bon and New Year. It is at either or both of these times that the couple may expect to visit the bride (or *yōshi*)'s family, and indeed, in the early years of their marriage, they remember their wedding by taking a gift to their go-between at these times. Thus while other practices associated with them serve to emphasise their differences, the bond created by marriage emphasises their similarity. Likewise, in many areas there is a clear opposition between Shinto and Buddhism, as between birth and death, village and household, but the institution of marriage provides a temporary ritual overriding of these differences as two households become interrelated. Adjustments must be made to the concepts of inside and outside for each family since marriage is the bringing of outside in, and as marriage links these two normally opposed categories, so it links many other oppositions.

Finally, marriage is also associated with that hazy middle area of divinatory activity mentioned as associated specifically with neither Shinto nor Buddhism, though individual practitioners may be affiliated with either. It is to such a person – in the Yame area referred to as the *ogamiyasan* – that people turn for advice about the prospect of compatibility or *aishō* for a particular couple. They may also seek advice about an auspicious date to hold the wedding, or an alternative date to hold a *karishūgen* if the date they have chosen is pronounced unlucky for some reason. The two brides who changed their given names slightly to improve the *aishō* with their husbands had received their advice, one from a Shinto specialist, the other from a Buddhist, although these allegiances seemed unimportant to the informants. Just as these specialists are concerned with the healing of illness, an affliction which threatens life and reminds of death, so they are also to be consulted at the time of marriage, which has associations with both creating life and caring for the dead. Marriage also has its period of dangers when numerous adjustments are being made to the social order. Until the wedding, there is uncertainty about the making of a match, about the agreement of the individual to take his new role in society, and about whether the match, once decided, will be a suitable one. Like the period during house-building, when the *ogamiyasan* is again consulted, there is concern about the redefinition of the household, and in the case of the marriage, its relations with other households. Once the wedding is completed, and particularly after a child is born to cement the union, the dangers gradually disappear.

In summary, marriage may be shown to play a 'pivotal' role in many important aspects of society. The two important social groups to which individuals belong are the village, described in Chapter 2, and the household, described in Chapter 3.[13] In both cases, individuals born into the groups usually spend the first half of their lives within them automatically. As they grow to be adults, they reach a period of decision about where and how they will spend the second half of their lives. For these groups, marriages represent the decisions of individuals to leave, join or remain in them, and once the decision is made, it is likely to be permanent, so that marriages determine the adult membership of both village and household. It also redefines relations between households and villages, which determines for future ceremonial who will be involved and to whom the individuals concerned will owe allegiance. In this chapter an attempt has been made to demonstrate that marriage in this society also plays an important role in temporarily overriding the universal opposition between life and death, just as it brings together male and female. It is vital to ensure the continuity of the household, which provides a link between man and the sacred, in this case the ancestors, an opposition related to and reinforced by that between Shinto and Buddhist worship. Little wonder that such a fundamental institution offers resistance to the sweeping tide of change.

Notes

1. Yaeko Shiotsuki, *Zukai Kankonsōsai (Illustrated Ceremonial)* (Kōbunsha, Tokyo, 1971), pp. 22, 27, illustrates how this folding should be done.

2. Hiroshi Fujisaki, *Kankonsōsai Jiten (Dictionary of Ceremonial)* (Tsuru Shobo, Tokyo, 1957), pp. 226-8.

3. Kiyomi Morioka, *Religion in Changing Japanese Society* (University of Tokyo Press, Tokyo, 1975), p. 6. The words in parentheses in the quotation are mine.

4. Cf. Fujisaki, *Kankonsōsai Jiten*, p. 147; Robert J. Smith, *Ancestor Worship in Contemporary Japan* (Stanford University Press, Stanford, 1974), p. 74.

5. Cf. John F. Embree, *Suye Mura* (University of Chicago Press, Chicago, 1939), pp. 252-3.

6. Ken Arai, 'New Religious Movements' in I. Hori *et al.* (eds.), *Japanese Religion* (trans. Yoshiya Abe and David Reid, Kodansha International, Tokyo and Palo Alto, 1972), pp. 89-90; Morioka, *Religion in Changing Society*, p. 5.

7. John F. Embree, 'Some Social Functions of Religion in Rural Japan', *American Journal of Sociology*, vol. 47 (1941), pp. 188-9.

8. Harumi Befu, 'Patrilineal Descent and Personal Kindred in Japan', *American Anthropologist*, vol. 65 (1963), pp. 1333-4.

9. Embree, *Suye Mura*, p. 183; Takao Sofue, 'Childhood Ceremonies in Japan', *Ethnology*, vol. 4 (1965), p. 152; Kunio Yanagida, *About Our Ancestors*, trans. Fanny Mayer and Yasuyo Ishiwara (Japanese Commission for UNESCO, Tokyo, 1970), p. 172.

10. Hitoshi Miyake, 'Folk Religion' in Hori *et al.* (eds.), *Japanese Religion*, p. 135.

11. Robert J. Smith, *Kurusu* (Dawson, Folkestone, 1978), p. 156.

12. Carmen Blacker, *The Catalpa Bow* (Allen and Unwin, London, 1975), p. 147.

13. Occupational groups may be considered more important in some people's lives than the village, and their weddings would probably illustrate this, one or more receptions being held for workmates.

APPENDIX: THE PRE-GREGORIAN CALENDAR AND SOME IMPLICATIONS FOR MARRIAGE

Although the Western calendar was adopted officially in Japan in 1872, previous schemes for marking the passage of time, most of which came originally from China, are still used in a variety of circumstances. Calculations based on these schemes determine auspicious and inauspicious days to carry out almost any endeavour, and details about the birth of pairs of individuals according to these schemes are said to make them compatible or otherwise for matrimony. The previous calendar used in Japan has been described by several writers in greater or lesser detail.[1] What follows is derived largely from these sources, although a good deal of information was also obtained from informants in the field.

Many writers refer to the sexagenary cycle based on the Chinese classification of time into 10 celestial 'stems' (*jikkan*) and 12 terrestial 'branches' (*jūnishi*), cycles which run concurrently to count years and days, so that the same combination of 'stem' and 'branch' returns only once in 60 days or years. The 10 'stems' are derived from a yin-yang cosmological scheme which holds that the universe is composed of five basic elements: wood, fire, earth, metal and water, each of which has two aspects, known in Japanese as the older brother (*e*) and younger brother (*to*), otherwise male (positive, light, warm, active) and female (negative, dark, cold, passive), yang and yin respectively. The 12 'branches' are each associated with a bird or animal of the Chinese zodiac, and follow the order: rat (*ne*), ox (*ushi*), tiger (*tora*), hare (*u*), dragon (*tatsu*), snake (*mi*), horse (*uma*), sheep (*hitsuji*), monkey (*saru*), cock (*tori*), dog (*inu*), wild boar (*i*).

The year itself was divided into lunar months, numbered from one to twelve, with an intercalary month of varying length added every few years to correct for the discrepancy with the solar year. These months had unofficial names associated with the seasons during which they came, or with customs practised during them. Details may be found in Clement.[2] Festivals were often held on the 15th day of a particular month so there was a good chance of a full moon for the evening celebrations. The year was also divided into 24 longer and 72 shorter periods associated with the expectation of a particular type of weather, and farmers worked within this framework in planning their activities.

240

Some of these divisions are still marked in a modern calendar since they include reference to the vernal and autumnal equinoxes, the summer and winter solstices, the beginning of spring and the hottest period of summer. Various customs are practised on particular days of this scheme, including the *setsubun* rites which mark the end of winter. The *shanichi* celebration takes place on the nearest day of 'earth in the *e* aspect' to the verbal and autumnal equinoxes, perhaps explaining the name 'earth spirit' for this deity.

Another scheme which is frequently considered is the Buddhist six-day week, which runs as follows:

> *sengachi* (early victory) when a venture started early is likely to succeed;
> *tomobiki* (pulling a friend) – a day to be avoided for funerals;
> *sakimake* (haste loses) when important ventures should be left until late;
> *butsumetsu* (Buddha's death) – an inauspicious day for anything;
> *daian* or *taian* (great safety) – a lucky day for anything;
> *shakkō* (red mouth) – a dangerous day when high noon is the only safe time.

Of these, the most auspicious day, *daian* or *taian*, is usually chosen where possible for celebrations associated with weddings. The Western seven-day week, adopted in schools in 1874 and more widely in 1876, named with the Japanese terms for the sun, moon and five planets (themselves named after the five elements), was also accorded degrees of auspiciousness for various ventures, but these are nowadays less often referred to than those of the six-day cycle. Details are to be found in Erskine and Fujisaki.[3]

There is also a horoscopic cycle of nine different combinations of the five elements and six colours, referred to by Erskine as the Nine Temperaments, which are attributed to days and years, and which are taken into consideration as part of the birth signs of a couple to determine whether or not they would be compatible for marriage. Details are to be found in Erskine and Fujisaki.[4] Specific combinations of the animals in the Chinese zodiac at the time of birth are also said to be compatible or otherwise, as are combinations of the five elements. This last involves certain combinations which produce mutual harmony, mutual prosperity or mutual destruction, in a manner related to the way the elements react together in fact. There are also more general prohibitions. A couple whose ages are separated either by four or by ten years should not marry, since the difference may also be read 'night eyes' (*yome*) or 'far eyes' (*tōme*), which would, according to a saying, be like 'the inside of an umbrella' where one knows nothing. Probably the most famous taboo for men is on marrying women born in the year *hinoeuma*, the active aspect of fire associated with the horse, which is said to give a female character with which no man could live. Consequently the birth rate is said to drop dramatically in such a year, and birth certificates are apparently often falsified to record a less drastic date of birth.

Apart from the choice of day according to the six-day Buddhist cycle, specific days in the sexagenary cycle are said to be especially auspicious for a wedding or other celebration. These are called *tensha* days and *tenichi tenjō* days, the former occurring once only in each season, the latter in periods of 16 days when a deity by the name of *tenichi* is said to return to heaven. Details of when these occur are to be found in Dixon and Fujisaki.[5] Certain other days and periods are said to be inauspicious. These include *hassen* days, which are periods in the sexagenary cycle, and other specific days known as *sanrinbo*, also especially to be avoided for house-building, since destruction of three neighbouring houses may result, *gomubi* and *tokunichi*, details of all of which are again to be found in Fujisaki and Erskine.[6] The latter also lists specific days to be avoided by people of particular birth signs.

Most people in Kurotsuchi have annual almanacs in the home which provide a great deal of information about good and bad days for various ventures, about the horoscopes and compatibility of people born at certain times, and also about another aspect of this subject, namely directions to be sought or avoided on particular days. Should further information be required, or clarification where doubts arise, the advice of a specialist is sought.

Notes

1. For example E. Clement, 'Japanese Calendars', *Transactions of the Asiatic Society of Japan*, vol. 30 (1902), pp. 1-82; 'Calendar (Japanese)' in J. Hastings (ed.), *Encyclopaedia of Religion and Ethics* (Edinburgh, 1910), Vol. III, pp. 114-17; W. Erskine, *Japanese Festivals and Calendar Lore* (Kyo Bun Kwan, Tokyo, 1933); H. Fujisaki, *Kankonsōsai Jiten (Dictionary of Ceremonial)* (Tsuru Shobo, Tokyo, 1957), pp. 32-41; B.H. Chamberlain, *Things Japanese* (John Murray, London, 1902), pp. 471-5; and J.M. Dixon, 'Japanese Etiquette', *Transactions of the Asiatic Society of Japan*, vol. 13 (1885), pp. 1-21.

2. Clement, 'Japanese Calendars', pp. 6-7; 'Calendar (Japanese)', pp. 114-15.

3. Erskine, *Japanese Festivals*, p. 189; Fujisaki, *Kankonsōsai Jiten*, p. 38.
4. Erskine, *Japanese Festivals*, p. 184; Fujisaki, *Kankonsōsai Jiten*, pp. 35-6.
5. Dixon, 'Japanese Etiquette', p. 15; Fujisaki, *Kankonsōsai Jiten*, p. 38.
6. Fujisaki, *Kankonsōsai Jiten*, pp. 35-9; Erskine, *Japanese Festivals*, pp. 172-3.

GLOSSARY

Use of Japanese words in the text has been limited to those for which there is no easy translation, although many words which have been translated are also given in Japanese, in parenthesis, the first time they are used.

This glossary brings together all the words which appear more than once in the text, for reference, and a few which are partially discussed in different places. Where a conventional translation of a word is mentioned, it is taken from Kenkyūsha's *New Japanese-English Dictionary*. Definitions of Japanese words, in Japanese, are sometimes given and these are taken from the *Nihon Kokugo Daijiten*, abbreviated here to NKD. At the end there is a list of Japanese historical periods referred to in the text, with the approximate dates according to Nelson's *Japanese-English Character Dictionary*.

Japanese vowels are pronounced as Italian or Spanish ones, being given double length where they are modified by a macron (e.g. ō, ū). Consonants are more or less as would be expected by an English speaker, although double consonants usually indicate an abrupt termination of the sound.

Written Japanese is usually a combination of logographs, which were originally imported from China in the fourth century AD, and a syllabic script developed in Japan itself. Normally the latter is used for word endings, particles and conjunctions, but any Japanese may be written entirely in the syllabic script (for example, in telegrams and primary school text-books), and the romanised version is a systematic transcript of this. The system used here is the modified Hepburn system. Since homonyms are not distinguished in this way the Japanese script has been provided for words entered in the glossary.

Part I

aijō 愛情: love; *see* pp. 116–17

aishō 相性: compatibility between spouses or potential spouses

atotsugi 跡継: successor

Bon 盆: midsummer festival for the dead

bunke 分家: branch house

buraku 部落: village

Burakumin 部落民: "*buraku* people"; euphemistic term for a Japanese pariah group

buri 鰤: yellowtail (fish)

butsudan 仏壇: household Buddhist altar

butsuma 仏間: room where the *butsudan* is kept

butsuzen 仏前: before the Buddhist image

chimeguri 血巡り: girls' age-mate groups

chōdohin 調度品: the bride's trousseau

chōji 弔事: an occasion of mourning

chōnai 町内: administrative section of a city

chōnaikai 町内会: village assembly

dai'an 大安: "great safety"; the most auspicious day in the 6-day cycle

daikoku bashira 大黒柱: the principal post in house construction; the inheriting son

en 縁: a notion of karmic destiny with regard to a relationship; *see* pp. 112, n. 65, regarding *chi'en* (地縁), "land-relation", and *ketsu en* (血縁), "blood-relation"; a wandering spirit with no family to care for it is said to be "without *en*" (*muen*, Smith 1975:41). *En* is mentioned if people meet in unlikely, coincidental circumstances. It is also required to be shared if a couple will marry (pp. 139–40).

engumi 縁組: marriage, or literally, the uniting of *en;* also applied to relations created by adoption

enmusubi 縁結び: the "tying up" or linking of *en; musubi* (結) has the alternative reading *ketsu,* the first part of *kekkon,* another word for "marriage."

enmusubi obi 縁結帯: a sash given as part of the betrothal gifts

fūfu 夫婦: (married) couple, husband and wife

fujinkai 婦人会: Housewives' Association (used with capital letters to distinguish the organisation from any other housewives' association)

geisha 芸者: professional entertainers, usually skilled at singing, dancing and the playing of traditional Japanese instruments

gokuraku 極楽: the Buddhist paradise

gozen 御前: the "front" room nearest the entrance in a Japanese house

hakama 袴: a traditional Japanese garment, resembling a divided skirt, worn by men on ceremonial occasions

hanamuke 餞: a parting gift, given especially before a wedding

hanashiai 話合い: discussion

harai 祓: a Shinto rite of purification

hatsu 初: first

hatsubon 初盆: the first Bon festival after a person has died

hatsumeinichi 初命日: the day approximately a month after a person has died which falls on the same date of the month as did the day of death

hibare 日晴れ: the end of a pollution period (elsewhere *hiaki, kiake*)

hi no hare 日の晴れ; see *hibare*

hirōen 披露宴: the "announcement feast" following a wedding ceremony

honja 本茶: "main tea"; the betrothal gifts as they are termed in some parts of Kyūshū

honke 本家: main house

honkyaku 本客: chief guests at a wedding ceremony

hotokesama 仏様: buddha; also applied to anyone who has died recently

ie 家: house or household; *see* p. 15ff. and Ch. 3

ihai 位牌: ancestral tablets

inkan 印鑑: a personal seal, used in Japan where signature would be used in the West

inkyo 隠居: retirement from the position of head of a household

ironaoshi 色直: the bride's change of dress at a wedding

ita no ma 板の間: a room with a wooden floor rather than *tatami* matting

iwai 祝: wedding or other celebration

ka 家: an alternative reading of *ie*

kafū 家風: "ways" of the house

kagemi 陰見: a hidden look, usually at a prospective spouse

kageutai 陰謡: a hidden *utai,* sung at wedding

kai 会: association or assembly

kairanban 回覧板: circulating notice board

kami 神: notion of deity; *see* p. 76, n. 31

kamidana 神棚: a Shinto "god-shelf"

kamon 家紋: house crest

kannushi 神主: Shinto priest

kanreki 還暦: "return of the calendar"; a celebration of attainment of the 61st year, the first return of the same year, according to the Chinese calendar, as that in which one was born

karishūgen 仮祝言: an interim marriage ceremony

kawamatsuri 川祭: river festival

kazoku 家族: family; see p. 107, n. 1

keiji 慶事: a celebration

keirōkai 敬老会: old people's association

kekkon 結婚: marriage; according to the NKD, *danjo ga fūfu to naru koto* (the conversion of a man and woman into a husband and wife), or *fūfu no en o musubu koto* (the linking of the *en* of a husband and wife); see also *enmusubi* and *kon*

kekkon shikijō 結婚式場: marriage hall

kettō 血統: blood, stock or family pedigree

kikiawase 聞合せ: see *kuchikiki*

kimeja 決茶: "decide-tea"; a gift to clinch an accepted proposal of marriage

kimono 着物: a Japanese garment—used as an English word

kimonzumi 鬼門隅: "the devils' gate corner"; northeast of a house

kinjo 近所: a neighbourhood group

kinjomawari 近所回り: "neighbourhood round"; the visit of a bride to her new neighbours after marriage

ko 戸: house, household, door

kō 講: a type of group or association; see pp. 68–9

kōden 香典: "incense money"; a mourning gift

kodomo 子供: child, children

kodomogumi 子供組: a children's group; previously an age-grade, now primary school pupils of a particular village

koi 恋: love in the sense of physical attraction, passion

kōkeisha 後継者: successor

kōku 校区: school zone

kōminkanchō 公民館長: head of the public meeting hall

kon 婚: marriage; according to the NKD, *fūfu no engumi o suru koto* (the making of the *engumi* of a husband and wife)

konbu 昆布: a type of seaweed used at celebrations and in Shinto rites

koshimaki 腰巻: petticoat

koshu 戸主: head of a household *(ie)*

kotobuki 寿: congratulations and wishes for longevity

kotowari 断わり: excuse, apology or refusal

kuchikiki 口開き: an investigation preceding a decision about a proposed marital alliance; see p. 133

kugicha 釘茶: "nail-tea"; see *kimeja*

kuizome 食初: "first-eating" (for a baby)

kuyō 供養: an ancestral memorial service

kyūjinin 給仕人: serving people at a wedding ceremony

machi 町: town; *see* p. 73, n. 7

matsuri 祭: festival, usually of a religious nature

meinichi 命日: the anniversary of a death, or the monthly return of the death date

miai 見合: a meeting of possible spouses for the purpose of mutual assessment

miya 宮: a Shinto shrine

miyamairi 宮参り: the shrine visit following the birth of a baby

mikka no mochi 三日の餅: "third-night rice-cakes"; a marriage rite of the Heian period

miko 巫女: female Shinto shrine attendants

mochi 餅: rice cakes

momoka 百日: "100 days"; first-eating rite celebrated about 100 days after the birth of a baby

mukashi no shinseki 昔の親戚: distant relatives, "relatives of yore"

muko 婿(聟): son-in-law, husband or bridegroom

mukoiri 婿入り: a reception for a bridegroom into his wife's household

muko-yōshi 婿養子: a son-in-law adopted as household successor

mura 村: village; *see* p. 73, n. 7

musubu 結ぶ: to tie up, link; see *enmusubi*

nakōdo 仲人: go-between, matchmaker

nēsan 姉さん: elder sister; also used as a term of deference by children

nikushin 肉親: "flesh-relation"

niisan 兄さん: elder brother; also used as a term of deference by children

nōkotsudō 納骨堂: "place for remains"; a building which houses the ashes of the dead

norito 祝詞: prayer chanted during a Shinto ceremony

noshi 熨斗; *see* p. 160

noshi no gi 熨斗の儀: the *noshi* rite

o 御: an honorific prefix; most of the following words could be used, less politely, without the 'o.' Exceptions are marked with a dot.

oba 伯(叔)母: aunt

obāsan 御祖母さん: grandmother; old lady

ọbi 帯: a belt or sash, especially that worn with kimono

ọgamiyasan 拝み屋さん: a diviner, shaman or holy man; of Buddhist or Shinto allegiances, with a knowledge of geomancy and other

Taoist lore

oji 伯(叔)父: uncle

ojiisan 御祖父さん: grandfather; old man

omedetai お目出度い: happy, auspicious

omedetō (gozaimasu) お目出度う: congratulations!

omiki 御神酒: a ceremonial drink of sake, especially following a Shinto rite

on 恩: a concept of debt, too great to repay in full

onegai shimasu お願いします: if you please; I request it

osekku お節句: certain annual festivals, particularly those for children

oyabun-kobun 親分・子分: a type of patron-client relation based on the parent-child relation as a model

oyakosakazuki 親子盃: a sharing of cups between bride or groom and the new parents-in-law

pairotto パイロット: "pilot"; the name given to the tea-field project on the hillside behind Kurotsuchi

ren'ai 恋愛: love, passion; *see* pp. 116–17

ryōtei 料亭: a traditional Japanese restaurant

rirekisho 履歴書: a personal history, curriculum vitae

sake 酒: Japanese rice wine; used as an English word in the text (i.e., not italicized)

sakaki 榊: *Cleyera ochnacea,* a plant used in Shinto worship

sakazuki 盃: a ritual sharing of cups; also a nest of three cups used for such a rite

san-san-ku-do 三三九度: "three-three-nine-times"; the sharing of cups as a rite of marriage

satoaruki 里歩き: a return home (dialect)

satogaeri 里帰り: a return home; *see* p. 189

seinen 青年: young people; youths

seinen daigaku 青年大学: "youth university"; *see* p. 58

seinendan 青年団: Youth Group (national organisation)

seinen shiki 青年式: celebration of the attainment of adulthood

sekihan 赤飯: rice cooked with beans, used on occasions of celebration

senzo 先祖: forebears or ancestors

senzo matsuri 先祖祭: a festival to remember common ancestors

setai 世帯: household

setsubun 節分: the traditional "end of winter"

shanichi 社日; *see* pp. 64, 77 and 241

shi 市: city; *see* p. 42

shichi-go-san 七五三: "7-5-3"; childhood ceremonies on 15 November

shichiya 七夜: the "seventh night" after a baby is born, when it is traditionally given its name

shimadai 島台: a decoration used at weddings or among betrothal gifts

shime-iwai 締祝: a closing celebration

shimenawa 注連縄(七五三縄): a straw rope which marks off a sacred area or object

shinboku 神木: a tree which is attributed sacred qualities

shinchiku iwai 新築祝: a celebration for a new house

shinseki 親戚: a relative; *see* pp. 106 and p. 112, n. 61

shinzen 神前: "before the *kami*"

shinzoku 親族: relatives; see *shinseki*

shison 子孫: descendants

shōbōdan 消防団: a fire-fighting corps

shōchikubai 松竹梅: a decoration including pine, bamboo and plum plants

shōgatsu 正月: New Year

surume 鯣: dried cuttlefish, used at celebrations and Sinto rites

tai 鯛: sea bream, used at celebrations

tamagushi hairei 玉串拝礼: the offering of a sprig of *sakaki* at a Shinto ceremony

tamashii 魂: soul or spirit

tan 反: a term of square measure, 1 tan = 993 sq. m.

tanjōbi 誕生日: birthday

tatami 畳: woven-rush matting used on the floors of Japanese houses

tekireiki 適齢期: appropriate age, particularly for marriage

tokonoma 床の間: an alcove where special objects are displayed

tomodachi 友達: friend; in local dialect, age-mate

tomobiki 友引: "friend-pulling"; a day in the six-day cycle to be avoided for funerals

tonari 隣: neighbour

tonarigumi 隣組: a neighbourhood group

tonari kinjo 隣近所: another kind of neighbourhood group

tōsan 父さん: father; *see* p. 86

tsugi no ma 次の間: "next room"

tsunokakushi 角隠: "horn-hider"; a bride's head-dress

ujigami 氏神: a guardian deity

utai 謡: extract from *Nō* plays sung on ceremonial occasions

wakamonogumi 若者組: a youth group found widely in pre-Meiji Japan

wakare 別れ: a separation; farewell party

wakashū 若衆: see *wakamonogumi*

wakashūyado 若衆宿: youth lodge where members of the youth group could spend nights together

yakudoshi 厄年: inauspicious ages

yobai 夜這(婚): the visit of lover to his sweetheart's house; *see* p. 24 and p. 34, n. 6

yome 嫁: wife, daughter-in-law, "woman of the house"

yomeiri 嫁入り): "*yome*-entering"; marriage; part of a wedding

yome-nusumi 嫁盗み: bride-stealing

yorokobi 慶び: a celebration, particularly following a marriage

yōshi 養子: an adopted child, particularly as successor or possible successor of a household; see also *muko-yōshi*

yubiwa 指輪: a ring

yuinō 結納: betrothal gifts

zagumi 座組: a goup of households with duties which concern the Shinto shrine

zashiki 座敷: the most formal room in a Japanese house

Part II

Where names have been used in the text to refer to historical periods they are of the duration shown below:

Nara 奈良:	AD 646 to 794
Heian 平安:	794 to 1185
Kamakura 鎌倉:	1185 to 1392
Muromachi 宝町:	1392 to 1568
Momoyama 桃山:	1568 to 1615
Edo or *Tokugawa* 江戸/徳川:	1615 to 1868
Meiji 明治:	1868 to 1912
Taishō 大正:	1912 to 1926
Shōwa 昭和:	1926 to present

BIBLIOGRAPHY

The following abbreviations have been adopted:

AA	*American Anthropologist*
AJS	*American Journal of Sociology*
CJ	*Contemporary Japan* (Tokyo)
EACS	*East Asian Cultural Studies*
FEQ	*Far Eastern Quarterly*
HJAS	*Harvard Journal of Asian Studies*
HO	*Human Organization*
JAOS	*Journal of the American Oriental Society*
JMF	*Journal of Marriage and the Family*
MFL	*Marriage and Family Living*
MK	*Minzokugaku Kenkyū*
MN	*Monumenta Nipponica*
P8ICAES	*Proceedings of the 8th International Congress of Anthropological and Ethnographical Sciences*
SC	*Social Compass*
SP	*Social Problems*
SWJA	*Southwestern Journal of Anthropology*
TASJ	*Transactions of the Asiatic Society of Japan*
TPJS	*Transactions and Proceedings of the Japan Society*
trans.	translated by

Amano, Fumiko 'Family Planning Movement in Japan', *CJ*, vol. 23 (1955), pp. 752-65.

Aoyama, Michio 青山道夫 'Gyakuenkon 逆縁婚 (Levirate Marriage),' in Emori (1976), pp. 192-8

Arai, Ken, 'New Religious Movements,' in Hori *et al.* (1972), pp. 98-104

Ariga, Kizaemon 有賀喜左衛門 *Nihon Kon'in Shiron* 日本婚姻史論 *(A Study of the History of Marriage in Japan)* (Nikkō Shoin 日光書院, Tokyo, 1948)

―― 'The Family in Japan', *MFL*, vol. 16 (1954), pp. 362-73

Asakawa, K. 'Notes on Village Government in Japan after 1600', *JAOS*, vol. XXX, no. III 259-300; vol. XXXI, no. II (1911), pp. 151-216

Baber, R.E. *Youth Looks at Marriage and the Family* (International Christian University, Tokyo, 1958)

Bacon, Alice M. *Japanese Girls and Women* (Gay and Bird, London, 1891)

Barrow, Sir J. 'Sketches of the Manners and Usages of Japan' *Quarterly Review*, vol. 52 (1834), pp. 293-317

Bartlett, C. 'Planning Japan's Families', *Far Eastern Economic Review*, vol. 54, no. 11 (1966), pp. 555-9

Beardsley, Richard K. *et al. Studies in Japanese Culture 1*, Occasional Papers No. 9 (Center for Japanese Studies, Ann Arbor, 1965)

— *Village Japan*, Phoenix edn (University of Chicago Press, Chicago, 1969)

Befu, Harumi 'Corporate Emphasis and Patterns of Descent in Japanese Family' in Smith and Beardsley (1962), pp. 34-41

— 'Patrilineal Descent and Personal Kindred in Japan', *AA*, vol. 65 (1963), pp. 1328-41

— 'Gift-Giving in a Modernising Japan', *MN*, vol. 23 (1968), pp. 445-56

— *Japan: an Anthropological Introduction* (Chandler, San Francisco, 1971)

— and Norbeck, Edward 'Japanese Usages of Terms of Relationship', *SWJA*, vol. 14 (1958), pp. 66-86

Benedict, Ruth *The Chrysanthemum and the Sword* (Secker and Warburg, London, 1947)

Bernstein, Gail 'Women in Rural Japan' in Lebra *et al.* (1976), pp. 25-49

Bishop, I.L. *Unbeaten Tracks in Japan* (John Murray, London, 1900)

Blacker, Carmen *The Catalpa Bow* (Allen and Unwin, London, 1975)

Blood, Robert O. *Love Match and Arranged Marriage* (The Free Press, New York; Collier-Macmillan, London, 1967)

Bownas, Geoffrey *Japanese Rainmaking and Other Folk Practices* (Allen and Unwin, London, 1963)

Brainbanti, Ralph 'Neighbourhood Associations in Japan and their Democratic Potentialities', *FEQ*, vol. 7 (1948), pp. 136-64

Brameld, Theodore *Japan: Culture, Education and Change in Two Communities* (Holt, Rinehart and Winston, New York, 1968)

Brannen, Noah S. *Sōka Gakkai: Japan's Militant Buddhists* (John Knox Press, Richmond, Virginia, 1968)

Caiger, John 'The Aims and Content of School Courses in Japanese History 1872-1945' in Edmund Skrzypczak (ed.), *Japan's Modern Century* (Sophia University and Tuttle, Tokyo, 1968), pp. 51-81

—— 'Ienaga Saburo and the First Post-War Japanese History Textbook', *Modern Asian Studies*, vol. 3, no. 1 (1969), pp. 1-16

Carey Hall, J. 'Japanese Feudal Law', *TASJ*, vol. 38 (1911), pp. 269-331

Casal, U.A. 'Some Notes on the Sakazuki and on the Role of Sake Drinking in Japan', *TASJ*, vol. 19 (1940), pp. 1-186

—— 'Incense', *TASJ*, Third Series, vol. 3 (1954), pp. 46-73

—— *The Five Sacred Festivals of Ancient Japan* (Tuttle and Sophia University Tokyo, 1967)

Chamberlain, Basil Hall *Things Japanese*, 4th edn, revised (John Murray, London, 1902)

Chang, Kenne H-K 'The Inkyo System in Southwestern Japan', *Ethnology*, vol. 9 (1970), pp. 342-57

Chikugo Kokushi 筑後国史 *(A History of Chikugo Province)* (Chikugo Iseki Kankōkai 筑後遺籍刊行会, 1926)

Chikushi, Yutaka 筑紫豊 *Nihon no Minzoku* 日本の民俗 *(Folklore of Japan),* No. 40 (Fukuoka, Tokyo, 1974)

Clement, Ernest 'Japanese Calendars', *TASJ*, vol. 30 (1902), pp. 1-82

—— 'Calendar (Japanese)' in James Hastings (eds.), *Encyclopaedia of Religion and Ethics*, (Edinburgh, 1910), Vol. III, pp. 114-17

Cornell, John B. 'Matsunagi, a Japanese Mountain Community' in Cornell and Smith (1969)

—— 'Individual Mobility and Group Membership: the Case of the Burakumin' in Dore (1971), pp. 337-72

—— and Smith, Robert J. (eds.) *Two Japanese Villages* (Greenwood Press, New York, 1969)

De Vos, George 'The Relation of Guilt toward Parents to Achievement and Arranged Marriage among the Japanese', *Psychiatry*, vol. 23 (1960), pp. 287-301

—— 'Social Values and Personal Attitudes in Primary Human Relations in Niiike' in Beardsley *et al.* (1965), pp. 53-91

—— *Socialization for Achievement* (University of California Press, Berkeley, Los Angeles and London, 1973)

—— and Wagatsuma, Hiroshi 'Value Attitudes toward Role Behaviour of Women in Two Japanese Villages', *AA*, vol. 63 (1961), pp. 1204-30

—— *Japan's Invisible Race* (University of California Press, Berkeley, Los Angeles and London, 1966)

Dixon, J.M. 'Japanese Etiquette', *TASJ*, vol. 13 (1885), pp. 1-21

Donoghue, John D. 'An Eta Community in Japan', *AA*, vol. 59 (1957), pp. 1000-17

—— *Pariah Persistence in Changing Japan: a Case Study* (University Press of America, Washington, DC, 1977)

Dore, R.P. 'Japanese Rural Fertility: Some Social and Economic Factors', *Population Studies*, vol. 7 (1953), pp. 62-88

—— *Land Reform in Japan* (Oxford University Press, Oxford, 1959)

—— *City Life in Japan* (University of California Press, Berkeley, Los Angeles and London, 1971)

—— *Shinohata: a Portrait of a Japanese Village* (Allen Lane, London, 1978)

—— (ed.) *Aspects of Social Change in Modern Japan* (Princeton University Press, Princeton, New Jersey, 1971)

Dorson, Richard M. (ed.) *Studies in Japanese Folklore* (Kennikat Press, Port Washington, New York, London, 1973)

Dykstra, Yoshiko Kurata 'Jizō, the Most Merciful – Tales from Jizō Bosatsu Reigenki', *MN*, vol. 33 (1978), pp. 179-200

Earhart, H. Byron *Japanese Religion; Unity and Diversity* (Dickenson, Belmont, California, 1969)

—— *Religion in the Japanese Experience* (Dickenson, Belmont, California, 1974)

Eliot, Sir Charles *Japanese Buddhism* (Edwin Arnold, London, 1935)

Ema, Tsutomu 江馬務 *Kekkon no Rekishi* 結婚の歴史 *(History of Marriage)* (Yūzan-kaku 雄山閣、Tokyo, 1971)

Embree, John F. *Suye Mura, a Japanese Village* (University of Chicago Press, Chicago, 1939)

—— 'Some Social Functions of Religion in Rural Japan', *AJS*, vol. 47 (1941), pp. 184-9

Emori, Itsuo 江守五夫 'Yobai to Tsumadoi' 「よばい」と「つまどひ」 in Emori (1976), pp. 68-79

—— (ed.) *Nihon no Kon'in: Dentō to Shūzoku* 日本の婚姻: 伝統と 習俗 *(Japanese Marriage: Tradition and Custom)* (Gendai no Esupuri 現代のエスプリ, No. 104, Tokyo, 1976)

Erskine, William *Japanese Customs: their Origin and Value* (Kyo Bun Kwan [sic], Tokyo, 1925)

—— *Japanese Festivals and Calendar Lore* (Kyo Bun Kwan, Tokyo, 1933)

Fueto, Toshio 不破藤敏夫 'Nōgyoson ni okeru kon'in mae no danjo kōsai no kanshū' 農漁村における婚姻前の男女交際の慣習 ('Customary premarital relations between the sexes in farming villages'), *Hōshakaigaku* 法社会学 vol. 4 (1953), pp. 102–10

—— 'The Discrepancy between Marriage Laws and Mores in Japan', *American Journal of Comparative Law*, vol. 5 (1956), pp. 256-66

Fujisaki, Hiroshi 藤崎弘 *Kankonsōsai Jiten* 冠婚葬祭事典
　(Dictionary of Ceremonies) (Tsuru Shobō 鶴書房, Tokyo, 1957)
Fukuoka-ken Shichōson Gappeishi 福岡県市町村合併史 *(A History
　of the Amalgamation of Cities, Towns and Villages in Fukuoka
　Prefecture)* (Fukuoka-kenchō 福岡県庁, Fukuoka, 1962)
Fukutake, Tadashi *Japanese Rural Society*, trans. R.P. Dore (Cornell
　University Press, London, 1972)
— *Japanese Society Today* (University of Tokyo Press, Tokyo, 1974)
Futabatei, Shimei *An Adopted Husband* (*Sono Omokage*), trans.
　Buhachiro Mitsui and Gregg M. Sinclair (Greenwood Press, New
　York, 1969)
Goh, Daigoro 'Family Relations in Japan', *TPJS*, vol. 2 (1895), pp.
　117-56
Goode, William J. 'The Theoretical Importance of Love', *American
　Sociological Review*, vol. 24 (1959), pp. 38-47
Goody, Jack, and Tambiah, S.J. *Bridewealth and Dowry* (Cambridge
　University Press, Cambridge, 1973)
Gubbins, John H. *The Making of Modern Japan* (Sealey, Service,
　London, 1922)
Hall, John W. *Government and Local Power in Japan 500-1700* (Prince-
　ton University Press, Princeton, New Jersey, 1966)
— and Jansen, Marius B. (eds.) *Studies in the Institutional History of
　Early Modern Japan* (Princeton University Press, Princeton, New
　Jersey, 1968)
Harada, Toshiaki 原田敏明 'Nyonin Kinsei' 女人禁制 ('Prohibitions
　on Women'), *Shakai to Denshō* 社会と伝承, vol. 2, no. 4
　(1958), pp. 162-71
—'Miya no za to Kabu' 宮の座と株 ('Shrine Organizations'),
　Shūkyō Kenkyū 宗教研究, vol. 36 (1963), pp. 1-12
Hartley, S.F. 'The Decline of Illegitimacy in Japan', *SP*, vol. 18 (1970),
　pp. 78-91
Hayami, Akira, and Uchida, Nobuko 'Size of Household in a Japanese
　County throughout the Tokugawa Era' in Laslett and Wall (1972),
　pp. 473-515
Hearn, Lafcadio *Japan: an Attempt at Interpretation* (Macmillan, New
　York, 1924)
Hendry, Joy 'A Japanese Wedding', *New Society*, vol. 41, no. 771
　(1977), pp. 68-9
Hill, Reuben, and König, René (eds.) *Families in East and West*
　(Mourton, Paris and The Hague, 1970)
Himeoka, Tsutomu 姫岡勤 'Hōken Dōtoku ni arawareta Fūfu no jōge

kankei' 封建道徳に表れた夫婦の上下関係 ('Husband-Wife Vertical Relationship according to Feudal Morals'), *Shakaigaku Hyōron* 社会学評論, vol. 4, no. 3 (1954), pp. 2–13

Hino, Lillian 'Twenty Japanese Proverbs', *Journal of American Folklore*, vol. 66 (1953), p. 18

Hirano, Kunio and Iida, Hisao 平野邦雄・飯田久雄 *Fukuoka-ken no Rekishi* 福岡県の歴史 *(History of Fukuoka Prefecture)* (Yamakawa 山川, Tokyo, 1975)

Hirayama, Toshijiro 'Seasonal Rituals connected with Rice Culture' in Dorson (1973), pp. 57-75

Holtom, D.C. 'The Meaning of Kami', *MN*, vol. 3 (1940), pp. 1-27

Hori, Ichiro *Folk Religion of Japan* (University of Chicago Press, Chicago, 1974)

— *et al.* (eds.) *Japanese Religion*, trans. (Yoshiya Abe and David Reid, Kodansha International, Tokyo and Palo Alto, 1972)

Horiguchi, Bob 'Inside the Weeklies', *The Japan Times Weekly*, vol. 17, no. 8, p. 4

Hozumi, Nobushige *Ancestor-Worship and Japanese Law* (Maruzen, Tokyo, 1913)

Inoguchi, Shōji 井之口章次 'Tanjō to Ikuji' 誕生と育児 ('Childbirth and Infant Care') in Omachi *et al.* (1962a), pp. 189–212; 'Sōshiki' 葬式 ('Funerals'), ibid., pp. 291–329

Inouye, Jukichi, *Home Life in Tokyo* (Tokyo, 1910)

Ishihara, Masaaki *et al.* (eds.) 石原正明 'Ritsu Itsubun' 律逸文 in Kuroita Katsumi (ed.), *Shintei Zōho: Kokushi Taikei,* 黒板勝見, 新訂増補・国史大系, Vol. XXII, Yoshikawa Kōbunkan 吉川弘文館, Tokyo, (1929), p. 117

Ishii, Ryōsuke *Japanese Legislation in the Meiji Era*, trans. and adapted by William J. Chambliss (Pan-Pacific Press, Tokyo, 1958)

Ishino, Iwao 'The Oyabun-Kobun: a Japanese Ritual Kinship Institution', *AA*, vol. 55 (1953), pp. 695-707

Isono, Fujiko 'The Family and Women in Japan', *The Sociological Review* (University of Keele), vol. 12, no. 1, pp. 39-54

Itō, Lucy S. 'Kō – Japanese Confraternities', *MN*, vol. 8 (1952), pp. 412-15

Iwasaki, Yasu 'Divorce in Japan', *AJS*, vol. 36 (1930), pp. 435-46

— 'Why the Divorce Rate has Declined in Japan', *AJS*, vol. 36 (1931), pp. 568-83

Izumi, Seiichi, and Nagashima, Nobuhiro 泉靖一・長島信弘 'Katoku Sōzoku kara mita Nihon no Higashi to Nishi' 家督相続から見た 日本の東と西 (East and West Japan and the Succession System'),

Kokubungaku Kaishaku to Kanshō 国文学解釈と鑑賞, vol. 28, no. 5, pp. 121-6

Izumimoto, Kigai 泉本季外 'Yomenusumi' 嫁盗み ('Bride-stealing') in Emori (1976), pp. 176-87

Japan *The Civil Code of Japan* (Ministry of Justice, Tokyo, 1972)
—— *The Civil Code of Japan*, trans. W.J. Sebald (J.L. Thompson, Japan; Butterworth, London, 1934)
—— *Statistical Handbook of Japan* (Bureau of Statistics, Tokyo, 1977)
—— *Statistical Yearbook* (Bureau of Statistics, Tokyo, 1977)
—— *The Constitution of Japan* Far Eastern Series 22 (Dept. of State Publication No. 2836, Washington, DC, 1947)

Johnson, Erwin, H. 'The Emergence of a Self-conscious Entrepreneurial Class in Rural Japan' in Smith and Beardsley (1962), pp. 91-9
—— 'Social Stratification in Rural Japan', *Ethnohistory*, vol. 15 (1968), pp. 328-51
—— 'Status Changes in Hamlet Structure Accompanying Modernization' in Dore (1971), pp. 153-83

Jōya, Mock *Japanese Customs and Manners* (The Sakurai Shoten, Tokyo, 1955)

Kamishima, Jirō 神島二郎 *Nihonjin no Kekkonkan* 日本人の結婚観 *(The Japanese View of Marriage)* (Chikuma Sōsho 筑摩叢書, Tokyo, 1969)

Kawasaki, Ichiro, *Japan Unmasked* (Tuttle, Tokyo, 1969)

Kawashima, Takeyoshi 川島武宣 *Kekkon* 結婚 *(Marriage)* (Iwanami Shoten 岩波書店, Tokyo, 1954)
—— and Steiner, Kurt 'Modernization and Divorce Rate Trends in Japan' Economic Development and Cultural Change, vol. 9, no. i (1960), pp. 213-40

Kitagawa, Joseph 'Master and Saviour' in *Studies of Esoteric Buddhism and Tantrism* (Koyasan, Japan, 1965)

Kitano, Seiichi 'Dōzoku and Ie in Japan' in Smith and Beardsley (1962), pp. 42-6
—— 'Dōzoku and Kindred in a Japanese Rural Society' in Hill and König (1970), pp. 248-69

Kitaoji, Hironobu 'The Structure of the Japanese Family', *AA*, vol. 73 (1971), pp. 1036-57

Knipe Mouer, E. 'Women in Teaching' in Lebra *et al.* (1976), pp. 157-90

Koyama, Takashi *The Changing Social Position of Women in Japan* (UNESCO, Paris, 1961)
—— 'Changing Family Structure in Japan' in Smith and Beardsley (1962), pp. 47-54

—— 'Changing Family Composition and the Position of the Aged in the Japanese Family', *International Journal of Comparative Sociology*, vol. 5 (1964), p. 155-61

—— 'The Significance of Relatives at the Turning Point of the Family System in Japan' in Halmos Paul (ed.), *Japanese Sociological Studies* (The Sociological Review Monograph 10, University of Keele, 1966)

Koyano, Shogo 'Changing Family Behaviour in Four Japanese Communities', *JMF*, vol. 26, no. 2 (1964), pp. 149-59

Küchler, L.W. 'Marriage in Japan', *TASJ*, vol. 13 (1885), pp. 114-37

Kurata, Ichiro 'Rural Marriage Customs in Japan', *CJ*, vol. 10 (1941), pp. 366-75

Laslett, Peter, and Wall, Richard *Household and Family in Past Time* (Cambridge University Press, Cambridge, 1972)

Lebra, Joyce 'Women in Service Industries' in Lebra *et al.* (1976), pp. 107-31

—— *et al. Women in Changing Japan* (Westview Press, Boulder, Colorado, 1976)

Lebra, Takie Sugiyama 'Reciprocity and the Asymmetric Principle' in Lebra and Lebra (1974) pp. 192-207; 'Intergenerational Continuity and Discontinuity in Moral Values among Japanese', ibid., pp. 90-116

—— and Lebra, William P. *Japanese Culture and Behaviour* (University of Hawaii Press, Hawaii, 1974)

Legge, James (trans.) *Li Chi Book of Rites*, ed. with Intro. and Study Guide by Ch'u Chai and Winberg Chai (University Books, New York, 1967), Vol. I

Lorimer, Norma 'Japan from a Woman's Point of View' in Sladen and Lorimer (1904)

Maeda, Takashi *Summary of Ane Katoku* (Kansai University Press, Osaka, 1976)

Mason, R.H.P., and Caiger, J.G. *A History of Japan* (Tuttle, Tokyo, 1975)

Masuoka, Edna Cooper *et al.* 'Role Conflicts in the Modern Japanese Family', *Social Forces*, vol. 41 (1962), pp. 1-6

Matsudaira, Narimitsu 'The Concept of Tamashii in Japan' in Dorson (1973), pp. 181-97

Matsumoto, Shigeru 'Introduction' to Japanese Religion in Hori *et al.* (1972), pp. 11-27

Matsumoto, Y. Scott 'Notes on Primogeniture in Postwar Japan' in Smith and Beardsley (1962), pp. 55-69

Maxson, Mary Lou 'Women in Family Businesses' in Lebra *et al.*

(1976), pp. 89-105

Mehra, A.N. 'Fertility Decline in Japan', *Eastern Economist*, vol. 51 (1968), p. 102

Minami, Ryōhei 南良平 *Konrei-shiki to kekkon no kokoroe* 婚礼式 と結婚の心得 *(On Marriage and the Marriage Ceremony)* (Taibunkan 泰文館, Tokyo, 1953)

Ministry of Labour, Japan *The Status of Women in Postwar Japan* (Women's and Minors' Bureau, Tokyo, 1956)

Miyake, Hitoshi 'Folk Religion' in Hori *et al.* (1972), pp. 121-43

Morioka, Kiyomi 'Religious Behaviour and the Actor's Position in the Household' in Morioka and Newell (1968), pp. 25-43

—— 'Préférence pour le mariage non-mixte parmi les Amidistes "Shin" du bouddhisme japonais', *SC*, vol. 17 (1970), pp. 9-20

—— 'The Changing Family and Buddhism in Post-war Japan', *EACS*, vol. 11, nos. 1-4 (1972), pp. 83-96

—— *Religion in Changing Japanese Society* (University of Tokyo Press, Tokyo, 1975)

—— and Newell, William H. (eds.) *The Sociology of Japanese Religion* (Brill, Leiden, 1968)

Morris, Ivan 'Marriage in the World of Genji', *Asia*, vol. 11 (1968), pp. 54-77

—— *The Nobility of Failure* (Secker and Warburg, London, 1975)

Morsbach, Helmut 'Aspects of Non-Verbal Communication in Japan', *The Journal of Nervous and Mental Disease*, vol. 157 (1973), pp. 262-77

—— 'Aspects of Japanese Marriage' in Marie Corbin (ed.), *The Couple* (Penguin, Harmondsworth, 1978)

Morse, Edward S. *Japanese Homes and their Surroundings* (Boston, 1886)

Murakami, Shigeyoshi 'New Religions in Japan', *EACS*, vol. 11, nos. 1-4 (1972), pp. 17-27

Murata, Kiyoaki *Japan's New Buddhism* (Walker, Weatherhill, New York, 1969)

McCullough, William H. 'Japanese Marital Institutions in the Heian Period', *HJAS*, vol. 27 (1967), pp. 103-67

McMullen, I.J. 'Non-Agnatic Adoption: a Confucian Controversy in 17th and 18th Century Japan', *HJAS*, vol. 35 (1975), pp. 133-89

Naito, Kanji 'Inheritance Patterns on a Catholic Island', *SC*, vol. 17 (1970), pp. 21-36

Nakagawa, Zenotsuke 'A Century of Marriage Law', *Japan Quarterly*, vol. 10, no. 2 (1963), pp. 182-92

Nakajima, Bun *Japanese Etiquette* (Japan Travel Bureau, Tokyo, 1955)

Nakane, Chie *Kinship and Economic Organization in Rural Japan* (University of London, The Athlone Press, London, 1967)

— 'An Interpretation of the Size and Structure of the Household in Japan over Three Centuries' in Laslett and Wall (1972), pp. 517-43

— *Japanese Society* (Penguin, Harmondsworth, 1973)

Nakayama, Tarō 中山太郎 *Nihon Kon'in Shi* 日本婚姻史 *(A History of Marriage in Japan)* (Shun'yō-dō 春陽堂, Tokyo, 1928)

Naoe, Hiroji 'A Study of Yashikigami: the Deity of House and Grounds' in Dorson (1973), pp. 198-214

Neel, James V. *et al.* 'The Incidence of Consanguineous Matings in Japan', *The American Journal of Human Genetics*, vol. I (1949), pp. 156-78

Nelson, Andrew N. *The Modern Reader's Japanese-English Character Dictionary*, revised (Tuttle, Tokyo, Rutland, Vermont, 1974)

Nihon Daijiten Kankōkai 日本大辞典刊行会 (Japan Dictionary Publishing Society) 日本国語大辞典 *(Nihon Kokugo Daijiten)* (Large Dictionary of the National Language of Japan) (Shōgakukan 小学館, Tokyo, 1976)

Norbeck, Edward 'Pollution and Taboo in Contemporary Japan', *SWJA*, vol. 8 (1952), pp. 269-85

— 'Age-Grading in Japan', *AA*, vol. 55 (1953), pp. 373-84

— *Takashima: a Japanese Fishing Community* (University of Utah Press, Salt Lake City, 1954)

— 'Yakudoshi, a Japanese Complex of Supernaturalistic Beliefs', *SWJA*, vol. 11 (1955), pp. 105-20

— 'Common Interest Associations in Rural Japan' in Smith and Beardsley (1962), pp. 73-85

— *Changing Japan* (Holt, Rinehart and Winston, New York, 1965)

— 'Little-Known Minority Groups of Japan' in Devos and Wagatsuma (1966), pp. 183-99

— 'Changing Associations in a Recently Industrialized Japanese Community', *Urban Anthropology*, vol. 6, no. 1 (1977), pp. 45-64

— and Befu, Harumi 'Informal Fictive Kinship in Japan', *AA*, vol. 60 (1958), pp. 102-17

Okada, Yoneo and Ujitoko, Sadatoshi *Shinto Shrines and Festivals* (Jinja Honchō, Kokugakuin University, Tokyo, 1958)

Omachi, Tokuzō 大間知篤三 'Izu Toshima no Ashiirekon' 伊豆利島 の足入れ婚 ('A Form of Bi-local Marriage on the Island of Toshima, Izu Province'), *MK,* vol. 14, no. 3 (1950), pp. 76-81

— *Kon'in* 婚姻 *(Marriage)* in Omachi *et al.* (1962a), vol. 3, pp.

175-202

—'Seinenshiki'青年式('Coming of Age') in Omachi *et al.* (1962b), vol. 4, pp. 227-46; 'Konrei' 婚礼 ('Marriage Ceremony'), ibid., pp. 247-74

—— 'Ashiire-kon' in Dorson (1973), pp. 251-66

—*et al.* (eds). *Nihon Minzokugaku Taikei* 日本民族学大系 *(An Outline of Japanese Folklore)* (Heibonsha 平凡社, Tokyo, 1962)

Ono, Sokyo *Shinto: the Kami Way* (Tuttle, Rutland, Vermont and Tokyo, 1969)

Papinot, E. *Historical and Geographical Dictionary of Japan* (Overbeck, Ann Arbor, 1948)

Passin, Herbert *Society and Education in Japan* (Columbia University Press, New York, 1965)

Paulson, Joy 'Evolution of the Feminine Ideal' in Lebra *et al.* (1976), pp. 1-23; 'Women in Media', ibid., pp. 209-32

Pelzel, John C. 'Japanese Kinship: a Comparison' in Maurice Freedman (ed.), *Family and Kinship in Chinese Society* (Stanford University Press, Stanford, 1970)

Pfoundes, C. 'On Some Rites and Customs of Old Japan', *Journal of the Anthropological Institute*, vol. XII (1882), pp. 222-7

Philippi, Donald *Kojiki* (trans.) (University of Tokyo Press, Tokyo, 1969)

Plath, David W. *The After Hours* (University of California Press, Berkeley, Los Angeles and London, 1964a)

—— 'Where the Family of God is the Family', *AA*, vol. 66 (1964b), pp. 300-17

Redesdale, Lord *Tales of Old Japan* (including translation of Sho-rei Hikki, a 'Record of Ceremonies' published 1706 by Hayashi Rissai) (Macmillan, London, 1908)

Reischauer, E.O. *Japan: Story of a Nation* (Duckworth, London, 1970)

Riviere, P.G. 'Marriage: a Reassessment' in Rodney Needham (ed.), *Rethinking Kinship and Marriage* (Tavistock, London, 1971)

Rohlen, Thomas P. *For Harmony and Strength* (University of California Press, Berkeley, Los Angeles, London, 1974)

Sakurai, Tokutarō 桜井徳太郎 *Kōshūdan Seiritsu Katei no Kenkyū* 講集団成立過程の研究 *(A Study of the Development of* Kō *Organization)* (Yoshikawa Kōbunkan 吉川弘文館, Tokyo, 1962)

—— 'The Major Features and Characteristics of Japanese Folk Beliefs' in Morioka and Newell (1968), pp. 13-24

Sano, Chiye *Changing Values of the Japanese Family* (The Catholic University of America Press, Washington, DC, 1958)

Sansom, G.B. *Japan: a Short Cultural History* (revised) (The Cresset Press, London, 1952)

Schull, W.J. and Neel, J.V. *The Effects of Inbreeding on Japanese Children* (Harper and Row, New York, 1965)

Segawa, Kiyoko 'Menstrual Taboos Imposed upon Women' in Dorson (1963), pp. 239-50

Seki, Keigo 関敬吾 'Nenrei Shūdan' 年齢集団 ('Age-Groups') in Omachi *et al.* (1962), pp. 127-74

Shibusawa, Keizō *Japanese Life and Culture in the Meiji Era*, trans. and adapted by Charles S. Terry (Obunsha, Tokyo, 1958)

Shimazaki, Chifumi *The Noh*, Vol. 1, *God Noh* (Hinoki Shoten, Tokyo, 1972)

Shimpo, Mitsuru 'Impact, Congruence and New Equilibrium' in Morioka and Newell (1968), pp. 54-72

Shiotsuki, Yaeko 塩月弥栄子 *Kankonsōsai Nyūmon* 冠婚葬祭入門 *(An Introduction to Ceremonies)* (Kōbunsha 光文社, Tokyo, 1970)

—*Zukai Kankonsōsai* 図解冠婚葬祭 *(Illustrated Ceremonies)* (Kōbunsha, Tokyo, 1971)

Silberman, Bernard S. (ed.) *Japanese Character and Culture: Selected Readings* (University of Arizona Press, Tucson, 1962)

Singer, Kurt *Mirror, Sword and Jewel*, ed. Richard Storry (Croom Helm, London, 1973)

Sladen, Douglas, and Lorimer, Norma *More Queer Things about Japan* (Anthony Treherne, London, 1904)

Smith, Robert J. 'Kurusu: A Japanese Agricultural Community' in Cornell and Smith (1969)

— 'Small Families, Small Households and Residential Instability' in Laslett and Wall (1972), pp. 429-71

— *Ancestor Worship in Contemporary Japan* (Stanford University Press, Stanford, 1974)

— *Kurusu* (Dawson, Folkestone, 1978)

— and Beardsley, Richard K. (eds.) *Japanese Culture: its Development and Characteristics* Viking Fund Publications in Anthropology No. 34 (Wenner Gren Foundation, New York, 1962)

Smith, Thomas C. 'The Japanese Village in the 17th Century' in Hall and Jansen (1968), pp. 263-82

— *et al. Nakahara* (Stanford University Press, Stanford, 1977)

Sofue, Takao 'Childhood Ceremonies in Japan', *Ethnology*, vol. 4 (1965), pp. 148-64

Steiner, Kurt 'Revisions of the Civil Code of Japan: Provisions Affecting the Family', *FEQ*, vol. 9 (1950), pp. 169-84

—— 'Popular Political Participation and Political Development in Japan: the Rural Level' in Ward (1968), pp. 213-47

Stoetzel, Jean *Without the Chrysanthemum and the Sword* (Columbia University Press, New York, 1955)

Storry, Richard *A History of Modern Japan* (Pelican, Harmondsworth, 1973)

Suenari, Michio 'First Child Inheritance in Japan', *Ethnology*, vol. 11 (1972), pp. 122-6

Sugiyama, Sadao, and Schull, W. 'Consanguineous Marriage in Feudal Japan', *MN*, vol. 15 (1960), pp. 126-41

Suzuki, Norihisa 'Christianity' in Hori *et al.* (1972), pp. 71-87

Suzuki, Takao *Japanese and the Japanese: Words in Culture*, trans. Akira Miura (Kodansha International, Tokyo, New York and San Francisco, 1978)

Takamure, Itsue 高群逸枝 *Nihon Kon'in Shi* 日本婚姻史 *(A History of Marriage in Japan)* (Nihon Rekishi Shinsho 日本歴史新書, Tokyo, 1963)

Takeda, Chōshū ' "Ancestor Worship" an Important Historic and Social Factor in Japanese Folk Buddhism', *P8ICAES*, Vol. 3 (1968), pp. 123-5

Takeuchi, Toshimi 竹内利美 *Satogaeri* 里帰り *(Homecomings) Nihon Shakai Minzoku Jiten* 日本社会民俗辞典 (Seibundō Shinkōsha, Tokyo, 1954), pp. 502-3

——'Kodomo-gumi ni tsuite' 子供組について ('The Children's Group'), *MK*, vol. 21, no. 4 (1957), pp. 61-7

Takimoto, Seiichi 瀧本誠一 *Nihon Keizai Taiten* 日本経済大典 (Tokyo, 1928)

Tamura, Naomi *The Japanese Bride* (Harper and Bros., New York and London, 1904)

Tamaru, Noriyoshi 'Buddhism' in Hori *et al.* (1972), pp. 47-69

Tanizaki, Junichirō *The Makioka Sisters*, trans. Edward Seidensticker (Grosset and Dunlap, New York, 1966)

Trewartha, Glenn T. *Japan: a Geography* (University of Wisconsin Press, Madison and Milwaukee; Methuen, London, 1970)

Tsuda, Sōkichi *An Inquiry into the Japanese Mind as Mirrored in Literature*, trans. Fukumatsu Matsuda (Japan Society for the Promotion of Science, Tokyo, 1970)

Tsurumi, Kazuko *Social Change and the Individual* Princeton University Press, Princeton, New Jersey, 1970)

Ueda, Kenji 'Shinto' in Hori *et al.* (1972), pp. 29-45

Ushijima, Morimitsu 牛島盛光 *Henbō suru Suemura* 変貌する須恵村

(Sue Mura in Transition) (Minerva Shobō ミネルヴァ書房, Kyoto, 1971)

—*Nihon no Minzoku* 日本の民俗 *(Folklore of Japan)*, No. 43 (Kumamoto, Tokyo, 1973)

van Gennep, Arnold *The Rites of Passage* (Routledge and Kegan Paul, London and Henley, 1977)

Varner, Richard E. 'The Organized Peasant: the Wakamonogumi in the Edo Period', *MN*, vol. 32 (1977), pp. 459-83

Vogel, Ezra F. 'The Go-Between in a Developing Society: the Case of the Japanese Marriage Arranger', *HO*, vol. 20 (1961), pp. 122-20

— *Japan's New Middle Class* (University of California Press, Berkeley, Los Angeles and London, 1963)

— 'Kinship Structure, Migration to the City and Modernization' in Dore (1971), pp. 91-111

— and Vogel, Suzanne H. 'Family Security, Personal Immaturity and Emotional Health in a Japanese Sample', *MFL*, vol. 32 (1961), pp. 161-6

Wagatsuma, Hiroshi, and Devos, George 'Attitudes toward Arranged Marriage in Rural Japan', *HO*, vol. 21 (1962), pp. 187-200

Wakamori, Tarō 'Initiation Rites and Young Men's Organizations' in Dorson (1963), pp. 291-304

Ward, Robert (ed.) *Political Development in Modern Japan* (Princeton University Press, Princeton, New Jersey, 1968)

Watanabe, Yozo 'The Family and the Law' in A.T. von Mehren (ed.), *Law in Japan* (Harvard University Press, Cambridge, Mass., 1963)

Yamanaka, Einosuke 山中永之助 'Meijiki no Gyakuenkon' 明治期の 逆縁婚 ('The Levirate Marriage of the Meiji Era'), *Hōseishi Kenkyū* 法制史研究, vol. 7 (1957), pp. 112–30

Yamegunshi 八女郡史 *(A History of Yame County)* (Yame-gun Yakusho 八女郡役所)

Yanagawa, Keiichi, 'The Family, the Town and Festivals', EACS, vol. 11, nos. 1–4 (1972), pp. 125–31

Yanagida, Kunio 柳田国男 *Kon'in no Hanashi* 婚姻の話 *(On Marriage)* (Iwanami Shoten 岩波書店, Tokyo, 1948)

—*Minzokugaku Jiten* 民族学辞典 *(Dictionary of Folklore)* (Minzokugaku Kenkyūjo 民俗学研究所, Tokyo, 1953)

— *Japanese Manners and Customs in the Meiji Era*, trans. and adapted by Charles S. Terry (Obunsha, Tokyo, 1957)

— *About Our Ancestors: the Japanese Family System*, trans. Fanny Mayer and Yasuyo Ishiwara (Japanese National Commission for UNESCO, Tokyo, 1970)

—and Omachi, T. 大間知 *Kon'in Shūzoku Goi* 婚姻習俗語彙
(Popular Terms associated with Marriage) (Minkan Denshō no
Kai 民間伝承の会, Tokyo, 1937)

Yoshida, Teigo 'Cultural Integration and Change in Japanese Villages',
AA, vol. 65 (1963), pp. 102-16

— 'Social Conflict and Cohesion in a Japanese Rural Community',
Ethnology, vol. 3 (1964), pp. 219-31

— 'Mystical Retribution, Spirit Possession and Social Structure in a
Japanese Village', *Ethnology*, vol. 6 (1967), pp. 237-62

Yoshino, Roger, and Murakoshi, Sueo *The Invisible Visible Minority:
Japan's Burakumin* (Buraku Kaiho Kenkyusho, Osaka, 1977)

INDEX